Praise for *Extraordinary Parents*

"Once again, Lynn Fielding is a master at using data to understand and improve learning for all students. Regardless of their own education, income or life experiences, parents want their children to succeed. This book provides them with powerful information that can be used to help them reach that goal."

—Cheryl Dell, Publisher,
Sacramento Bee

"At last parents have a practical guide as they assume their vital role in overseeing the education of their children. Using the strategies outlined in *Extraordinary Parents* they will bestow on their children life long opportunities and benefits."

—Paul Rosier, Executive Director,
Washington Association of School Administrators

"Because of this book, I have put one of my children in Sylvan. If I had read this book five years ago, I would have known what to do to have avoided that and saved $5,000."

—Stacey M., single parent
of a five-and eight-year-old

"It feels like you're sharing all the 'secrets in the system.' This book contains all the strategies I need to prepare my children to excel in their education from cradle to college."

—Alison G.,
parent of three

"I needed this information in the '90s for my sons. The A's they earned in middle school did not follow them through high school or college. Now I understand why, and what I could have done to boost their confidence and achievement."

—Patty K., mother of four
grandmother of two

"The sweep of this book is immense—from cradle to kindergarten and from kindergarten to college. The data underscores the absolutely pivotal role of parents in their child's successful education."

—Evelyn Pelletier, Tennesssee PTA,
State President 2005-2007

"Every child in America should be raised like this! I would buy this book for any pregnant mother. I always use to give a special children's book at a baby shower, but this will be better. Every one entering middle and high school should read Part Two. This is a GPS for preparing your child for college and the rest of life."

—Teresa H., mother of two
grandmother of four

"Your early chapters address the myth that kids who start behind catch up in a year to two. It places grave and life altering responsibility with parents from birth to kindergarten. It's sobering information.

With my own kids, I felt at peace with public education during elementary school but from the sixth grade on my experience was beyond frustrating. This book would have been pivotal in giving me the tools and confidence to make some important changes that could have improved my kid's lives. I NEEDED YOUR BOOK!"

—Debra B., mother of two

"What the book *gives* (to its everlasting credit) is *hope*. 'Gee, I *can* make a difference in my child's future. If I do the right things, there will be money for her college, *and* she'll be able to get in.'"

—Carl V.,
business leader

"My bright fourth grader wants to be a research scientist. Lynn gave him the book to read. He has started teaching letters and sounds to his three-year-old brother, practicing reading with his second grade sister and has asked me to transfer him into a nearby and more competitive school district."

—Seberita S.,
parent of three

EXTRAORDINARY

PARENTS

Choosing Your Child's Future: A year by year guide from cradle to college

Lynn Fielding

To my own extraordinary parents

Herman J. Fielding

1917-

Della Maude Dial Fielding

1914-2007

To obtain additional copies and quantity discounts or for permission to reproduce parts of this material please contact:

The New Foundation Press
114 Vista Way
Kennewick, WA 99336
Phone (509) 551-3226
Fax (509) 783-5237

Library of Congress Catalog Card Number: 2009934573
ISBN: 9780966687538
Printed in the United States of America

The following are registered trademarks: The Children's Reading Foundation.® Explore® and Plan® are registered trademarks of ACT, Inc.

Acknowledgements

I wish to acknowledge the contributions of those whose efforts made this book possible.

The READY! for Kindergarten material, although modified here, has been the result of the significant efforts of many, including Nancy Kerr, Virginia Paine, Tonia Kostorowski, Beverly Abersfeller, Steve Halliday, and Janie Easton.

Data from Northwest Evaluation Association has been used through the book and material from Holt, Rinehart and Winston, and McMillan McGraw-Hill was used to develop the curriculum guides in Appendix D.

A variety of educators reviewed and made valuable contributions. They include my co-authors of earlier books Nancy Kerr, President of the Children's Reading Foundation and Paul Rosier, Executive Director of the Washington Association of School Administrators; Kennewick administrators David Bond, Greg Fancher, and Marlis Lindbloom; Kennewick School Board Directors Dawn Adams, Ed Frost (retired), and Dan Mildon; and other esteemed colleagues Mary Rosier, J. E. Stone (President, Education Consumers Foundation), Ginger Hopkins, a Vice President of NWEA and Carl Hauser, senior researcher, NWEA.

Drafts of the book were reviewed by a host of young parents and others whose opinions have been invaluable, including Lisa Bokenkamp, Deb Bowen, Wendy Fielding, Jared Fielding, Alisson Gilbert, Yasmine Gilbert, Patti Kessie, Kat Miller, Melissa Neal, Evelyn Pelletier, Brittany Phillips, Leo and Cheryl Smigelski, Connie and Warren Smith, Erin Tomlinson, Kristine Toth, and Carl VanHoff. These reviewers generously offered a range of advice about an evolving project, while continuing to express faith in the final outcome.

I express heartfelt thanks to my editors Lavina Fielding Anderson and Monica Fiscalini; graphic designer Daniel Van Tassell; and advisor A. Melody. Special thanks to my typesetter and assistant Kat Miller for expertly managing countless tasks related to the research, editing, and design of this book. All met amazing deadlines throughout the entire process with exemplary grace and refreshing wit.

And most of all, I express love and appreciation to my wife and children, who have stoically endured this two-year writing process with unfailing support and encouragement.

About Lynn Fielding

- 22 years (1987 to present) as a school board director of Kennewick, Washington, school district (15,000 students)
- 14 years as a director and co-founder of the Children's Reading Foundation (1995 to present)
- Eight years as a director of the Washington State School Directors Association
- Seven years (2002 to present) as a director of Northwest Evaluation Association (NWEA), a testing company serving more than 2,500 U.S. school districts
- 28 years as a business attorney with an advanced law degree from Georgetown University in Taxation and CPA (Maryland)
- 31 years of parenting four children with Wendy, his wife

Other publications include co-authoring:

- *The 90% Reading Goal* (1997)
- Initial *READY! for Kindergarten* lessons (2002-2003)
- *Delivering on the Promise* (2004)
- *Annual Growth for All Students, Catch-Up Growth for Those Who Are Behind* (2007)

Lynn presents throughout the United States at conferences on early education, accelerated academic growth in public schools, and school governance to create extraordinary achievement in educational organizations and individuals. He is most easily contacted through newfoundationpress@gmail.com.

TABLE OF CONTENTS

PART ONE: *From Cradle to Kindergarten*   11

Chapter

1	Your Child and the Race	12
2	From Cradle to College	17
3	READY! for Kindergarten	31
4	Three Rules and Four Limitations	36
5	Birth to One	41
6	Age One to Two	53
7	Age Two to Three	67
8	Choosing a Preschool: A Checklist	82
9	Age Three to Four	85
10	Age Four to Five	97
11	Accelerated Reading and Math	112
12	Living with Regret	118

PART TWO: *From Kindergarten to College*   121

13	Entering Kindergarten: Where Is My Child?	123
14	Elementary School: Annual Growth, Catch-Up Growth	129
15	Gifted and Talented	141
16	Dark-Blue Targets for Grades Two to Eight	147
17	Middle School: Annual Growth, Catch-Up Growth	153
18	Sharing the Journey	163
19	The Middle School College Work Book For College	167
20	Financing Postsecondary Education	175
21	High School: Annual Growth, Catch-Up Growth	185
22	Choosing High School or Less	193
23	Choosing Some College	203
24	Getting Through Your Four-Year University	213
25	The Extraordinary Parenting Maxims	224
	Appendices	228-257
	Index	258-262

PREFACE

This is an invitation to extraordinary moms and dads.

Extraordinary parents smooth the pathway of their children. They hold visions for their infants, weave expectations around them, and guide with firm hands their tottering young feet down pathways and toward objectives that sometimes only they can see.

Extraordinary moms and dads do ordinary things. Few of the things are particularly hard. What is extraordinary is you do them over and over again every day. You do those ordinary things for years and do not lose focus or interest. That's what is hard.

Holding that vision from cradle to kindergarten is hard. Kindergarten starting points determine whether children, with ordinary growth, will start ahead or start behind. Starting ahead means your children will feel good about themselves, will look forward to going to school, and will make the effort to stay ahead. Extraordinary parents give that gift to their children.

Holding that vision from kindergarten through college is what you do next. The path is already smoothed. The vision is already in place. Your children are already ahead without the burden of difficult catch-up growth. Your children usually stay ahead as your skillful parenting supports their high levels of academic achievement and personal goals. Your skill and dedication, by itself, may determine whether your child will have a university experience.

This is an invitation to be extraordinary parents.

PART ONE

From Cradle to Kindergarten

Although I've been involved in public education as a parent and an elected official for more than thirty years, perhaps the most important fact about it dawned on me slowly: *Some students start kindergarten two years ahead, others at grade level, and others up to three years behind their classmates.* The academic skill level of your child on the first day of school has a huge impact on the rest of your child's educational career and the trajectory of the rest of his or her life. If your child starts ahead, he gets a strong start. If he starts behind, he struggles when he starts. And the good news is that for most parents, you pretty well get to choose where your child starts.

Part One explains the five-year range in reading and math ability that exists at virtually every grade level, where it originates, and how that range impacts whether your child will get into a four-year university (chaps. 1-4). More importantly, we will explore together the targets, tools, and activities at each age from birth to five that will help your child start kindergarten ahead (chaps. 5-12). These chapters will change the way you look at parenting, showing you how to smooth the way for your child during the crucial birth-to-five years.

To avoid the awkwardness of "he or she" in dealing with parents and children, I switch from masculine to feminine pronouns section by section or, if more convenient, paragraph by paragraph.

Grandparents can play a powerful role in the lives of grandchildren, especially when parents are distracted by making a living or are single. Grandparents, other significant relatives, and caregivers should read themselves into passages where I refer to moms, dads, and parents.

At an average adult reading speed of about 300 words a minute, including sidebars, comment boxes, and footnotes, and spending three minutes on each figure or table, you can read Part One in about three hours.

CHAPTER ONE

YOUR CHILD AND THE RACE

"Parents can position their child for academic success long before the first day of kindergarten. A vibrant life of learning begins at birth."
—Nancy Kerr, National President,
The Children's Reading Foundation

Imagine a twelve-and-a-half-mile race. Imagine 100 runners lined up and ready to go. But in this race, 20 runners are standing on the starting line. They are suited up in green. The rest are either ahead or behind the starting line. Twenty runners wearing blue start a mile ahead. Two miles ahead in the distance are another 20. Mindy, wearing dark-blue, is one of those two miles in front of the starting line. Now imagine another 20 runners, dressed in yellow, positioned a mile behind the starting line. Ten, wearing orange, are poised two miles behind. A final 10 runners in red start three miles behind. Tony is one of those wearing red. Those who have previously run fastest are positioned farthest ahead. Those who have previously run slowest are farthest behind. Once everyone is in position, the gun goes off. Everyone starts running. Everyone gives his or her best effort.

3 miles
BEHIND

2 miles
BEHIND

1 mile
BEHIND

It's really not a very fair race. A snapshot of the runners at the first mile and almost every mile thereafter shows them running in almost the same order as they started. Mindy and most of the runners who start ahead with her are still ahead. Tony and most of the runners who start behind with him are still behind.

Almost no one realizes that Tony and those who started behind with him run just as far, just as fast, and in the same amount of time as Mindy and those who started ahead.

We say that Mindy and the dark-blue crowd with her—who start out ahead and stay ahead—are the fastest runners. And why not? The dark-blue runners are ahead at every milepost in the race. Almost no one realizes that Tony and those who started behind with him run just as far, just as fast, and in the same amount of time as Mindy and those who started ahead.

Speed
Of course, not everyone keeps running at the same speed during the entire race. A few runners get stronger as the race continues and move up in the pack. Some runners have fans cheering enthusiastically for them while others run on their own. Some runners lack stamina and focus. Without staying power, they start to fade. Events that occur off the track—such as a divorce, moving, an accident that requires hospitalization—may cut speed. Speed is important because, if the runners who are behind aren't moving at a faster rate than the rest of the pack, they will never catch up. Speed is also important because runners who do not maintain their speed lose ground. Some of those who start ahead will start dropping back. Some of those who are already behind will fall back farther. Once the average pace is determined, it is easy to watch individual runners shift forward and backward within the pack.

START   1 mile   2 miles
                         AHEAD   AHEAD

So yes, speed is important. In school, just as in a track meet, it's essential for students trying to catch up. And the hopeful message is that such catch-up growth is truly possible with targeted, smart, consistent effort.

Starting Points and Speed

But speed simply modifies or maintains the advantage of the most important factor: the runner's starting point. Let's suppose that the average speed of the pack is six miles an hour. Let's suppose that Tony (running in red), who started a discouraging three miles behind the line, is scorching along— running eight miles an hour, or a third faster than the average six-mile-an-hour pace. Even at that impressively accelerated rate, his gain is too slow in relationship to his disadvantage. By mile three, Tony will catch the orange runners. By mile six, he will catch the yellow runners. By mile nine, he will catch up to the green runners in the middle of the pack. By maintaining sprinting speed, in 12 miles he will overtake the blue runners. But this race ends at 12.5 miles. He will never catch Mindy and the others in dark- blue.

It takes an *extraordinary* difference in speed—or in school, the rate of learning—over an extended period of time to eliminate a five- to six-year difference in starting points.

In order for red runners starting three years behind to catch up to the green, grade-level group by mile three, they have to run *twice* as fast. They have to cover six miles while the grade-level group is running three miles. If they continue this spectacular performance, they could catch the dark-blue runners at mile six. This rare event occurs with a few very talented runners or normal runners in an extraordinary training program.

The twelve-and-a-half-mile race also trains runners for life after the race. It is also a qualifying race for other races that follow. If your runner finishes poorly or drops out altogether, the post-race opportunities are fewer, shorter, and less lucrative. Finish in the upper third of the pack and the opportunities increase. If your runner finishes in the top 10% of the pack, great race opportunities abound at the university level.

As we have seen, a runner can finish well by running an average race if she starts with the blue runners. On the other hand, if the runner starts with those in yellow or still farther back, she must run at a truly impressive pace in order to finish well.

It takes an extraordinary difference in the rate of learning over an extended period of time to eliminate a five- to six-year difference between starting points among entering kindergarteners.

Finishing well is important, even for athletes who are better sprinters, javelin throwers, or pole-vaulters and whose inclinations and individual skills are therefore wholly misaligned with the requirement of this race. Their future opportunities are also affected by how well they do.

When it comes to the race for knowledge, the interesting part, of course, is that as a parent **you can pretty well decide where your child starts.** He can start with the Mindys who start ahead and generally stay ahead. He can start with the Tonys who are one, two, or three years behind. Extraordinary moms and dads give their child this edge.

CHAPTER TWO

FROM CRADLE TO COLLEGE:

"Sometimes a truth is so simple and obvious that it eludes detection for years."

—*Dan Yankelovich*[1]

As a parent, what do you say when someone asks, "What do you want for your child after high school?"

"Go to college," you'll say.

Ask high school freshmen what they'll do after high school.

"Go to college," 95% of them will say.

Yet despite the overwhelming unanimity of this aspiration, only one in three (34%) of U.S. students will enroll in a four-year university directly out of high school. Two in three (66%) will not.

As a knowledgeable parent, you can dramatically alter these outcomes for your child, especially when you start at birth. The balance of this chapter, using a few simple diagrams and charts, summarizes this book. It puts in your hands the hinge on which your child's future swings: use of those precious preschool years.

---

[1] Dan Yankelovich, "How Public Opinion Really Works," *Fortune Magazine*, October 1992. Yankelovich is cofounder, with former Secretary of State Cyrus Vance, of Public Agenda, the nonprofit research foundation that published the seminal educational research *First Things First* in 1994.

From birth to kindergarten, youngsters learn at vastly different rates. That is why there is such a wide range of skill levels among kindergarteners the first day of school. Their early learning and achievement rates are primarily a function of the opportunities and activities that you as their parents provide for them.

"...it is common to find within a kindergarten classroom a five-year range in children's literacy-related skills and functioning."

Dr. Jeni Riley[2]

If your child is average, he will make five years of language and pre-literacy growth in those first five years. He will start the race at "grade level" dressed in green. About 20% of children are in this group (Fig. 2.1).

Other children make less cognitive growth during the five years before kindergarten:

- Some make only *four* years of growth in their first five years of life, starting kindergarten a year behind the statistically average child. Their growth is shown in yellow.
- Others make *three* years of growth (shown in orange). They start kindergarten two years behind.
- Still others make *two* years of pre-literacy and language growth (shown in red). These students, like Tony in Chapter 1, start kindergarten three years behind.

On the upper end of the spectrum, some students make more growth during the five years before kindergarten.

- Your child could make six years of growth in her first five years of life, starting kindergarten one year ahead (blue).
- Your child could make seven years of growth (shown in the dark-blue). He could start two years ahead with Mindy.

As extraordinary moms and dads, and following the guidance in chapters 3-12, you can pretty well choose the reading and language achievement path on which your child will start kindergarten. It is an exciting opportunity as well as a significant responsibility. Either way, however, the level of achievement with which your child enters kindergarten will pretty well be the results of your parenting decisions and actions.

---

[2] Joint Position Statement of the International Reading Association and the National Association for the Education of Young Children: *Learning to Read and Write: Developmentally Appropriate Practices for Young Children* adopted May 1998 quoting Dr. Jeni Riley of the University of London. Fifteen national associations either endorsed or supported the concepts of the Joint Position Statement.

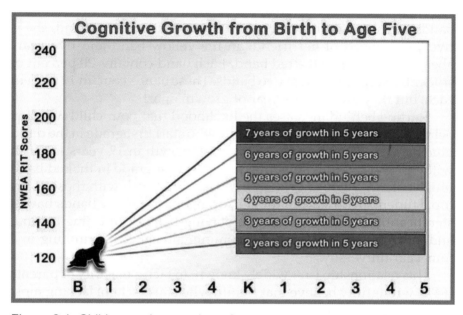

Figure 2.1. Children make anywhere from two to seven years of pre-literacy and language growth from birth to age five.[3]

[3] The RIT scale shown on the left or y-axis is the work of the Northwest Evaluation Association (NWEA). The RIT scale is a substantially equal interval scale where each point of growth along the interval is equal to every other point of growth and allows students to be compared not only to other students at the same grade level but students with similar academic proficiency at different grade levels. NWEA, a not-for-profit organization which provides over 2 million assessments a year in more than 2,500 of the nation's 13,862 school districts, has used this scale for the last 30 plus years. *The five-year span at kindergarten is an extension of NWEA data which shows the five-year span at the beginning of second grade* consistent with Dr. Riley's research and Joint Position Statement of the International Reading Association and the National Association for the Education of Young Children(note 3). It is based on NWEA's published data using the test scores gathered from the fall and spring of 2003 and 2004. It shows the average reading scores of 2.3 million students for the 90th (top line) percentile, 70th, 50th, 30th, 15th and 5th (bottom line) percentiles from the beginning of second grade through the beginning of eleventh grade.

Between birth and age five is the only time in life where students of the same age grow at substantially different rates. Your child starts school farthest ahead in the dark-blue band and farthest behind in the red band. Each of the bands is one academic year apart in elementary school.

There is a five-year range between the top and bottom reading bands. If your child is at the midpoint in the dark-blue band, she is two years ahead of her friends in the yellow band and five years ahead of students in the red band. Each band contains 20 percent of students except the lowest two bands. These bands contain 10 percent each, but they are still one year of growth apart.

Starting behind increases the likelihood that your child will stay behind. The math is simple. Students who start first grade in the dark-blue band must only make 12 years of growth in 12 years to finish with those at the top. Students who start first grade in the red band must make 17 years of growth in 12 years to finish with those at the top. Students who start in the red, orange, and yellow bands have a significantly increased chance of staying behind, finishing behind, and/or dropping out, and only a minimal chance of enrolling in a four-year university.

This relationship isn't widely known. In fact, a majority of parents (64%) wrongfully believe that a child who starts school lacking most of the necessary skills "will be able to catch up to other children within a year or two."[4]

On the other hand, assuring that your child starts ahead increases the likelihood that he will stay ahead, finish ahead, and enroll in a four-year university if he chooses. Starting ahead smoothes the path for him, perhaps for the rest of his life.

Your child's initial starting point advantages (and disadvantages) can be seen when the red, green, and blue achievement bands are extended through elementary, middle, and high school (Fig. 2.3).

Now that the relation between color and achievement is clear, I'll avoid repetition from this point on by referring to students by their color, color bands and occasionally as color paths, color pathways, or potentials.

---

[4] Thrive by Five Washington. Report on Opinion Research. March 2008, 3. Also available at http://thrivebyfivewa.org/.

Band Names	Relationship to Grade Level	% of Students Represented
Dark Blue	2 Years above Grade Level	Top 20%
Blue	1 Year above Grade Level	Next 20%
Green	Grade Level Skills	Middle 20%
Yellow	1 Year below Grade Level	Next 20%
Orange	2 Years below Grade Level	Next Lowest 10%
Red	3 Years below Grade Level	Bottom 10%

Figure 2.2. The relationship of the bands to each other.

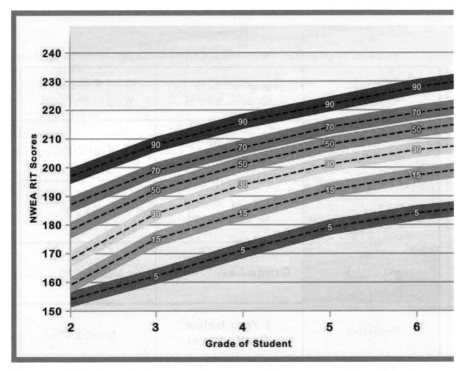

Figure 2.3. Northwest Evaluation Association fall reading achievement scores from 2nd grade through 11th grade for 2003-2004.[5]

This chart shows how the bands, formed by the beginning of kindergarten, persist through elementary, middle, and high school. Because the academic paths remain virtually unchanged all the way from beginning to end, a year of academic growth each year, wonderful as that is, will keep your child in the same band she started in.

---

[5] The graph is compiled from published data of the NWEA using the test scores gathered from the fall and spring of 2003 and 2004. It shows the average reading scores of 2.3 million students for the 90th (top line) percentile, 70th, 50th, 30th, 15th and 5th (bottom line) percentiles from the beginning of second grade through the beginning of eleventh grade. See *RIT Scale Norms, for Use with Achievement Level Tests and Measures of Academic Progress,* September 2005, Appendix A, Fall Reading RIT Score to Percentile Rank Conversion, 76. Lynn Fielding has been on its board of directors since May 2002. More information about this graph appears in Appendix B.

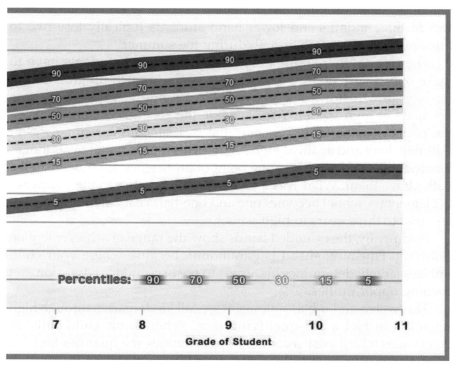

Percentiles: 90 70 50 30 15 5

Grade of Student
7   8   9   10   11

- Notice that the difference between the top and bottom bands stays about the same (44 RIT points plus or minus two points) from the beginning of second grade through 11th grade.
- Notice also that the one-year difference between each band also persists through elementary school.

Check it out for yourself. Look at the scores running down the left hand side of the graph. Put your finger on the RIT score of 198. This is where beginning second-graders in the dark-blue band (90th percentile) achieve. Then, move your finger across horizontally until it intercepts the red band (5th percentile). You can see that students in the red band finally achieve that same RIT score of 198 at the beginning of 10th grade, some eight years later.

If you repeat the exercise measuring horizontally from one band just to the one below it, you can see that there is about a year of growth between each band at second, third, and fourth grade with only a few exceptions.

Students who start ahead have an easier time staying ahead in school. Furthermore, top band students typically gain an additional two to three months and lower band students typically lose two to three months of reading growth during the summer.

There is another subtle advantage. High band students have to make only a year of growth each year, with no catch-up growth. But reading growth slows at every pathway in middle school and slows yet again at high school. That is, while the vertical distance between the paths remains fairly constant, the *horizontal distance* increases at middle school and again at high school. This means that it takes longer for students to achieve the same point of proficiency as students in the path above them. What was a year separation between the pathways in elementary school becomes one and one-half years in middle school and two to three years in high school.

And finally, the extended bands show the range of achievement on finishing. Finishing ahead is paramount, because where your child finishes largely determines his access to post-secondary education and training opportunities.

The twelve-and-a-half-mile event we call kindergarten through high school is in fact a pre-qualifying race. Where your child finishes determines which post-secondary opportunities she qualifies for.

You may want your child to attend a four-year university, but the limited number of available seats for freshmen results in a selection process based on preparation. There are 1.2 million freshman seats in our four-year universities but an average of

> *Finishing ahead is paramount, because where your child finishes largely determines his access to post-secondary education and training opportunities.*

3.7 million students at each age from birth through age eighteen. At birth, your child's odds of enrolling in a four-year university are one in three (Fig.2.4). To rephrase this message conversely, two out of every three children will **not** be able to enroll in a four-year university directly after high school. These proportions have changed very little over the last 35 years.[6]

Where you live is also a factor in this equation. Students in certain states have greater (or lesser) access to higher education. Figure 2.5 shows the odds of enrolling in a four-year university depending on the

---

[6] The percentage of enrolled freshmen in four-year universities in 1970 was 29.8% calculated from data in U.S. Bureau of the Census, *Historical Statistics of the United States: Colonial Times to 1970, Part 1*, p. 383, Series H, 700-715.

Figure 2.4 National probability at birth of enrolling in a four-year university directly out of high school.[7]

Total number of freshman seats
available at four-year universities   1,277,700

Number of students at each grade level   3,752,200

Odds at birth of your child enrolling as
a freshman in a four-year university   One-in-three (1:3)

Figure 2.5 State probability at birth of enrolling in a four-year university directly out of high school.[8]

1:5   in Nevada, California, Arizona, Alaska, Wyoming, and Mississippi
1:4   in Texas, Washington, New Jersey, Florida, Hawaii, and New Mexico
1:3   in Maryland, Illinois, Oregon, Oklahoma, Arkansas, Missouri, Michigan, and Connecticut
1:2.5 in South Carolina, Idaho, Alabama, North Carolina, Ohio, Minnesota, Tennessee, Colorado, Kansas, Virginia, Georgia, Maine, and Kentucky
1:2   in New York, Louisiana, Nebraska, Iowa, Wisconsin, Utah, New Hampshire, Delaware, Pennsylvania, Montana, South Dakota, Indiana, Massachusetts, and West Virginia
1:1.4 in North Dakota and Vermont
1:1.1 in Rhode Island

---

[7] These odds are calculated using the actual freshmen admitted and enrolled in four-year universities as the numerator and the average number of eighth grade students in the U.S. Department of Education Common Core Data base retrievable from http://www.nces.ed.gov/ ccd/bat/ from 2001 through 2006 as the denominator. The number of enrolled freshmen is calculated using 2004 data reported in the U.S. News and World Report, *Ultimate College Guide 2006* (Napier, IL: Sourcebooks, Inc., 2005).

[8] See Appendix B for a by-state breakdown of enrolled students and available freshman seats.

state you live in. Students are allowed to apply to schools in other states, but the high cost of out-of-state tuition may restrict your child's choice of university.

So who gets the seats? You can see the answer in the percentage of students in each of the six colored achievement bands. They are those in the lighter left area of each color band (Fig. 2.6).

If your child is in the top 10% (top one-half of the dark-blue path), she can attend a four-year university if she wants and 98% of students like her do.[9] Her higher achievement translates into higher ACT and SAT scores.[10] After the top half of the dark blue band, the percentage of students who enroll in a four-year university drops precipitously for each lower achievement band:

- 63% of those in the lower dark-blue band (80th to 89th percentiles)
- 44% of those in the blue band (60th to 79th percentiles)
- 25% of those in the green band (40th to 59th percentiles)
- 12% of those in the yellow band (20th to 39th percentiles).

In fact, few students in the three lowest achievement paths even bother taking the SAT or ACT. Given their achievement levels, there are few university seats available. Community colleges, a more likely postsecondary training opportunity, rarely require the ACT or SAT.

---

[9] Ninety-eight percent of those enrolling as freshmen at four-year universities report being in the top 10%. Percentages of each reading achievement band thereafter are based on class standing of enrolled college freshmen students using 2004 data reported in the U.S. News and World Reports, *Ultimate College Guide, 2006 Edition* (Napier, IL: Sourcebooks, Inc., 2005). Where universities did not report the high school class standing of their incoming freshmen, both class standing and freshman enrollment of those universities were removed from the calculations. Enrollment by band was derived from the data points available from the 90th, 75th and 50th percentiles.

[10] Until recently, nearly all major colleges used the scores from either the ACT or SAT to compare the academic performance of students. The ACT is a 3.4 hour test, costs $31-$46 and has a 1-16 point range on each of the math and reading portions of its tests. A majority of college-bound students take the SAT on the east and west coasts and in Texas. A majority of students take the ACT in the interior states, a total of 1,300,000 nationwide in 2006. The current SAT is called the SAT Reasoning Test, is four hours long, and costs $45. It has a 200-800 point range on both the math and critical reading portions of the test. Recently it added a writing section.

Students in the *top half* of the dark-blue band will score between 1250 and 1600 on the SAT and between 27-36 on the ACT. The achievement difference between the 90th percentile and the 10th percentile eventually translates into more than a 15-point difference on the language and math portion of the ACT and nearly an 800-point difference on the language and math portion of the SAT.

See Chapter 19 for a way to use the achievement bands prior to high school to approximate future SAT and ACT college entrance scores.

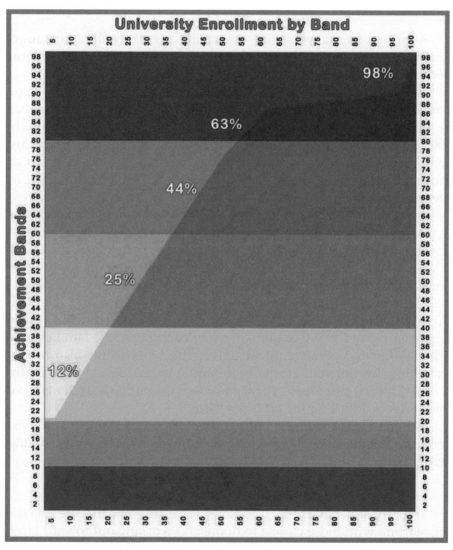

Figure 2.6. Percentage of students enrolled in a four-year university the year following high school by achievement band.

Pause to Think About It

At birth, your baby has one chance in three of enrolling in a four-year university after graduating from high school, with some variation depending on the state you live in.

However, by kindergarten, the odds change. If your child begins kindergarten in the top half of the dark-blue band—and assuming that he stays there—his new odds of university enrollment are virtually 100%. If he's an average student in the middle of his class, operating competently at grade level (green path), his chances of getting one of those college freshman seats have dropped to 25%. If he's operating in the red and orange potentials, his odds drop nearly to 0%.[11] These percentages also vary slightly from year to year. When more students in the upper pathways are accepted and enroll in a four-year university, fewer seats are available for students in the lower pathways. Conversely when students in the lower bands take more of the seats, fewer seats are available to upper-band students.

There are exceptions for the wealthy, noteworthy, and talented. Private schools generally find room for full-tuition students whose parents can pay $40,000 or more per year or those whose families may bring status and prestige. Most university departments also recruit exceptionally talented students in single areas like science, math, writing, sports, and music. Perhaps 10% of the nation's students have these factors adjusting the odds for them.

But you've just read the house odds for perhaps 90% of students, controlled by the ratio between four-year university seats and incoming students.

Some Frequently Asked Questions

You probably have some questions. Here are some that are asked a lot, starting with those closest to home and working out toward large social issues.

1. My children are already in grade school and middle school. Is it too late for them to catch up? It's never too late. Human beings really are lifelong learners, from birth to death. You can make a difference starting now.

---

[11] Naturally, the odds are lower for enrolling in better universities and higher for getting into less competitive universities.

2. **We're not rich. We can't afford fancy educational toys or private tutors. What can we do?** You're going to love this answer because it's the best news of all. It takes little money especially in the early years. You can do this job with time—parental time—to optimize your child's learning potential. It takes consistent time and it takes systematic time. The tools of learning are readily available and inexpensive. Your child learns best in the context of trusting and respectful relationships, frequent and positive interactions, and a loving and safe environment. Money helps but it's more about spending time than money.

3. **I don't want to turn education into a grim race—my child against every other child in her class—or turn into a nag as a parent.** Then you'll like our first rule, in the birth-to-five chapters. "It has to be fun!" Children are born learning, they love to learn, and they love their parent's undivided attention. It is their life-task to understand how their world works and how to manage it. Parents, by their positive actions and attitudes, infuse their child with a lifelong zest and quest for knowledge.

4. **I love children and oppose depersonalizing them into sets of numbers and statistics.** Adults who love children work to improve individual learning as well as the systems which create that learning. Numbers and statistics are the tools that baseline and indicate individual and system growth. So adults who care about children also care about statistics. It is the new data about early childhood growth and brain development that is driving new learning strategies. The birth to five frameworks I discuss let you choose activities based on the needs, interests, and temperament of your child, along with your family's values and culture. It's the most personalized learning environment possible.

5. **Why haven't I heard any of these facts before?** You are not alone. At my seminars, the superintendents sit on one side of the aisle with their arms folded saying, "I'm not disputing the data, but if this were so, I should have heard about it before now." On the other side of the aisle sit the early childhood specialists and kindergarten teachers who say to them, "Where have you been for the last decade?" and "Come to my classroom if you want to see the five-year range." Until recently, the assessments of most testing organizations, with the exception of the NWEA, could not accurately measure students two or three years below and two years above grade level.

6. **If everybody is working to get their child achieving as far above grade level as possible, won't this just inflate the achievement**

levels so we're right back where we started? Yes, 100% effort by 100% of parents would raise achievement levels everywhere. What a wonderful problem that would be! The United States would be internationally competitive. But the cold reality is that, for the next couple of decades, your child will be functioning inside our current system defined by these six achievement bands. If you are going to match her achievements to her ambitions and potential, you will have to work inside this system.

7. **It seems really unfair that the handful of parents who know this information can work the system to their advantage. Don't we believe in equality of opportunity?** There's no question that the American education is democratic, idealistic, and inspiring. There's also no question that it could work much better. But fixing the system isn't the job this book is trying to tackle.[12] My job here is to provide equality of information and help make it work for your child. That is where you as parents come in.

In Conclusion

As a concerned parent, you've likely already jumped ahead to the logical conclusion of making sure the probabilities are in your child's favor. And that's what the rest of the book is about:

- Starting your child in the highest pathway possible at kindergarten (chaps. 3-12), and
- Maintaining and improving his relative position each year during elementary school (chaps. 13-16), middle school (chaps. 17-20), high school (chap. 21), and finally,
- Matching your child's interest, finances, and abilities to all of his post-secondary training opportunities. Some certification programs, trade, technical and community college degrees may actually be more appropriate and cost-effective than four-year liberal arts programs (chaps. 22-23). Four-year universities need to pass the same matching criteria (chap. 24).

When you understand the probabilities, you give your child her best chance of an appropriate, meaningful education.

---

[12] Books in which we have tackled the job of system reform include *The 90% Reading Goal* (Kennewick, WA: New Foundation Press, 1998), *Delivering on the Promise* (Kennewick, WA: New Foundation Press, 2004), and *Annual Growth for All Children, Catch-Up Growth for Those Who Are Behind* (Kennewick, WA: New Foundation Press, 2007). Each is co-authored by Lynn Fielding, Nancy Kerr, and Paul Rosier.

CHAPTER THREE

READY! FOR KINDERGARTEN

"Getting your child ready for kindergarten is the indispensable first step in getting him or her ready for college."
—Paul Rosier, Ed.D., Executive Director,
Washington Association of School Administrators

So, how do you make sure that your child begins kindergarten on the dark-blue path? One way is to pay someone to do it for you. Nannies with early childhood education training. Exceptional child care. Montessori academies using a time-tested curriculum. Pricey pre-schools. Continually enriched language, social, and problem solving environments.

The other approach is to do it yourself. You and your spouse can identify the outcomes, figure out the steps, gather the most effective materials, divide up the work, and dive in.

Most parents use a common-sense combination of the two approaches, consistently reading to, talking with, and interacting with their child from birth to age five, and supplementing their own efforts with a high-quality pre-school at age three and/or four.

Whether you are going to outsource the job, do it yourself, or use a combination of approaches, you need a clear understanding of the process. You need some sense of the level of commitment that is required for the different achievement bands. And you need to understand and aim for the specific skills and abilities that characterize the level at which you want your child to enter kindergarten. Figure 3.1 shows the green (grade-level) goals for an entering kindergartener.

Incoming Kindergarten Targets

Letters and Sounds
1. Speaks fluently and in complete sentences with a vocabulary of about 5,000 words.
2. Recognizes and names 10-15 alphabet letters and their sounds.
3. Hears and repeats beginning and ending sounds in words.

Math
4. Counts in order from 1 to 20.
5. Recognizes numbers and quantities to 10.

Social
6. Settles into new groups or situations.
7. Concentrates on a task for 5 minutes.

Bi-lingual
8. Comes to school speaking English, if other languages are spoken at home.

Figure 3.1. Major Incoming Kindergarten Targets (green path) calibrated at the 50th percentile and at grade level. These skills are not legal requirements for entering kindergarten. Rather they are "targets" and benchmarks to aim for as you guide your child's cognitive and social-emotional development.

Notice the focus on skills that support reading and math. Reading is the fundamental academic skill your child will use to acquire her education. Eighty-five percent of her curriculum will appear in words: textbooks, whiteboards, handouts, and computer screens. She will use words to transcribe information into class notes, take spelling tests, and write reports. Reading is critical in math acquisition as well. There are far more words than numbers in even simple math books.

Figure 3.1 shows the eight basic skills an average kindergartener should have on entrance. In turn, each of these areas has three to five sub-goals, a total of 25 in all. How can you help your child acquire them?

Chapter 5 describes development from birth to age one, beginning with the 25 age level targets your baby can typically achieve by the time he turns one. The targets are grouped by the kinds of activities that you can use for teaching them.

- Reading and writing (targets 1-4)
- Listening and speaking (targets 5-8)
- Visual matching and naming (targets 9-15)
- Math and reasoning (targets 16-20)
- Social and emotional development (targets 21-25)

Each chapter describes activities you can play and tools you can use so your child will acquire each of the skills. The corresponding number or numbers appear in brown italics after the paragraph describing the activity that teaches the target. Each chapter concludes with a skill continuum to help you observe whether your child has mastered the needed skills. This simple assessment parallels the targets and also includes skills for one year ahead. By referring back to the age level targets, you can see the goal for the activities.

Each of the birth-to-five chapters is organized in the same manner to simplify the steps. More importantly, the chapters are written in your child's voice. He will describe the learning activities, how each activity will occur for him from his point of view, and what he will learn. Each succeeding chapter follows the same pattern of targets, learning activities, and skill assessments.

The targets and assessments are the backbone of this approach, and have been developed by The Children's Reading Foundation® for its READY! for Kindergarten program.[1] I have reordered and occasionally reworded them (with permission), and suggest that they may be the best birth-to-five benchmarks currently in existence. They are, however, 50th percentile benchmarks. Years from now, there may be really good 90th percentile and 70th percentile benchmarks for children at ages one, two, three, and four. However, until that occurs, the most reasoned approach is to use READY!'s 50th percentile targets and accelerate your child's growth a little each year so that she achieves the targets a year ahead of normal growth (blue band), or two years ahead of schedule (dark-blue band) by the beginning of kindergarten. Each chapter will suggest an appropriate rate of acceleration.

The daily implementation of this program centers around reading aloud 20 minutes a day with an additional 5 to 10 minutes spent in purposeful play.

---

[1] In the interests of full disclosure, I freely admit my bias as a co-founder and current director of this organization.

Reading Aloud 20 Minutes a Day

Reading aloud with your child at least 20 minutes every day from birth transfers the patterns of formal language, grammar, and a fairly complex vocabulary to your child. It introduces three times as many rare words as you use in normal conversation while at the same time reinforcing high-usage words.

> *The daily implementation of this program centers around reading aloud 20 minutes a day with an additional five to ten minutes spent in purposeful play.*

Reading aloud also develops phonemic awareness which is the ability to hear the little differences between sounds (such as "d" and "p"), comprehension, imagination, and general knowledge. With this enjoyable activity, your child's brain is literally wired to eventually learn to read. And reading is the gateway skill for nearly all subjects and opportunities in school.

The 20 minutes does not have to be all in one sitting or in one place, especially when your child is little. Repetition in a safe and secure environment are essential elements of how your young child learns best. Sitting on your lap and hearing you read her favorite book over and over again capitalizes on your child's optimal learning style. Make it the most important 20 minutes of your day.

Purposeful Play, Five to Ten Minutes a Day

Another 5 to 10 minutes are devoted to activities which teach the targets, weaving four kinds of simple learning activities—in addition to reading and writing—into everyday moments.

- *Visual matching and naming activities* help your child recognize alphabet letters and their sounds, numbers with their names and quantities, geometric shapes, and colors.

- *Listening and speaking activities* help your child use rapid learning centers in the brain by singing and chanting to memorize the ABC's and numbers to 30. These activities also develop the ability to hear the ending and beginning sounds in words, an essential first step to reading and communication.
- *Math and reasoning activities* enhance your child's aptitude for sorting and pattern recognition, as well as addition and subtraction concepts.
- *Social and emotional development* assure that your child will be ready to "settle in" at kindergarten, make friends and fully participate in a wide range of experiences.

Consider interweaving throughout these minutes the techniques developed by Glenn and Janet Doman to teach your tiny child to read and do math at ages one, two, and three. The Doman techniques are described in Chapter 11.

The READY! for Kindergarten curriculum is described at www.readyforkindergarten.org. Traditional presentations of each target and tool is available in age level kits which include DVDs with PowerPoint slides featuring embedded videos demonstrating essential activities.

From this point, I'm assuming that you and I have the same goal: for your child to enter kindergarten two years above grade level—starting in the dark-blue pathway. Not only are the college enrollment odds better, but your child's path each year is easier. All she has to do is make a year of growth each year to stay in the dark-blue band. When students start at a lower achievement level, they have to make the same annual growth plus they have to catch up the years that they are behind. Not an easy path. Not a lot of fun either.

Additional copies of Extraordinary Parents *are available by using the order form in Appendix A at page 228, online at www.readingfoundation.org or www.newfoundationpress.com, and at your local bookstore.*

Some students will struggle to learn in traditional public schools. These children may not start in the dark-blue band, but starting kindergarten as far ahead as possible will help them as well.

It is now time to introduce you to the three simple rules and four limitations in getting your child ready for kindergarten.

CHAPTER FOUR

THREE RULES AND FOUR LIMITATIONS

The Rules

Teaching your child between birth and age five is not "school at home." It's a natural process of discovery. Here are three simple rules for being your child's best and most effective teacher.

Rule 1. FUN.

It's got to be fun. You want your child to embrace learning as enjoyable, not as drudgery. The mind of a young child is vulnerable and shaped by the role models in his life. If, during the 20 minutes of reading aloud and the 5-10 minutes of purposeful play, it ceases to be fun for your child—STOP. If it ceases to be fun for *you*—STOP. If you're the sort of person who is always grumpy or never has fun with children, seek professional help. Your child deserves it. But when you stop, plan when you will start again.

Rule 2. DANCE.

Learning is an interactive dance. You start out leading with your child following. Later, your child may take the lead and you follow. Move with him into the energy of the moment, and then gradually reassume the lead. Keep harmony with the rhythm and pace he sets. Each child, each day, may have his own rate and energy for learning.

Rule 3. ADJUST.

Whatever target you teach will require skills either above or below your child's existing level. Adjust what you teach to her level. A good rule of thumb is that she should be successful at the activities at least 80% of the time. You will need to adjust the level of complexity and the amount of repetitions accordingly.

Remember to apply these three rules and you will do just fine.

The Limitations

Your child's learning has four limitations that you should know and respect.

1. Genetics. Your child's first limitation is that the fundamental wiring in his brain is controlled by his DNA. From conception onward, the basic structure of his brain develops with increasing complexity according to an internal architecture and timetable that is independent of anything you do.

An example of this layered complexity is myelination. Information processing and body control results from electrical impulses that pass along hundreds of millions of linked neurons in the brain. These neurons (they're axons actually) need to be insulated by a white substance called myelin, much as ordinary electrical wires need to be coated by plastic. Electric impulses passing through neurons not yet coated with insulation can be slowed, become unreliable, or simply short out before they get where they are intended to go.[1] Myelination begins before birth and proceeds in different parts of the brain at different times. It enables the sequential developmental process of hearing, vision, large and then small motor control, and later cerebral cortex control.

"Over the past decade, scientists have learned so much more about how young minds work. Children's brains develop much faster than educators ever imagined. Now we know the early years are the foundation for all future learning."
Nancy Kerr, National President,
The Children's Reading Foundation

In the construction industry, you can pressure the contractor to install the wall insulation or wiring earlier or faster. As a parent, there is nothing you can do to speed up the installation of myelin or the timing of any other deep-brain wiring. You must be patient. Putting more pressure on the child will not help.

2. IQ. The second constraint is similar to clock speed in computers. That is, some computer processers and brains work faster than others. In the 1990s, PCs advanced through a series of versions that processed

---

[1] Myelination is a process which starts before birth and continues, albeit at a slower rate into mid-life. Inadequate myelination contributes to or worsens disorders such as autism, attention deficit/hyperactivity disorders, and schizophrenia, as well as the high incidence of impulsive behaviors in some teenagers. "Myelination, a process uniquely elaborated in humans, arguably is the most important and most vulnerable process of brain development as we mature and age," says Dr. George Bartzokis, professor of neurology at UCLA's School of Medicine and director of the UCLA Memory Disorders and Alzheimer's Disease Clinic. Retrieved on October 26, 2008, from http://www.futurepundit.com/archives/003141.html.

the same information with increasing speed. In people the measure of the processing speed is called IQ or Intelligence Quotient. IQ is essentially the speed with which we and our children process verbal and mathematical information. IQ is an important factor, but parenting has a far greater impact on the initial starting band in kindergarten than IQ for most children.[2]

3.   **Parenting.** Your child's third constraint is the skill and creativity with which you can respond to her assessment information contained

> *The following chapters share age-sequenced skills modified from READY! for Kindergarten, a program developed by The Children's Reading Foundation. Parents and organizations interested in using these targets, tools, and training materials for parents or child care providers can contact READY! at (509) 396-7700, or visit its website at www.readyforkindergarten.org.*

in the targets at the chapter beginnings and in the skill continuums at their ends. During the young years, most of the assessments are observational so she does not even realize that her abilities are being measured. Little children love spending time with their favorite adults, but they do not particularly like being tested. The assessment information that you provide to your child should consistently be that you are delighted with her and with what she is learning and doing.

---

[2] READY! focuses on achievement, not IQ. Research supports gains of only 3-4 IQ points from early intervention, but such gains, while statistically significant, are invisible in the classroom. Be careful about exotic claims from early childhood interventions, such as 8-20 point IQ gains, returns of $4.37 for every dollar invested prior to age five from "sleeper" effects, social benefits accruing after age 16, and taking advantage of "developmental windows" before they "close." Proponents of these claims often miscite four studies in their support.

In the 1966 *Milwaukee Project* (35 black children deemed at risk based on impoverished economic circumstances and mothers' initial IQ below 70), initially reported gains of 25 IQ points; but these gains had dropped to 10 points by age 12. Achievement in reading and math for both control and intervention groups was inexplicably similar for both groups and, even more strikingly, showed the intervention group as one to two years behind by the fourth grade.

In the early 1970s *Abecedarian Project* (107 impoverished black children, whose mothers had IQs lower than 70), the IQ in the intervention group increased 18 points over the control group in the first six months, but thereafter declined to an increase of 8 points by age five despite interventions conducted six hours a day, five days a week, 50 weeks a year. IQ further declined to three-point gains by age eight.

The Infant Health and Development Program (1985-88) focused on low birth-weight babies and found that little sustained IQ effect resulted from the early intervention.

The Perry Preschool Project (123 impoverished black children with IQ scores of 70-85) showed an IQ increase of 11 points between the intervention and control group by kindergarten; but by second grade, the difference was slight and, by fourth grade, was virtually nonexistent. These studies are reviewed in a variety of places including John T. Bruner, *The Myth of the First Three Years* (New York: Free Press, 1999), 144-80.

Adjusting the activities and the repetitions to cater to your child's strengths and to strengthen his weaknesses is a very personalized effort. With practice and thoughtfulness, you will become smarter and better about adjusting what you do and how you do it. Yet the choice is not between optimal action or no action at all. Responsible parenting requires clear expectation and acting to reduce inconsistencies between those expectations and your child's behavior. In the long term, your child will be better off for having been directed down the right path, even with parenting techniques that may be short of perfect. Don't beat yourself up if you make mistakes. Fix them.

4. Choices. The fourth limitation is this. Of all of the potential abilities you could choose to develop in your child (extraordinary hearing, accelerated reflexes, or hitting a thrown object), you are choosing to focus on skills that will enhance your child's performance in our 21st-century education systems. This book limits its focus to the small set of activities that ramp up literacy, math, and social skills from the cradle to kindergarten, through the public schools and to college. Other perspectives and skills are valuable, but this book isn't about them.

And Now The Age Level Targets

Now it is time to explore the age level targets. Every child will reach every one of these targets. Your child will be no different. Some children will reach the goals earlier, and some will reach them later. Timing matters. In reaching the targets earlier, you are using the same strategies as professional elementary school teachers to advance your child's early development.

The age level target chapters use the voice of your child to address Mommy, Daddy, and "you." As elsewhere, grandparents and other caregivers should read themselves into these passages as well.

CHAPTER FIVE

BIRTH TO ONE

"From the simplest cell to the most complex organism, a new life unfolds in one of two ways: it either defends itself against a hostile environment or it opens, expands, and embraces its world. It does not do both at the same time and its environment is the primary driver of that decision."
—Bruce Lipton, Ph.D.,
Author of the *Biology of Belief,*
2006 Best Science Book of the Year

I am your child, and I am born learning.[1] My brain is like a little sponge absorbing all the sounds and sights, emotions and intonations of those around me. I learn best through repetition and imitation. I may not understand it all. I may not be able to reproduce it immediately; but within a few hours of birth, I am watching you and am working purposefully to emulate your simple face, tongue, and lip movements.[2] Model for me this year what you want me to do when I am one and two. Sing the songs, chant the numbers, say the nursery rhymes, and use the colors, numbers, and positional ("up," "across") words that you want me to learn. I am absorbing the grammar, vocabulary, inflection, and the happy (or upset) energy of the back-and-forth social interactions I see and hear through the filters of my own little personality.

---

[1] This chapter and those that follow are drawn and adapted from the READY! for Kindergarten curriculum, used by permission. "I am your child, and I am born learning" is the first sentence in the excellent series of videotapes available from Parents' Action for Children at its website: http://iamyourchild.org.

[2] Alison Gopnik, Andrew N. Meltzoff, and Patricia K. Kuhl, *The Scientist in the Crib: What Early Learning Tells Us about the Mind* (New York: HarperCollins, 1999), 29.

READY! for Kindergarten

Reading & Writing

1	Seeing Clearly	My eyes smoothly follow an object, tracing an "H" and "cross" (+) in the air." I focus near, then far.
2	Comprehending Books	I hear books read to me for 20 minutes a day, perhaps in five minute segments.
3	Knowing Print Concepts	I point to a book during story time. I know if pictures are right side up.
4	Copying, Tracing, Printing	I hold a writing tool in my fist and scribble.

Listening & Speaking

5	Singing, Chanting, Rhyming	I am sung to daily, including ABC and number songs. I like simple nursery rhymes and poems.
6	Saying Sounds in Words	I react differently to various sounds.
7	Hearing Spoken Words	I hear my parents speak to me, often using "parentese," about 30 times an hour.
8	Developing Verbal Skills	I babble/vocalize using different sounds, volume, and inflection to convey meaning.

Visual Matching & Naming

9	Naming Colors	I hear my parents say the names of colors during the day.
10	Matching Letter Shapes	I see interesting shapes around my crib and home. I recognize the faces of my family.
11	Naming Letter Shapes	(None for this age)
12	Saying Letter Sounds	I watch my parents' mouths as they emphasize a letter sound.
13	Recognizing Sight Words	I hear my parents naming common objects.
14	Matching Number Shapes	(None for this age)
15	Geometric Shapes	I play with objects in a variety of shapes.

Math & Reasoning

16	Counting	I hear my parents count out loud during the day.
17	Sorting Items	After eight months, I may group a few objects by color or type with assistance.
18	Adding and Subtracting	I understand the concept of "more" food and play.
19	Making Patterns	My parents play predictable games with me using patterns (e.g., 3 kisses; 2 claps).
20	Spatial Relationships	I hear simple position words, such as up/down, in/out.

Social & Emotional

21	Relating to Others	I feel connected to family and caregivers by their eye contact, words, and gentle touching.
22	Attention Span	I focus for a short time when others interact with me.
23	Following Directions	I enjoy turn-taking games, like peek-a-boo.
24	Taking Responsibility	I am very dependent on my family. I may cooperate during routines.
25	Emotional Well-Being	I feel secure because my needs for food, comfort, love, and care are being met. I show self-soothing strategies.

I do not stay tiny very long. In the first 12 months, I will almost triple in weight. My eating, sleeping, and diaper-changing patterns will finally settle down, only to be interrupted by the pain of teething. Roller-coaster hormones and systematic sleep deprivation may take you, my mild and playful parents to the edge of your tolerance levels. So keeping your long-term goals for me in view is really important.

Think of the first 12 months as increasing my ability to see, hear, reason, and interact with others. Think of these targets and the simple activities to achieve them as baby steps that increase in complexity each month for me. You will be able to fit most of these exercises into our everyday routines, because it is important for me to experience them with great regularity. I will not learn these skills the first time; but if you repeat them daily, I will have heard them hundreds of times by the end of my first year.

I will call you "Mommy" and "Daddy" and the rest of the time I will say "you" because I want to include both of you.

On the left-hand page are the targets for my first 12 months. At the end of this chapter is the READY! for Kindergarten Skills Continuum to help you assess where I am, how successful you have been, and how you might adjust your efforts to better help me. Activities to achieve these targets are developed in the following pages.

Physical Development: Eyes and Ears

My vision at birth is limited. I distinguish between faces and between bright and dark. My eyes focus best at 8 to 10 inches. This just happens to be the distance from my eyes to your face when you hold me in the crook of your arm. I start to follow moving objects at 8 to 12 weeks. I watch your face when you talk to me at 10 to 12 weeks. I notice and watch my hands at 12 to 16 weeks. I start looking for the toys I drop at 32 to 38 weeks.

During my first six weeks of life, I move my eyes by moving my head. Then the six muscles in each of my eyes strengthen to move with increasing fluidity. I track the brightly colored object or even my pacifier that you use to make slow, wide "H" movements and slow, wide crosses in the air. You watch the movement of my pupil in each eye, checking that both eyes are moving smoothly and simultaneously. You practice with me daily until they do. You tell me that my head will move very little by the time I am one. "Lazy eye," where one of my eyes lags behind the other when I am tracking objects, is a fairly common condition. It generally corrects itself with continued exercise, but it may require professional help if it continues after I am age two. *[1] The bracketed number indicates that the preceding paragraph(s) or sentence explains activities that correspond to an age-level target, in this case Target #1. This practice will continue throughout this and the next chapters.*

Daddy checks each eye separately by gently covering one of my eyes with his hand. If I am blind or have lost vision in one eye and it is not corrected in the first two years, my "good eye" could commandeer all of the brain cells in the back of my skull that control vision. If this happens, even when the condition is repaired, my "bad" eye still won't be able to see. Daddy also checks for pinkness, redness, and lots of tearing. You check carefully for irritation when I constantly rub my eyes. The color of my eyes may change as I get older but it usually stabilizes by the time I am one.

Visual Matching

As I grow older, my ability to focus expands about a foot a week until I can focus well at 10 feet at three or four months. I see large objects better than small ones and rounded corners rather than sharp ones. I look at the sheets of paper with wide, black horizontal lines and vertical lines that you put around my crib. I like the bull's eye, too! *[10]*

I love to see faces. Seeing faces triggers a response that lights up my new brain. Seeing my own face in a mirror helps me learn that I have a nose, eyes, and mouth just like you do. Playing peek-a-boo delights me. Not only do I get to look at faces, I get to practice patterns. By six months, I am entranced by a plastic-covered picture album of my family. When you buy mobiles for me, please check to see how they look when I am flat on my back (where I usually am) and not how they look to you from beside my crib. *[10]*

My vision is critical to reading. Eighty-five percent of my future public school curriculum will be delivered by reading. It will be far easier to read and learn to read if my ability to see is as close to perfect as possible.

Listening and Speaking

My hearing is well developed at birth, more than most of my other senses. I will turn toward a noise because the sound reaches one ear a fraction of a second before it reaches the other. I immediately recognize Mommy's voice, and I respond to nursery rhymes that you read or sang to me while I was in the womb. *[5]* I am startled by loud, sudden noises. [6] In fact, really loud noises and blaring music can permanently damage my delicate hearing.

My auditory learning process is simple. You look at the targets that involve hearing and

My hearing is complicated. My ability to hear varies by ear. If there is a problem, its location is important (whether outer or middle ear, inner ear, cranial nerve, or central auditory processing disorder of the brain). These variables may affect the range, frequency and nature of any hearing loss. See www.asha.org/public/hearing/testing/assess.htm.

speaking for the next three years. Then you say, sing, read, and chant each day the things that you want me to be able to say, sing, read, and chant. You sing the ABC song to me daily, chant the number song, and play some soft, complex music daily. Daddy recites the 6 to 10 simple nursery rhymes that you want me to know by the time I enter kindergarten. [5] You show me and name common objects, [13] saying the color of many of them. [9]

You both talk to me regularly in "parentese" (intuitively speaking softly and sweetly, emphasizing the vowels which are the hardest sounds for me to hear). [7] I watch how Daddy's mouth moves to make the sounds. [12] Me, I just babble and vocalize, experimenting with different sounds, volume, and inflection in my attempt to be understood. [8]

Mommy looked online and found out how to sign some of my favorite words. Now she is teaching me and I love it. At 10 months, I can do simple hand gestures and signing is an easy way for me to

First Signing Words: *more, eat, milk, drink, bath, bed, book, yes, cold, hot*

communicate my basic wants. My frustration diminishes when I can communicate concepts such as more, eat, milk, drink, bath, bed, book, yes, cold, and hot.

Reading and Writing

You read to me while I am snuggled in the crook of your arm and gazing up at your face. You started reading aloud to me when you started talking to me, the day I was born. My attention span may initially last only a few minutes so dividing the reading time into smaller, more frequent sessions makes sense. [2]

Within a short time, I will become more active, pointing to the book, registering a protest if the pictures aren't right side up, and wanting to feel and handle the book and chew on it. By eight months, I may prefer

turning pages to listening to you; and by a year, I will point to pictures that I know. I like one-to-a-page pictures because too much detail is incomprehensible to me. When I gaze intently at one page, you give me as much time as I want. You know that reading is about engaging me, not about covering lots of ground. [3] Near age one, I can grip a large crayon in my fist and scribble, making random marks on paper. I love "painting" with water, making large, exuberant brush strokes. [4]

Math and Reasoning

I hear Daddy counting aloud. [16] You use spatial-relation words like "up," "down," "in," and "out" repeatedly. [20] I will not learn these words the first time, but I will by the five hundredth or thousandth time. Daddy counts my "one nose" and "one, two eyes" and my "one, two, three, four, five little toes." You kiss and tickle me and clap in patterns of twos and then threes, so that even when you wait after two kisses, I know that there is still one more coming.☺ Patty-cake and peek-a-boo are interactive, but they are also about mathematical patterns. [19]

I have learned the important mathematical concept of "more"— more food, more hugs, more time with my mommy and daddy. [18]

You bring home really interesting toys. You trace their shape with my finger saying, "This is a square block," and "This is a round ball with some red and yellow and blue on it." In the early months, I'm just trying to pick the toys up and move them around. [15] By eight months, I may be able to group a few of them by their color or their shape with a lot of coaching. [17]

But the really important thing during the first year is that Mommy and Daddy are

> *READY! for Kindergarten is a complete program of tools, training, and activities to do at home with your child based on the targets. Learn more at* www.readyforkindergarten.org.

emotionally bonding with me, and I am bonding with them.

Social and Emotional: Bonding *[21] - [25]*

The Dance. The early years are when you learn to dance with me, the wonderful back-and-forth cooing, the tiny eye flirtations, the leading and following, the taking turns, and generally having a wonderful time. Part of the dance is first mirroring my emotions when I am sad or hurt or very happy and then responding to them. This first year is when you lay the foundation for my social adeptness and create long-lasting emotional connections with me.

More than 40,000 of my heart's cells are neurons clustered in ganglia forming axon-dendrite connections just like in my brain. With this "little brain" in my heart, I process information independently of my brain or nervous system. It learns, remembers, feels, senses, and sends messages. Complex interdependent communications exist between my heart neurons (which also extend throughout my body to my organs and muscle tissue) and to the part of my brain affecting my perceptions, mental processes, feeling states, and performance in profound ways. My heart connections are important.[3]

> *My Ten Emotions*
> *Happiness*
> *Distress*
> *Interest*
> *Sadness*
> *Anger*
> *Surprise*
> *Disgust*
> *Fear*
> *Embarrassment*
> *Shame*
> *www.talaris.org*

In addition, my heart also produces an electrical field about 60 times greater in amplitude and 5,000 times greater in strength than the electrical activity generated by my brain. The neurocardiologists suggest that my heart signal may affect your brainwaves. As we become more connected and emotionally coherent, we become more sensitive to the subtle electromagnetic signals sent by each other. That is why I like it when you hold me.

Body Language. You are learning to read me. This is good because we are going to spend a long time together. Our elaborate dance is far easier if you can read my "cues," anticipate my needs, and avoid the equivalent of stepping on my toes. I will learn to love you and form a lifelong attachment to you.

If you watch my eyes for the first five years, you will learn to read my emotional state at a glance. This is an especially useful skill to have when I am a teenager. My eyes, hands, head, and body movements telegraph my emotions to anyone who is observing.

---

[3] J. Andrew Armour and Jeffrey L. Ardell, eds., *Basic and Clinical Neurocardiology* (New York: Oxford University Press, 2004) vii.

Safe and Secure. My first year is when I learn that I am safe and loved and that the world is a secure place for me. When I am secure, nourishing blood with lots of oxygen in it floods the outer quarter-inch of my brain (cerebral cortex) where my higher-level thinking occurs. If I don't feel secure during this first year, I may learn that the world is an angry, frightening place that will hurt me. When I need to be prepared for pain, my blood flows concentrate near my brain stem where survival responses like my heart and breathing rates are controlled. After I have a frightening experience, it may take 40 minutes for significant amounts of blood to return to the outer levels of the brain where my higher-level thinking occurs.

A great investment for me and you at this age is a rocker-glider, the current version of an old-fashioned rocking chair. Rock me and stroke my head and back to soothe me. I like it and it teaches me how to soothe myself. This skill will be useful well into my elementary and middle school years.

Choose to be Happy.[4] It's hard for me to be contented and happy when either of you are angry. So please choose to be happy as much as possible.

Happiness is about choosing positive "self-talk." Self-talk is the endless chatter that goes on inside our brains. It mirrors how you define your world and defines mine as well. Self talk can be happy, playing out incidents of a healthy birth, your dreams for me, and cheerful relationships. Negative self-talk is consistently destructive, full of fear, replaying ugly fights, practicing angry statements, and reliving incidents of "not-good-enough." It makes negative self-images and negative behaviors stronger.

---

[4] The window for choosing happiness is tiny. In the first three- to six-tenths of a second between an "event" and Mommy or Daddy's response, you get to choose how to act. If that half-second passes without your making a conscious choice, then you probably react unthinkingly instead. The reaction is frequently negative—angry or impatient—and repetitive. You may blame how you are feeling on others, sometimes me. ☹ On the other hand, happiness is a choice which you generally make in that first fraction of a second. Almost no one blames someone else for their happiness. Except me, of course. I am deliriously happy because of my wonderful parents. ☺

It is easier for me to bond with a happy parent, so I need you to choose to be happy by replacing negative self-talk (if that's part of how you're currently treating yourself) with positive self-talk. Awareness of it, paying attention to it, and writing it down are the first steps to changing it. An unofficial emotional target may be for me to rarely hear angry arguing or yelling during my first 24 months.☺

Consider Breastfeeding.[5] Breastfeeding, for six months if not a full year, has numerous benefits. Experts have long known that breast-fed babies tend to have higher IQs than those who are not. They don't know why. Some suggest that the fatty acids present in breast milk result in better myelination in my brain.[6]

Inside my Brain. Other breaking news is what is going on inside my head. During my first year, my brain nearly triples in size—to about 70% of adult size. Waves of electrical energy pulse through my brain every second, creating new connections between my neurons. Today I cannot distinguish a single alphabet letter. Yet with your help and using a series of simple tools and activities, I will soon be processing impulses from my eyes, sending signals to my lungs to draw a breath, and telling my tongue to form certain shapes. These are the skills necessary to speak and to read aloud when I am older.

Daily Routines

Preparing me to start ahead in kindergarten is easier when the activities are embedded into our family lifestyle, using a series of everyday moments. Some elements of a daily routine might look like this:

Feed. Feeding, especially breastfeeding for Mommy and bottle-feeding for Daddy, is one of the best times to bond with me. It is a great time to be present and emotionally available for me, sweetly saying why you love me.

Touch. Bonding also occurs by touch—stroking my skin, hugging cheek to cheek, and even showering together.

---

[5] "Pedatricians and parents should be aware that exclusive breastfeeding is sufficient to support optimal growth and development for approximately the first six months of life and provides continuing protection against diarrhea and respiratory tract infection. Breastfeeding should be continued for at least the first year of life and beyond for as long as mutually desired by mother and child." American Academy of Pediatrics, "Breastfeeding and the Use of Human Milk – Policy Statement," *Pediatrics* 115, no. 2 (February 2005): 496-506. Retrieved on February 12, 2009, from http://aappolicy. aappublications.org/cgi/content/full/pediatrics;115/2/496.
[6] Karen Prior and Gayle Pryor, *Nursing Your Baby* (New York: Collins, 2005) 99, 141, 207. See Chapter 4 for a definition of myelination.

Check. Using my pacifier and tracing an 18-inch high "H" and a "cross" in the air is a good time to watch and check my eyes. Routinely check my eyes and ears for good health.

Scaffold. Changing my diaper gives you a chance to "scaffold." When you scaffold, you ask a question, get a smile, a nod, or a grunt, and then provide an answer. You ask how many toes and fingers I have and then you count them for me. Just talking to me is good, too. Talk about the blankets, crib, diaper, pacifier, decorations in my room, and your day. Sing the ABC and number songs. Say nursery rhymes.

Read. I like it when you read to me several times a day, holding me in your arms or lap. As I get stronger, I will try to hold the book and put it in my mouth. By 12 months, I'll be turning pages.

Show. While I am lying in my crib on my back, draw my attention to the brightly colored mobile and crib shapes displayed around me. Say the colors as I look at them.

Talk. Take me on an "object walk" through the house. Name common objects and their colors as we stroll along together.

Sing. Your voice is magic to me. I like it when you sing and rock me or we dance around the room. When you sing the ABC song, I know I will have a dry diaper by the time you're done. When you are pushing me in a stroller or I am riding in a car seat remember that I can't see you. Keep talking or play engaging songs in the car and sing along with them so I can hear your voice. Doing this capitalizes on my well-developed hearing.

The skills continuum, featured on the following page, lists the milestones I should achieve by the *end* of my first year. It also shows you what is ahead for me next year.

READY! Skills Continuum

	Birth to Age One	Age One to Two
Reading, Writing, Listening, & Speaking		
Listening to Books	I listen to you read 20 minutes a day to me in short segments. I help turn pages.	I read 20 minutes a day in short segments. I answer "Where is" questions by pointing.
Rhyming	I am sung to daily (ABC and number song) and hear nursery ryhmes and poems.	I sing parts of ABC and number songs with others. I hear nursery ryhmes.
Hearing Language	I hear my parents speak to me about 30 times an hour using "parentese."	I hear my parents speak to me about 30 times an hour.
Spoken Words	I babble using sounds, volume, and pitch.	I use single-word speech, learn two-four words a day, and imitate some animal sounds.
Visual Matching & Naming		
Colors	I hear my parents say the names of colors during the day.	I hear the names of colors. I can point to three colors; yellow, blue, and red.
Letter Shapes	I recognize familiar faces. I see interesting shapes around my crib and home.	I see my first initial everywhere at home. I match three shapes: curves, lines, and V's CURVE LINE V ⌒ I V
Sounds in Words	I react differently to various sounds.	I repeat the last word in rhymes with assistance.
Letter Sounds	None at this age.	
Number Shapes	None at this age.	I can match number shapes 1 to 3.
Math & Reasoning		
Geometric Shapes	I play with objects in a variety of shapes.	I play with shape toys, although I seldom match correctly.
Counting	I hear counting aloud.	I hear counting of one, two, and three.
Patterns	My parents play predictable activities with me using patterns (e.g., 3 kisses; 2 claps).	I recognize sequence words "before" and "after." I arrange objects in lines.
Social & Emotional Development		
Relating to Others	I use eye contact, sounds, and gestures.	I feel loved and safe when my parents respond quickly to me.
Attention Span	I focus on others for a short time.	I focus briefly on tasks.
Follows Instructions	I enjoy interactive games (peek-a-boo).	I am beginning to obey one-step directions (e.g., Please get your coat.")
Emotional Well-Being	I show self-soothing strategies.	I begin to control my impulses. I show emotions with my face, words, gestures.

CHAPTER SIX

AGE ONE TO TWO

"What people call genius is little more than the ability to focus on the same problem for twenty years."

—Albert Einstein

I am leaving the emotional cocoon of my first year. Until a few months ago, this bubble encompassed only me, my mommy and daddy, and my siblings. This year I am into "things"—things I can now clearly see, things I can grasp and hold, things I can crawl and toddle to, and things I can put in my mouth, shake, and throw down to the floor.

Physical Development: Eyes and Ears

Daddy continues to practice with me. You trace an "H" and "cross" in the air with me daily for a couple of months until my eyes track smoothly. You check my ability to focus on my pacifier when it is close, about 10 inches away from my eyes, and when it is far way, about 10 feet away from me. [1_]¹

Mommy points out visual details in the objects around me, especially things that are red, blue, and yellow. [9] I am becoming a little "copy cat," mimicking your gestures, smiles and trying to say your words.

I am learning by imitation from thousands of gentle repetitions of the activities I see in a safe, supportive environment. When Mommy

---

¹ Numbers in brackets next to activities correspond to the number in the left-hand column of the age level targets charts.

READY!
for Kindergarten

Reading & Writing

1	Seeing Clearly	My eyes smoothly follow an object tracing an "H" and cross (+) in the air. I focus near, then far.
2	Comprehending Books	I hear and see books read to me for 20 minutes a day. I can answer "Where is…" questions by pointing.
3	Knowing Print Concepts	I point to three parts of a book: the book, page, picture. I help turn pages.
4	Copying-Tracing-Printing	I scribble up/down (14 mo.), then in circles (24 mo.).

Listening & Speaking

5	Singing, Chanting, Rhyming	I sing parts of ABC and number songs with others. I frequently hear nursery rhymes.
6	Saying Sounds in Words	I can say the last word in familiar rhymes, with assistance.
7	Hearing Spoken Words	I hear my parents speak to me abut 30 times an hour.
8	Developing Verbal Skills	I say one-two word sentences. I learn 2-4 words a day (16 months). I imitate some animal sounds.

Visual Matching & Naming

9	Naming Colors	I hear the names of colors. I can point to three colors: red, blue, yellow.
10	Matching Letter Shapes	I match three shapes: curves, V's, and lines.
11	Naming Letter Shapes	I see my first initial displayed around my home.
12	Saying Letter Sounds	I easily repeat vowel sounds.
13	Recognizing Sight Words	I point to familiar objects, if you ask me.
14	Matching Number Shapes	I match number shapes from 1 to 3.
15	Geometric Shapes	I play with shape toys, although I seldom match correctly.

Math & Reasoning

16	Counting	I hear my parents count objects (e.g., 1-2-3 crackers). They use numbers in everyday routines (e.g., 2 shoes, 3 stairs).
17	Sorting Items	I sort objects by color or size sometimes.
18	Adding and Subtracting	I understand more and none (all gone).
19	Making Patterns	I recognize simple sequence words like "before" and "after." I arrange objects in lines.
20	Spatial Relationships	I understand simple position words, such as up/down, in/out, over/under.

Social & Emotional

21	Relating to Others	I feel loved and safe because my parents respond promptly to my needs. They smile and cuddle me.
22	Attention Span	I can pay attention to what others are looking at or pointing to.
23	Following Directions	I am beginning to obey one-step directions (e.g., "Please get your coat.")
24	Taking Responsibility	I often cooperate during daily routines. I like to help.
25	Emotional Well-Being	I show a range of emotions with my face, words, gestures. I am beginning to control impulses.

points and names, I point and name although my lungs, voice box, tongue, and lips are still struggling to make all those exquisite sounds.

Things I may do that show my eyes are developing within a normal range include:
- *I use both hands together and individually.*
- *I visually steer my hands.*
- *I look for and identify pictures in books.*
- *I hold objects close to my eyes to inspect them.*
- *I point to objects or people using words like "look" and "see."*

—The Optometric Extension Program Foundation, www.oepf.org.

Visual Matching and Naming

Mommy and Daddy have started to play a game with colored cards with me. The cards are four inches by six inches. There is nothing on the cards, just the color. I sit on your lap. You put down a yellow card on a table or next to us on the bed and say,

"This card is yellow."

Then you put down two other cards, like another yellow card and the red card and you say, "Which of these cards is the same color as the yellow card?"

At first it was hard. I wasn't paying attention to the color. The cards were the same size and had the same shape, and there wasn't any real difference. Suddenly, when Mommy helps me by holding the cards up to other yellow things, I could see it and *I point* to the second yellow card. [9]

I was ecstatic! Mommy shrieked and gave me lots of hugs. Each time it got easier, and I got better and could point faster and more accurately. Daddy names the colors of lots of things now, so I hear colors all the time and am starting to see "color." Daddy and Mommy then used red as the target card, and when I could point to red, you started using blue, *introducing just one color at a time.* I still don't know what color is, but I know it when I see it.

Yesterday we had yellow day. Mommy gave me a yellow banana, dressed me in my yellow shirt, and put on her yellow shoes. We used our yellow bath towels. I point to yellow cars and yellow arches and everything else I see that is yellow.

After I got good at the color game, we started to play another game with the big cards. These cards had black spots on them. We played the game just like the color cards. Daddy would lay down a card with three black spots on it (half-inch round dots).

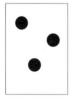

Then you lay down two more cards one with one dot and another with three dots and say, "Which of these cards is the same as the first card?"

Hard again. Very hard. All the dots were black. Then Daddy puts some Cheerios on the center of the dots, and suddenly I see more Cheerios and only one Cheerio. I am finally learning to see quantities. Amounts of things. [18] I think Cheerios and I will have a special relationship as I grow up. ☺

After I got good at the color and the "dots to three" game, we started to play another game with the big cards. We used cards that had black squiggles on them. At least, that's what they looked like to me. Daddy would lay down a card with a black squiggle on it.

3

Then you lay down two more cards each with different squiggles on them and and say, "Which of the these cards is the same as the first card?"

3   **1**

Again, I didn't know! So you point out the little differences—how the line on the first card was like just one of my fingers and how the lines on the other cards were more curved like an ear and he would point to the right one for me. Soon I started to see the difference between the squiggles and could point to it for myself. I don't know the names of the squiggles or what they mean, but my eyes are getting better at matching their shapes. It's like I am embedding little templates in my brain so I can match what I have seen in the past with what I am seeing now. [14]

We make shapes with my body. We make a "V" with my arms, an curve by holding my arms over my head and then arcing my whole body until my hands almost touch my toes, and a line by standing very straight and tall with my arms by my sides. By the time I am done, I can feel the difference between the line, the curve, and the "V." [10]

One of my favorite games is the *Mystery Bag*, which is always introduced with great fanfare. Daddy made two sets of a "curve," a "V," and a "line" from wood, and Mommy made a sturdy cloth bag.

You then show me the curve and give it to me to hold. I keep a copy of the "curve" (my target shapes) outside the bag so I can keep seeing and feeling it. You put the second curve into the Mystery Bag with a medium-sized rock. Then I put my hand into the bag and feel. Which one is the "curve?"

After a while, my fingers learn to feel the difference between the curve and the rock, and then later between the rock and the line, and last of all between the rock and the "V."

> *READY! for Kindergarten is a program of tools, training, and activities that support your child in reaching these targets. Age-level kits are shipped three times a year. www.readyforkindergarten.org.*

When this game becomes easier for me, you make it a tiny bit harder, putting three and four objects instead of two into the bag. I still get it, but it takes a little more time. Then you start adding similar objects like a toothbrush and a butter knife with the line. The Mystery Bag is one of my favorite games, especially with the hugs and kisses and happy words and laughing voices when I get it right. I like the celebrating.

This game helps my eyes see the differences as well. Although I don't know it, the touching is embedding in my brain the three shapes that occur almost everywhere and from which all the upper and lower-case alphabet letters can be made.

Mommy points out to me the curves on the corners of tables, soft seated swings at parks, the edge of my car seat, and the arches at McDonald's. I see lines on shirts and doorways. I see V's on roof lines and yield signs. I am starting to see these shapes everywhere. [10]

Mommy has taped up the first letter of my first name where it is easy to see but just out of reach by my high chair, on the refrigerator, and in my bedroom. You use four-inch high letters printed on six-inch tall cards. Dad holds me as we walk through the house, and I repeatedly point this letter out to him. Because I have seen this shape so many times, I learned it easily. Besides, it is the first letter of my favorite word in the whole world. [11] I also point to familiar objects. At first Daddy points to objects and says, "This is a bed. This is a window. This is a door." Now he says, "Where is the bed?" and I point to it. "Where is the window?" I point. "Where is the door?" I point again! [13]

By the way, I love these games. We always stop before I stop having fun or if I'm grumpy or distracted. It's never more than just five minutes anyway.

Listening and Speaking

My first words, besides "ma ma" and "da da," will occur near 12 months. In the six weeks after I produce my first word, I usually say 25 more words. I'll probably have a speaking vocabulary of 200 words by 16 to 24 months, adding 10-20 new words a day.[2] I use one-word sentences like "up" for "please pick me up," and "more" for "please give me more juice." [8]

Daddy recites lots of simple nursery rhymes to me, a vital first step as I distinguish between the tiny sounds that make up words and learn to say them myself. When Daddy asks,

> A fifteen-decibel hearing loss is enough to cause an academic impairment for a child Even if a child has normal hearing in one ear, but a hearing loss in another, the child is at 10 times greater risk for academic failure.

"Wouldjalikeadrinkavmilk?" he has used about 21 separate little sounds (phonemes) in a little over a second, each of which I must detect, match with previously learned sounds, and nod yes within another two seconds.

I like it when Mommy and Daddy speak slowly and distinctly to me and say the words very clearly, especially on the part of the alphabet song that goes "l, m, n, o, p." [5]   I am starting to hear the ending sounds which is one of the easiest of the phonemic awareness skills, and I can say the last word in familiar rhymes with a little help. [6]

---

[2] Learn more by checking out the Timeline at www.talaris.org.

Daddy sings the alphabet song and points to each of the letters on a long ABC strip lots of times each week. Mommy is saying many of the words she wants me to be able to say later. She is singing the songs and saying the nursery rhymes this year that she wants me to say next year. [5]

Sometimes we go on a "listening walk" outside to hear tiny sounds, like distant traffic, or insects, or the wind. She is careful to safeguard my hearing by avoiding loud noises (jets, jackhammers, boom boxes, barking dogs, car horns, TV volume, etc.), and takes my earaches very seriously.

While my speaking vocabulary may be very small, my recognition vocabulary is very large. I have taken the first step toward learning the 5,000 to 7,500 or so words I will know when I enter kindergarten. I will have heard 46 million words by kindergarten spoken directly to me. Some of my classmates won't be so lucky. They will arrive at kindergarten having heard only 26 million words spoken to them while still others will come having heard only 13 million words. Mommy talks to me 30 times an hour when I am awake, modeling the new research. [7][3]

It is especially useful when Mommy narrates our daily activities ("Now we're unfolding your socks"), asking questions ("Shall we put your sock on your right foot first?", tickling my foot), and scaffolds by asking questions and then "helping" me answer them ("Yes, on the right foot!"). Scaffolding will go on for a year or more until I can mostly answer questions by myself. It is like training wheels for bikes. Mommy uses "parentese," where she speaks slowly to me and emphasizes the vowels so I am now repeating the vowel sounds. [12] Parentese is not baby talk. Baby talk models the wrong thing for me to imitate because it changes the sounds of normal speech and grammar: "Oh, do you have pretty brown eyes?" not "Oh, does 'oo have pitty, pitty brown eyes?"

Reading and Writing

Every day Mommy and Daddy read to me 20 minutes, asking me "Where is . . .?" questions that I gleefully answer by pointing. You use big voices and little voices and whispers and your full-of-wonder-and-hope voices and questioning voices and sometimes even your singing

---

[3] Betty Hart and Todd R. Risley, *Meaningful Differences in the Everyday Experience of Young American Children* (Baltimore, MD: Paul H. Brookes Publishing, 1995), 198.

voices. You have more different voices when we read than at any other time! [2]

Reading time is good time because Mommy and Daddy hold me, and I get to snuggle, relax and chatter. I like to see the same book over and over again. Without even knowing it, I am learning to focus and extend my attention span. [22]

The books I like best have lots of repeated words and patterns so I can "chime in," such as Mother Goose rhymes and rhyming stories. Books I can touch and feel are ideal. I may gnaw on the pages, and even drop

books, pick them up in funny ways, and use both hands to turn pages. So sturdy, thick, cardboard pages let me learn how to handle books and keep them safe at the same time. I like interactive books with flaps or other moving parts which I may gently pull apart. Simple colorful illustrations and very short text are best for me. I don't understand pictures with lots of detail or long story plots. Wordless books inexplicably cost more than books with words, but you make up great stories to go along with the pictures. You get these book ideas at www.readingfoundation.org. [3]

"Children become readers on the laps of their parents."
Emile Buchwald

I can point to a book when you ask me. I can also point to the pages and the pictures. While we are on pointing, I love when Daddy plays the "Where is . . .? " game with me.

"Where is your nose?"

"Where are your toes?"

"Where are your blue (brown, green) eyes?"

Writing is really fun although I still don't quite understand why walls and floors are off limits but newspapers and paper bags are okay. I start at 12 months with a large half-inch thick crayon that I hold in my fist. I make scribbling patterns to begin with. At around 15 months, I start scribbling up and down. At 18 months, I scribble left and right. By 24 months, I can scribble round and round. [4]

Math and Reasoning

I hear Mommy and Daddy count everything–like my toes, my bites of food, and socks. You especially like to count from one to three. My favorite is when I hear Daddy count one-two-three blocks as you stack them just before I gleefully knock them down, which I know is my job. [16]

I am learning significant math concepts during meal times. I am learning that dessert comes *after* vegetables and *before* I get down from my high chair. [19] *More* is a particularly useful concept to know about dessert, and *all gone* is a very sad concept about cookies. [18]

I sometimes sort my blocks and clothing by color, with my parents help. [17]   I am still more interested in "experiencing" the socks which means feeling, tasting, smelling, and throwing them rather than sorting them. I play with shape toys and puzzles, although I seldom match the shapes correctly. [15]

We play another game with a plastic butterfly where the butterfly flies *up, down, in, out, over,* and *under* me. I hear my parents tell me where the butterfly is as I learn a few of the 40 positional prepositions that describe spatial relationships. [20]

When it's not fun, my parents stop. When it's too hard, they adjust. But all the time, they continue the endless, interactive dance with me–responding to me, leading me, following me.

Social and Emotional

I feel loved and safe because my mommy and daddy respond promptly to my needs. You cuddle and smile at me. Sometimes Grandpa pretends to be a boat. He holds me facing away from him on his lap, with his arms snuggled around me. Then he rocks me gently like a boat on the water as he sings to me. Then he says, "Oh no, a storm is coming. I will hold you tight so you won't fall out of the boat." And he sings the song again in a louder storm voice and the rocking increases, and he snuggles me closer.

"Oh no, we have hit a rock, we are going down. I will save you," he says and lifts me on to his shoulders to save me and carries me to the dinner table or to bed. [21][4]

I am a little person, and I cannot remember three- or four–step sequences of instructions. I have finally trained my mommy and daddy to give me one-step instructions. A one-step instruction has only one request. "Eat your cheese," or "please sit down," or "wave good-bye to Grandma." One-step instructions are a lot easier for me to understand and do. Now that Daddy gives me one instruction at a time, he thinks I am much more obedient. [23] ☺

I respond well, or at least better, when I know what to expect. When our daily schedule is the same, it is predictable for me. It is easier for me to cooperate during the daily routines. I know that after I eat breakfast, I play in my bath, then you get me dressed, and after lunch I'll take my nap.

I like to help, pretending to do housework, closing the refrigerator door, pushing the start button on the dryer, putting the spoons away when unloading the dishwasher, and trying to push the vacuum cleaner.

---

[4] Becky A. Bailey, *I Love You Rituals* (New York: HarperCollins Publishers, 2000) 190-91, recounting her experience with her grandfather. She suggests an alternative ending, saying, "The storm is over, the sea is calm. Sing the song once more, returning to your gentle rocking and calm voice." Her book is an excellent resource for developing rich emotional practices within your home.

I love it when my mom celebrates what I do. It's important that I know when my behavior is pleasing to Mommy and Daddy so I can repeat it. Some cultures do not approve of verbal praising or displays of affection, but a smile works in every language, especially mine. [24] I feel great when Daddy looks deep into my eyes and tells me he loves me lots and lots.

I am experiencing a wide range of emotions and am learning how to deal with them. Just being able to name these emotions helps me sort them out and begin to understand them. Mommy made a "sad" puppet and a "happy" puppet out of two mid-sized paper bags, drawing the eyes and nose on the bottom and using the fold as the mouth. As I approach my second birthday, Mommy introduces more names for complex emotions like "frightened" and "frustrated." I really like it when the puppets talk to me about my feelings. After I can name the emotion, I get better at controlling it. [25]

Using the READY! Skills Continuum

The skills continuum on the following page is an easy way to observe and measure my development. I will develop at different rates for different skills than my brothers and sisters and cousins. What you should watch for is consistent growth over time. Over like the next 20 years! That is what extraordinary is. Or genius. Patiently sustaining a 20-year vision! ☺

There will be more difference in performance between ages three and four and ages four and five than from birth to age one and one to two. The years from birth to age three are critical years, however, in which my emotional and verbal foundations are being laid.

> *When I achieve the one- to two-year-old targets at 24 months I am generally on course to enter kindergarten in the green band, in the blue band when I achieve them four months earlier and in the dark-blue band if I achieve them eight months earlier, although measurement at this age is soft at best with large amounts of variation.*

READY! Skills Continuum

	Age One to Two	Age Two to Three
Reading, Writing, Listening, & Speaking		
Listening to Books	I read 20 minutes a day in short segments. I answer "Where is" questions by pointing.	I supply words and discuss characters during our 20 minute reading time. I answer "Why?" questions.
Rhyming	I sing parts of ABC and number songs with others. I hear nursery ryhmes.	I can say parts of serveral rhymes. I sing/chant ABC and number songs.
Hearing Language	I hear my parents speak to me about 30 times an hour.	I hear my parents speak to me about 30 times an hour.
Spoken Words	I use single-word speech, learn two-four words a day, and imitate some animal sounds.	I understand 2,000-3,000 words, say two-four owrd sentences, and repeat short phrases.
Visual Matching & Naming		
Colors	I hear the names of colors. I can point to three colors; yellow, blue, and red.	I know six colors; yellow, blue, red, green, black, white.
Letter Shapes	I see my first initial everywhere at home. I match three shapes: curves, lines, and V's **CURVE LINE V**	I know the first letter of my first name. I match distinctively different letter shapes including: a-d-m-t-v.
Sounds in Words	I repeat the last word in rhymes with assistance.	I repeat ending sounds that rhyme. I clap or jump the syllables of names with help.
Letter Sounds		I can sound the first letter in my name.
Number Shapes	I can match number shapes 1 to 3.	I can match number shapes 1 to 6.
Math & Reasoning		
Geometric Shapes	I play with shape toys, although I seldom match correctly.	Circle Square Triangle Rectangle
Counting	I hear counting of one, two, and three.	I count by rote (memory) to five.
Patterns	I recognize sequence words "before" and "after." I arrange objects in lines.	I make two-step color patterns like yellow, purple, yellow, purple
Social & Emotional Development		
Relating to Others	I feel loved and safe when my parents respond quickly to me.	I play side-by-side with others and I use "please" and "thank you."
Attention Span	I focus briefly on tasks.	I focus on an activity with an adult for short periods of time.
Follows Instructions	I am beginning to obey one-step directions (e.g., Please get your coat.")	I remember and follow two-step directions.
Emotional Well-Being	I begin to control my impulses. I show emotions with my face, words, gestures.	I name basic feelings of myself and others.

CHAPTER SEVEN

AGE TWO TO THREE

"...in an average hour together, some parents spent more than 40 minutes interacting with their child, and other parents spent less than 15 minutes. Some parents responded more than 250 times an hour to their child, and others responded fewer than 50 times. Some parents expressed approval and encouragement of their child's actions more than 40 times an hour and others less than 4 times."

—Drs. Betty Hart and Todd R. Risley, Researchers[1]

I am your child at the terrible two's. For me, it is an exciting and stimulating age. I am young, recently mobile, and ready to go. Think of me as a 16 year-old with my first driver's license, new wheels, and a whole world calling. I can walk, run, and even jump. I have fully functioning vision and reasonable hand-eye coordination. I am intent on becoming my own person and a grown-up human being. As you might imagine, my least favorite words are "no" and "you can't."

Physical Development: Eyes and Ears

My vision and hearing are how I learn about the world. Fortunately, Mommy and Daddy know it's important to identify problems early. Every three months, you check several things about my eyes. You first hold up a small toy and say, "Watch this." Then you draw the shape of a big "H" and then a "cross" in the air, while observing whether both my eyes follow the movements smoothly and together. You then watch as I scan the room, noticing that my eyes stop momentarily and then move to a new spot. The stopping is normal and helps my brain adjust to the shifting scene as my eyes move. I can now track objects without

---

[1] Betty Hart and Todd Risley, *Meaningful Differences in the Everyday Experiences of Young American Children* (Baltimore, MD: Paul H. Brookes Publishing, 1995), 10.

READY!
for Kindergarten

Reading & Writing

1	Seeing Clearly	My eyes follow an object tracing an "H" and cross (+) in the air. I focus near then far, and on my field of vision.
2	Comprehending Books	During our 20 minute reading time, I supply words and discuss characters. I answer "Why" questions.
3	Knowing Print Concepts	I identify 10 print concepts: the previous three, plus title, author, cover, words, letters, top of page, bottom of page.
4	Copying-Tracing-Printing	I trace shapes with my finger or crayon. I copy shapes made by others.

Listening & Speaking

5	Singing, Chanting, Rhyming	I sing/chant ABC and number songs. I am familiar with several nursery rhymes and can say parts of them.
6	Saying Sounds in Words	I repeat the ending sound in words that rhyme. I clap or jump the syllables in familiar names, with assistance.
7	Hearing Spoken Words	I hear my parents speak to me about 30 times an hour.
8	Developing Verbal Skills	I say two-four word sentences. I understand 2,000-3,000 words. I repeat short phrases and imitate animal sounds.

Visual Matching & Naming

9	Naming Colors	I know six colors: red, blue, yellow, green, black, white.
10	Matching Letter Shapes	I match distinctively different letter shapes, including a-d-m-t-v
11	Naming Letter Shapes	I identify and say the name of the first letter of my name.
12	Saying Letter Sounds	I say the sound of the first letter of my name.
13	Recognizing Sight Words	I see labels on common objects in my home.
14	Matching Number Shapes	I match number shapes from 1 to 6.
15	Geometric Shapes	I identify and match circles, squares, rectangles, triangles.

Math & Reasoning

16	Counting	I count to five from memory.
17	Sorting Items	I sort objects by one characteristic or classification (e.g., color, shape, type).
18	Adding and Subtracting	I recognize groups of objects to three. I know big/small; more/less, all/none.
19	Making Patterns	I make two-step color patterns (e.g., red-blue, red-blue).
20	Spatial Relationships	I know 10 preposition words (position words).

Social & Emotional

21	Relating to Others	I play side-by-side with other children. I use "please" and "thank you."
22	Attention Span	I play independently or focus on an engaging activity with an adult for short periods of time.
23	Following Directions	I remember and follow step-step directions.
24	Taking Responsibility	I like encouragement when I "help" with tasks. I am beginning to develop self-help skills and self-confidence.
25	Emotional Well-Being	I name the feelings of myself and others. I respond well to being re-directed to appropriate activities.

moving my head at all–I just move my eyes. That's good because when I go to school I'll be able to read sentences without moving my head back and forth. [1][2]

Then you check to make sure I can see things close-up (within reach) and then see distant details (things about 10 feet away.) You hold a toy about 12 inches away and cover one of my eyes. You ask me questions about the toy to make sure I am really looking at it. Next, you remove your hand and notice how much my eye has to move to focus on the object up close. A little movement is okay; but if my eye drifts out quite a bit, you talk to my pediatrician about it. [1]

Each morning you carefully wipe my eyes free of night time mucus that could scratch the lenses of my pupil. You don't let me use scissors or pencils unless you are sitting right next to me. And of course, you protect my eyes from all safety risks, such as sharp corners on furniture, toxic chemical products, blowing sand or grass clippings, bright sunlight, and more.

You talk to me about things that are red and green and we practice at the stoplights. You tell me that some children cannot tell the difference between red or green or can only tell the difference when it is really obvious. Doctors can tell mommies and daddies about this, you say.

Daddy is always alert to my hearing, too. You protect me from loud noises because my hearing is so delicate and easily damaged. Sometimes you speak softly behind me to see if I notice. It might be a game, but it also might be a way of checking how well I hear. If I'm pulling at my ear, that signals that I might have an infection and you call my doctor immediately. At bath time, you gently clean the outside crevices of my ears and peek to see if I've put anything inside. Our family rule is no music, power tools, TV, arguments, or rambunctious play that is very much louder than a normal speaking voice because it could be dangerous to my eardrums.

Visual Matching and Naming
I am learning a lot of things this year using matching. Last year, I learned to match numbers 1, 2, and 3. This year, I am learning to match six colors [9], six alphabet letters (the first letter in my name and five other letters) [10], six numbers (1 to 6) [14], quantities of dots to six [18],

---

[2] Numbers in brackets next to activities correspond to the number in the left-hand column of the age level targets charts.

and seven shapes (curve, V, line, triangle, circle, square, and rectangle) *[15]*. It seems to me that things come in sixes and sevens this year. Next year it will be the nines. I will match dots cards with groups of dots from one to nine, *[18]* match nine colors, *[9]* and geometric shapes. I am beginning to see these letters, numbers, colors, and shapes everywhere I go. It's easy with the game pieces my parents got from the READY! program.

After I can match all the letters, numbers, dots, colors, and shapes, then I learn the other stuff about them, like their name and quantity. *[15]* We still play the game with colored cards, using the same easy, matching process we used when I was a one-year-old. The four-inch by six-inch cards contain no words or shapes, just a beautiful color.

We sit on the floor. Usually I sit in your lap and you put a green card in front of me.

Beside the green card, you put two other cards: another green and a red one.

You slowly move the first card back and forth–next to the other green card and pause; then next to the red card and pause. While doing this, you say, "Point to the card that is the same as the one in my hand." You help me with little clues. I point and when I get it right, you cheer for me. *[9]* You say, "That's right! These cards are green." This is easy for me because I learned red, yellow, and blue last year, so it is simple to learn more new colors now. This year you add green, black, and white, although there is no reason to stop with three colors if I'm enjoying the game.

> Making the matching cards will be easier if you do them all at the same time. Gather paper, scissors and colored markers or crayons. Or print templates at www.readyforkindergarten.org/parents Make four, 4"x6" cards for each concept.
>
> **Four each:**
> Colors (6)   Letter (my first initial)
> Dots (1-6)   Letters (a-d-m-t-v)
> Numbers (1-6)   Geometric shapes (7)

At first you ask me to point to the card that is the same, and then you tell me the name of the color. Later, you give me the card and say, "Put this card next to the card that is the same." I can do it! [9]

You may be moving systematically through increasingly complex targets, but me? I'm just having fun playing with you.

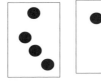

Another day we play the game with dot cards. You put a couple of dot cards on the table. Then you give me a card that is exactly like one of the cards on the table, and say, "Which card on the table is like the card in your hand?"

It's amazing how my brain can recognize quantities as easily as shapes. I make a match and giggle. After I get good at this game, Daddy turns the cards sideways or upside down so they look different. He does not count the dots for me. The dots are not arranged in equidistant patterns like dice or dominos. I just look and see. Numbers are about quantities. That is why Daddy teaches me quantities first. [18]

A bigger step for me is learning to match (but not yet name) different looking letters. You made pairs of cards with these letters: a-d-m-t-v which you said you downloaded on the computer and printed from www.readyforkindergarten.org. These letters are good for training my

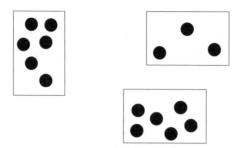

eye, since each shape is distinctively different from the other. First you guide me in choosing between two choices; and once I'm successful doing that, you put down more cards. By age three I can point to the matching letter shape from among five choices. [10]

I am also matching numbers from 1 to 6, [14] and I recognize the geometric shapes of the curve, line, V, circle, square, triangle and rectangle. [15] Tracing the shapes on the cards with my finger helps me to match them. Playing matching games trains my brain and eyes to work together to quickly spot differences. Mommy and Daddy are careful not to play all of these games at the same time.

You say, "Look at this card." You help me trace the shape with my finger.

m

Then you put down two other cards, another "m" and the first initial of my name (let's say it's "D"), and say "Which of these shapes are the same?" [11]

The game is the same when we play it with geometric shapes. The shapes are fun because the cards are actually cut (or drawn) in the shape. "The name of the shape I am holding is called a circle," Mommy says. "Can you say circle? Where does the circle go?"[15] You hand me the card and I put it by the triangle. "Let's look. Does this shape look like this one?" Mommy asks while she holds the circle next to the triangle. "Or this one? This one, that's right," you answer. Silly me. Now I see the difference.

 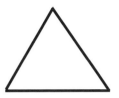

Matching is easiest for me when Daddy makes the shapes at least three to four inches tall on cards that are at least six inches tall. I see best when the shapes are bold and simple and when the colors are strong and distinct, like black, green, blue, or red on white paper. Matching games let me spend time with my favorite people in a happy way. Mommy keeps cards in her purse so we can play while riding the bus or waiting at the doctor's office. Just a few minutes a day is all it takes. It's fun and I want more!

Visit www.readyforkindergarten.org/parents to download sets of the alphabet letters, colors, dots, numbers, and shapes. Glue printed templates to stiff papers and cut to make individual cards for matching.

The first letter of my name is still posted around our home. Daddy carries me so I can point to it and say its name plus its sound. [12] In addition, we pick three items to label. You make three strips of paper and write one word on each page: bed, door, books. Then we tape the words to the objects. You call these signs "sight words." Just by looking, I know that those letters make a word and what that word means. Soon I ask you to make more sight words. The words are "I", "love", and "butterflies." "Butterfly" is actually a really easy word for me. I don't sound it out. I don't know the letters. I just know it's the longest set of squiggles that Daddy shows me. When I say all three words together, and ask, "Is this reading?" you just smile. [13]

Reading and Writing

During my 20 minutes a day story time, I enjoy books about families, potty training, my nighttime fears, my feelings, and places that I go, like the doctor's office or child care center. I like books about colors, counting, ABC's, and shapes and use my matching cards when we read them. I'm really interested in books about real things like wild animals, semi-trucks, and sports. Between the www.reading foundation.org website, *The Read Aloud Handbook* by Jim Trelease, and the local library my parents have lots of ideas for good books.

We often read a new story along with a few of my favorites that you read over and over again. I enjoy knowing what is coming next– I can anticipate and predict. I like the sounds of rhyming text, and stories that repeat the same sentences with just one- or two-word differences. Sometimes you leave out words. Then I have to tell you. Sometimes you talk about the

Information and pricing about pre-packaged curriculum on DVD, along with toys that make learning fun, available at www.readyforkindergarten.org.

characters and ask me about details on the page you just read. I help with some of the words, tell which characters I like best, and answer "why" questions. These are all good ways to make reading fun and valuable for me. [2]

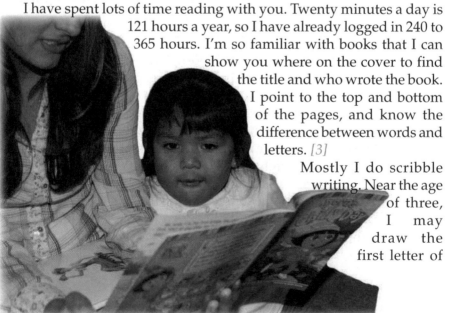

I have spent lots of time reading with you. Twenty minutes a day is 121 hours a year, so I have already logged in 240 to 365 hours. I'm so familiar with books that I can show you where on the cover to find the title and who wrote the book. I point to the top and bottom of the pages, and know the difference between words and letters. [3]

Mostly I do scribble writing. Near the age of three, I may draw the first letter of my name. I learn how by tracing. You draw my first initial on scraps of paper and I trace it with my crayon. It's not exactly the same, but we both clap because it's my letter! In the store or while reading, when we see my initial, you say, "There's your letter!" and I trace it with my finger. Outside, you draw my initial in the sand box and I trace over it. Inside, you make a sand pan by putting sugar or salt on a cookie sheet. Then you draw a shape for me to trace – lines, curves, v's, letters and numbers. You guide my finger until I can do it myself. The "sand" lets me make mistakes and experiment repeatedly. This is fun! *[4]*

Listening and Speaking

When I am almost three, you play *Odd Word Out* with me. You say three words: "cat, fat, dog." Two of the words have the same ending sounds and one word doesn't. I repeat the words, and I can hear that "dog" is the odd word. Next you say three more words, "ball, cow, tall," and when I repeat them I can hear that "ball" and "tall" sound alike and that "cow" doesn't match. You are careful to use rhyming words that don't start with the same sound (like "chair, cherry, hair") because that really confuses me. *[6]*

run, fun, carrot	spoon, moon, fork	tooth, four, core
can, dog, fan	stay, two, tray	penny, walk, talk
sit, card, mitt	main, kite, train	some, little, come
three, day, pay	this, look, book	dots, pots, me

When you say nursery rhymes, you place extra emphasis on the rhyming words. I am getting better and better at hearing and repeating the ending sounds in the nursery rhymes. I am familiar with five to six nursery rhymes well enough to say parts of them myself.[3] Guess what else I can do? I clap or jump each syllable in familiar names, with your help. When we say my friend Jason's name, we say "Ja" at the same time we clap, and then we clap again when we say "son." *[6]*

Daddy says, "I spy with my little eye something red." You want me to guess what you see. I look around and then discover what you are looking at. "Car!" I say and point. We also play *Extend My Sentence.* You say, "The animal across the street is a . . ."

---

[3] "Children who know eight nursery rhymes by heart by the time they're four years old are usually among the best readers by the time they're eight." Mem Fox, *Reading Magic* (New York: Harcourt, 2001), 85.

and I say, "Big dog."

You say, "If I saw that big, white dog in the park I would . . ."

and I say, " . . .bring it home with us." [7]   ☺

In the morning and at lunch, I wash my hands for as long as it takes you to sing the ABC song. For dinner I wash my hands while you chant the number song (also to the tune of the ABC song). I join in on a few numbers! [5]

And have you heard all the words I can say? I can name lots of things including my body parts (18 to 24 months) and combine words in a meaningful way (24 to 26 months). I use about 500 words now, can imitate several animal sounds, and repeat short expressions accurately. Naturally, "bad" words are the easiest for me to learn! [8]

I am adding 10 to 20 new words a day and naming familiar people. What is really happening, of course, is that I have heard you reading aloud and using these words for years. The sounds and meaning of these words are already embedded in my neurons. It is just the last part that is occurring now–my saying the words aloud in a short sentence.

One thing that has made a really big difference is the 30 times an hour you talk to me. Most of the time when you talk to me, I try to answer back. It is part of the dance. Sometimes you just say out loud everything you are doing so I hear lots and lots of words. With all of this practice, I can easily put two to four words together. This is good because I have cousins who are talking more, but you and my pediatrician say that the rule is that I do not need to be checked for developmental delay if I am speaking in sentence fragments that have at least as many words as I am old. [7]

Math and Reasoning

I can count from one to five by rote (by memory). Rote counting uses the same part of my brain that I use for singing. I can show my age with my fingers, when I can get them to work. [16] None of this is hard for me. It's play! I count my crackers for my snack: one, two, three. [18]

In fact when I look at things, I can just "see" that there are three crackers or two orange sections. I am also getting better at sorting. I sort by one thing—like color or shape, but it is still too tricky to sort by two characteristics like a color *and then* a shape. [17]

I know that a pattern is not a pattern unless it repeats itself. I see two-step patterns on my shirts and socks. I repeat two-step sound patterns, too. Making patterns with the color cards took a little time for me to figure out. I kind of got the hang of it by watching Mommy and then making some patterns together.

You say "red card . . . then blue card" while you lay down the red card . . . then the blue card.

Then you say "red card . . . then blue card" and lay down another red card and another blue card just below the first red and blue card. Because I am sitting on your lap, I easily see the columns of cards.

You give me the cards and we say together "red card . . . then blue card" as I lay them down. You have me put down a red card and then a blue card.

Then right under it, we put down another red card and then a blue card as we say it together. We do this until we run out of cards. After a little while, I can do it myself. That is pretty easy.

Then instead of putting them in columns, we start making the pattern with the cards all in a long row. It is harder to see the pattern when it is in rows instead of columns, but either way I learn that "it is not a pattern unless it repeats itself." [19]

I learn to point to shapes that are round, square, and have three angles. [15] I know the difficult mathematical concepts of "big," "small," "more," "less," "all,"and "none," and I practice my skill with these concepts every time we have cheese cubes and raisins at snack time or dessert. ☺[18] Every so often, we play "Where is the butterfly?" Using a plastic butterfly, you move it around and talk about its location. "The butterfly is *under* the table, and now it is landing *on* the table. It's flying *around* the table and then going *across* the room to fly *over* your head." Then the butterfly goes in new places, and you say that the butterfly is "*under*" me, and "*on*" me. I repeat "*under*" and "*on*," and Daddy tells me that I will know these words next year.

Another fun way we use prepositions is playing the *Itsy Bitsy Spider* where I practice *up* the spout and *down* the drain. [20] And we sing *The Ants Go Marching* where I practice ". . . one *by* one, *down* *to* the ground *to* get *out* of the rain. Dum, dum, dum."[5]

> "With few exceptions, the more parents talked to their children, the faster the children's vocabularies were growing and the higher the children's IQ test scores at age three and later."
> Betty Hart and Todd R. Risley[4]

I like the "dum, dum dum" part best although Mommy tells Daddy he will live to regret teaching me this song. Daddy says that understanding position words prepares me to do math in school.

---

[4] Betty Hart and Todd Risley, *Meaningful Differences in the Everyday Experiences of Young American Children* (Baltimore, MD: Paul H. Brookes Publishing, 1995), 10.
[5] Words, tunes and directions for these poems and many more are available at www.niehis.nih.gov/kids/musicchild.htm

Social and Emotional

Occasionally, I enjoy activities with other children my age. It's fun to just play side-by-side. Because I sometimes feel anxiety when my mommy is out of sight, it's easier for me to be with other children in familiar settings—at family gatherings and reunions, library story times, Sunday School class, family meals with guests, and at our neighborhood park. [21]

I am beginning to play by myself for short periods of time, and I can focus on an engaging activity with an adult. [22] Wooden blocks, nesting cups, simple puzzles and colored stacking rings are activities you help me with and which extend my ability to concentrate.

I am also learning to follow two-step instructions. "Wash your hands and then dry them." "Put on your shirt and then get your shoes." I can remember two things, but remembering three things is tougher. We play games that help me practice following directions. One game is *Simon Says* where Simon says, "Jump, then turn around once," or "Touch your nose and clap." We also play *Red Light, Green Light* where

Daddy says, "Pick up your teddy bear." When I start to pick up my teddy bear, he says, "Red light." I stop. Then he says, "Green light" and I start again. [23] Stop, go, stop, go . . . silly Daddy.

I like recognition and praise when I "help" with appropriate tasks. Daddy says, "You are so thoughtful," and "You are getting really good at remembering to put your toys away." I just love it when Mommy puts her arms around me and says that I give the best hugs in the whole world, and then hugs me tightly. It makes me feel very happy and secure. [24] I am beginning to show more kindness to others, but I am mostly still concerned with my own needs.

I am getting better at naming what I feel, and I can guess how other people feel, too. Daddy plays "faces" with me. He does happy, sad, angry, puzzled, and many other kinds of expressions. I try to imitate them and make guesses about how others feel when they make these faces. Mommy and Daddy are great at re-directing me. When I say, "Cookie! Cookie now!" You say, "I am hungry, too. Let's go find a healthy snack." You offer alternatives to my frequent demands, and I respond well. This avoids the confrontations and frustrations that occur when I hear "no."

Really, the terrible two's are not so terrible after all. With the help of my parents, some tools, and activities, I am thriving and understanding concepts appropriate for my age. I have the skills of a typical two-year-old, and I'm on track to be prepared to enter school with the skills of a five-year-old. [25]

When I achieve the two- to three-year-old targets at 36 months I am generally on course to enter kindergarten in the green band, in the blue band when I achieve them six months earlier and in the dark-blue band if I achieve them ten months earlier, although measurement at this age is soft at best with large amounts of variation.

READY! Skills Continuum

	Age Two to Three	Age Three to Four
Reading, Writing, Listening, & Speaking		
Listening to Books	I supply words and discuss characters during our 20 minute reading time. I answer "Why?" questions.	I listen to you read 20 minutes a day to me in short segments. I answer "How" and "What" questions.
Rhyming	I can say parts of serveral rhymes. I sing/chant ABC and number songs.	I recite four-five nursery rhymes. I sing/chant ABC and number songs independently.
Hearing Language	I hear my parents speak to me about 30 times an hour.	I hear my parents speak to me about 30 times an hour.
Spoken Words	I understand 2,000-3,000 words, say two-four owrd sentences, and repeat short phrases.	I understand 3,000-4,000 words. I say four-six word sentences. I accurately repeat sounds I hear in words. I ask and answer questions.
Visual Matching & Naming		
Colors	I know six colors; yellow, blue, red, green, black, white.	I can match and name nine colors; yellow, blue, red, green, black, brown, orange, white, purple.
Letter Shapes	I know the first letter of my first name. I match distinctively different letter shapes including: a-d-m-t-v.	I know and name the letters in my first name (six-seven letters) and I match similar letter shapes: a-c-e-o-s; b-d-g-p-q; m-n-r-u.
Sounds in Words	I repeat ending sounds that rhyme. I clap or jump the syllables of names with help.	I repeat the beginning sounds of words. I clap syllables of names, with help. I make up nonsense rhymes.
Letter Sounds	I can sound the first letter in my name.	I know the sound of letters in my first name.
Number Shapes	I can match number shapes 1 to 6.	I can match number shapes 1 to 9.
Math & Reasoning		
Geometric Shapes	Circle Square Triangle Rectangle	Star Diamond Parallelogram Plus Oval Heart
Counting	I count by rote (memory) to five.	I count by rote (memory) to 10.
Patterns	I make two-step color patterns like; yellow, purple, yellow, purple	I can extend two-step patterns like; red, blue, red, blue
Social & Emotional Development		
Relating to Others	I play side-by-side with others and I use "please" and "thank you."	I play cooperatively with other children and share occasionally.
Attention Span	I focus on an activity with an adult for short periods of time.	I complete short tasks through sustained effort.
Follows Instructions	I remember and follow two-step directions.	I remember and follow two-step directions and I undertand basic safety rules.
Emotional Well-Being	I name basic feelings of myself and others.	I show emotional control sometimes, and I am learning not to hurt others.

CHAPTER EIGHT

CHOOSING A PRESCHOOL: A CHECKLIST

"Making the decision to have a child is momentous. It is to decide forever to have your heart go walking around outside your body."
—Elizabeth Stone

Many of my friends are already in some form of daycare. Child care centers often offer preschool classes, as do other businesses, agencies, and co-ops. Even if you are not working outside our home, you may decide to enroll me in preschool for one or two years before kindergarten to augment the social and pre-academic skills you are already teaching me at home. Here is a common-sense checklist of what to look for.

Safety and Fun
1. Is this a safe place—safe neighborhood, safe yard, safe house or facility, and safe people for me?
2. What is the ratio of children to adults?
3. Is this a place where I will have fun?

Academic Rigor
4. Does this preschool administer pretests and posttests to its students? If the answer is no, you should probably keep looking.
5. Are its assessments in the areas of literacy, math, and social adjustment or do they focus on less important areas? What are the students' initial achievement levels? What kind of growth does the program create?
6. Are the teachers trained for the age level of students that they teach?

7. Circle the the skills that you think I'll develop as a result of attending this preschool using the 25 READY! targets shown in Chapter 10. Are you satisfied with the probable outcomes?
8. When you observe typical outcomes of the preschool's "alumni," are those results green, blue, or dark-blue path results?
9. What kind of academic credentials do the adults have?

Cost

10. How much does this preschool cost? Can you afford this preschool for one or two years?
11. Is the location convenient? What is your time worth? How much does travel to this program add in monetary terms and subtract from your discretionary time?
12. What is the cost difference between your number one and number two choice? Does the difference in programs justify the difference in the price?

Verifying How You Know What You Think You Know

13. Have you spent at least a full school day observing the program? Observing gives you better information than listening to administrators describe their program. Observing for a full day generally means you are there in the spring preceding the fall enrollment.
14. Have you reviewed actual copies of the assessments this preschool uses? Do the assessments check for letter and sound recognition, beginning and ending sound recognition and production, and most of the other incoming kindergarten targets?
15. Have you spoken with parents whose children attended this preschool and are now in kindergarten or first grade? What is their evaluation of their child's level of preparation?

Intuitive Check

16. Do you feel that this program and these adults are a good fit for your child?
17. Now spend 10-15 quiet minutes mentally visualizing and emotionally "scanning" the different aspects of the neighborhood, premises, adult educators, curriculum, and the other children. Pay attention to any tension in your body. Does the program that you have chosen pass the "gut check"?

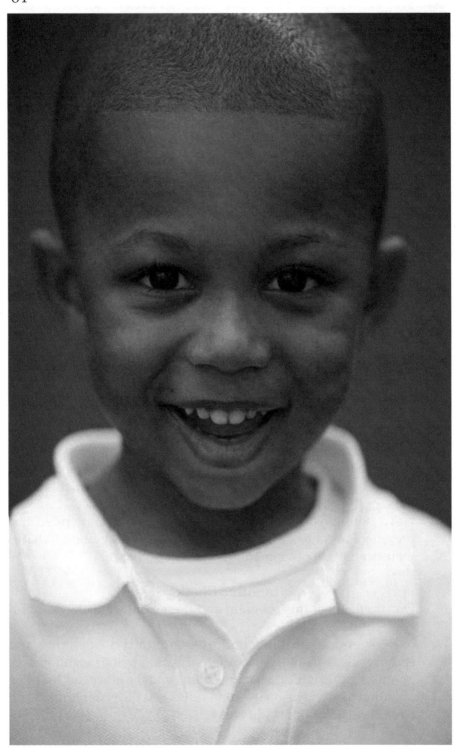

CHAPTER NINE

AGE THREE TO FOUR

"The future belongs to those who see the possibilities before they become obvious."

—John Scully, former CEO,
of both Pepsi and Apple

I am your three-year-old child. I am curious, capable and full of energy. I'm very much my own little person, and I like to please you and do what you do. I am learning to share with my playmates, and I frequently imitate my older siblings, cousins, and friends. In addition to all the activities you are doing with me in our home, you may be considering preschool to give me an extra little boost academically and socially (chap. 8).

Physical Development: Eyes

Mommy is still checking my vision regularly. In addition to the "H" and "cross" you draw in the air, and checking my ability to focus near and far, you watch to see if either of my eyes wanders—when covered—from the object that I am looking at (field of vision). You also check my ability to see details at a distance. For the distance detail game, you ask me to describe details like shapes or colors in a picture that is 15 feet away. You do this by covering one of my eyes, then the other, so you know if I see the same out of each eye. Because instruction delivered by my school teachers will often occur more than 15 feet away from me, most optometrists agree that this game is very important. [1][1]

A fall or blow to the back of my head may affect my vision, Mommy knows. That is where 20 million receptors from my eyes connect to 20 million neurons in my brain so Mommy and Daddy are very protective

---

[1] Numbers in brackets next to activities correspond to the number in the left-hand column of the age level targets charts.

READY! for Kindergarten

Age Level Targets
Age Three to Four

Reading & Writing

1	Seeing Clearly	My eyes correctly respond to the "H", cross, near-far, field of vision, and distant details tests.
2	Comprehending Books	During our 20 minute reading time, I anticipate what comes next in familiar books. I give 3-4 word answers to "What" and "How" questions.
3	Knowing Print Concepts	I know 15 print concepts: the prior 10, plus (1) first page, (2) last page, (3) print represents spoken sounds, (4) meaning comes from words, (5) pictures help meaning.
4	Copying-Tracing-Printing	I trace and/or copy letters, numbers, and simple geometric shapes.

Listening & Speaking

5	Singing, Chanting, Rhyming	I sing/chant ABC and number songs independently. I can recite 4-5 rhymes.
6	Saying Sounds in Words	I repeat the beginning sound of words. I clap or jump the syllables in familiar words, with assistance. I make up nonsense rhymes.
7	Hearing Spoken Words	I hear my parents speak to me about 30 times an hour.
8	Developing Verbal Skills	I say 4-6 word sentences. I understand 3,000-4,000 words. I accurately repeat sounds I hear in words. I ask and answer questions.

Visual Matching & Naming

9	Naming Colors	I know 9 colors: red, blue, yellow, green, orange, purple, brown, black, white.
10	Matching Letter Shapes	I correctly match letters in similar shape families: a-c-e-o-s; b-d-g-p-q; h-m-n-r-u.
11	Naming Letter Shapes	I identify and name all the letters in my first name (6-7 letters).
12	Saying Letter Sounds	I say the sounds of all the letters in my first name (6-7).
13	Recognizing Sight Words	I recognize the meaning of labels on 5 common objects in my home.
14	Matching Number Shapes	I match number shapes from 1 to 9.
15	Geometric Shapes	Geometric Shapes: I match and name 13 shapes: line, curve, circle, V, square, rectangle, triangle, diamond (rhombus), oval (ellipse), pentagon, octagon, star, heart.

Math & Reasoning

16	Counting	I count in order to 10. I show my age with my fingers.
17	Sorting Items	I sort quickly by color and shape. I order items from large to small.
18	Adding and Subtracting	I recognize groups of objects to 6. I know greater than, less than, equal to. I can do simple addition and subtraction with objects.
19	Making Patterns	I begin to copy patterns and create 2-step color patterns (AB, AB) and 3-step sound sequences (ABC, ABC).
20	Spatial Relationships	I know 20 prepositions and do simple puzzles.

Social & Emotional

21	Relating to Others	I play cooperatively with other children. I am learning to share.
22	Attention Span	I accomplish simple tasks through sustained effort.
23	Following Directions	I easily remember and follow 2-step instructions. I understand basic safety rules.
24	Taking Responsibility	I help dress myself, put toys away and do simple chores. I take care of my toileting and hygiene needs.
25	Emotional Well-Being	I am learning to name and appropriately express emotions. I may show empathy for the feelings of others. I am learning not to hurt others.

of my head and neck. Come to think of it, you are actually pretty protective about all of me—never shaking me, always strapping me in my car seat, and padding sharp corners where I play.

Reading and Writing

I love it when you read to me. I get to sit on your lap or cuddle close to your side, hold the book, and turn the pages. This is some of the best one-on-one time that I get, and it is wonderful time for me. Mommy and Daddy are using more ways to involve me in what we are reading. We stop to talk about what has already happened, and I guess what might happen next. I like answering questions. Questions that ask "what

> Check out book titles for me, reading tips, and a video demonstration at www.readingfoundation.org

and why", like, "What would we do if the big bad wolf knocked on our door?" and "Why do you think the house of sticks blew down so easily?", make story time interesting and also help me learn to think. Retelling the beginning, middle, and end of stories helps me to develop my memory and my comprehension. [2]

You must wonder why I want to hear my favorite book for the hundredth time. I am endlessly practicing, much like a high-performance athlete perfecting my jump shot, so to speak.

It's helpful when you comment, ask, and respond to what I say and then wait six to eight seconds for me to produce a response.[2] I know that eight seconds is a really long time, but my mind works like a computer sending a document to a printer. It takes a little time to form my mental response and for it to thread its way

> Comment and WAIT
> Ask.........and WAIT
> Respond...and WAIT

through all of the neural pathways and come out my mouth as words. But it is great exercise for my growing brain. [2]

Asking me about the parts of the book helps engage me as well. I have learned to identify the first and last pages, and that the story you read comes from the letters. When I see the word cards we have made for objects around our home, I know what they say and that they are

---

[2] The "Comment, Ask, Respond" formulation is based on work by the Washington Research Institute, (telephone (206) 285-9317), and utilizes the research of Grover Whitehurst, then professor of education at State University of New York at Stony Brook. Dr. Whitehurst served as U.S. Under-Secretary of Education and then as the first director of the Institute of Education Sciences headquartered in Washington, D.C., from 2002 to 2008.

like the words in our books. I know that letters stand for sounds and the sounds make words. *[3]* I pretend to write on paper. I practice making the scribbles myself by copying or tracing the letters of my first name. It seems that when my hand gets better drawing the letters, my eye notices the details of the letters better, too. This practice is great for the letters, numbers, and geometric shapes I am learning. *[4]*

Listening and Speaking

Mommy and Daddy talk to me constantly throughout our daily routines even while we are dressing or driving in the car. It is a dance. Each time you speak to me, I answer, which gives me lots of practice. Austin Powers may have pioneered the concept of a "mini-me" in the movies, but I am the original "mini-me." I have been learning your vocabulary, your inflection, your speech patterns, and your gestures since birth. I am *your* "mini-me!" *[7]*

By age three, I have heard the ABC song and watched my daddy point to each of the letters on the ABC strip hundreds times. It is the same with the number song. I can sing these songs by myself. *[5]* Singing and chanting accesses a part of my brain where remembering is easier. This is why I can rote count to 10 so easily. Daddy is rote-counting to 30 this year so I will be able to do it next year. *[16]*

I can recite four or five nursery rhymes and am delighted to perform for you. Memorizing these little poems helps me to learn three essential skills I need to read—hearing the ending sounds of words (rhyme), hearing the beginning sounds in words, and clapping or jumping the individual syllables in familiar words. *[6]*

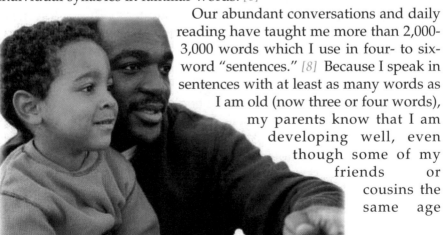

Our abundant conversations and daily reading have taught me more than 2,000-3,000 words which I use in four- to six-word "sentences." *[8]* Because I speak in sentences with at least as many words as I am old (now three or four words), my parents know that I am developing well, even though some of my friends or cousins the same age

PHONEMIC AWARENESS

Talk to me and I will learn to speak, but I will not necessarily learn to read. To read well, I need to learn that spoken language is made up of individual words, which are made up of syllables which, in turn, are made up of the smallest units of sound call phonemes. I need to "hear" the 43 tiny sounds (phonemes) that are the building blocks for our million English words. Learning to hear the difference between an "m" and an "n", or between "b" or "p" or "g", is essential for me to match the right sound to the right shape in learning to read. Developmental steps I will complete by the end of kindergarten and during first grade include:

- Saying ending sounds that rhyme like running, laughing, skipping.
- Hearing beginning sounds (alliteration), like silly, Sam, singing.
- Identifying the beginning, middle, and final sounds in words.
- Clapping syllables in a word.
- Clapping phonemes in a word.
- Blending sounds to make a word: "a" + "t" = "at."
- Substituting one phoneme for another: change "h" in "hot" to "p."
- Deleting phonemes from words: omitting the "c" in "cat."
- Separating sentences into words.
- Separating words into syllables.
- Separating syllables into phonemes.

may already speak in longer   sentences.

Visual Matching and Naming

After printing my first name and putting it up at my eye level, Mommy repeatedly draws attention it. "Where is your name?" you ask. "What does this word say?" or "I think this word is the best name in the world, but I don't know what it says. Do you?" After a month, I can recognize, say, and point to my name. Mommy then reintroduces the first letter of my name that I learned last year. When you print this letter and tape it near the entire name, I point and touch the letter that matches. *[11]*

You then print the other letters and introduce them the same way, one at a time. After I can match all the letters, Mommy begins to make the sound of the first letter and helps me until I can too. You continue until I learn the sound of each of the letters, one at a time. *[11]* Then last of all, I learn the name of each letter. Training my eye to recognize unique shapes uses a different part of my brain than learning to attach the sound and a name to the shape. This simple sequencing helps me.

I learned to match these very different shapes as a two-year-old: a, d, m, t, v.

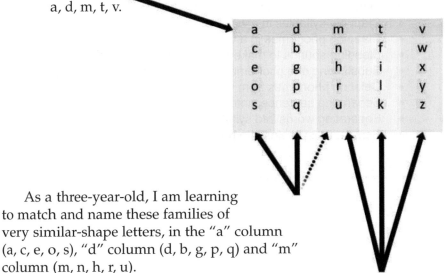

a	d	m	t	v
c	b	n	f	w
e	g	h	i	x
o	p	r	l	y
s	q	u	k	z

As a three-year-old, I am learning to match and name these families of very similar-shape letters, in the "a" column (a, c, e, o, s), "d" column (d, b, g, p, q) and "m" column (m, n, h, r, u).

As a four-year-old, I will learn to match and name the family of letters in the "m" column again (m, n, h, r, u), the "t" column (t, f, i, l, k), and "v" column (v, w, x, y, z). *[10]*

I like matching lots of letters now, even the really tricky ones. I can match all the letters in my name, say their letter names, and say their sounds by looking at cards with letters one to two inches high. [12] I can match alphabet letters, even when they are grouped in "families" that look alike and could be confusing — like a-c-e-o-s and d-b-g-p-q. No way could I have done this a couple of years ago, but the five minutes a day of purposeful play is paying off.

We play the same matching game as we have since I was two. I sit on Daddy's lap and you lay down the target letter. Then you lay down a second copy of the target letter and one of the other "family" letters. You help me with little clues like, "The first one goes all the way around in a circle. Which of these two goes all the way around in a circle?" When I get it right, you cheer for me. [11]

We find letters in alphabet soup and alphabet cereal. We make letters using canned cheese on crackers, and Daddy makes my pancakes in letter shapes. Learning letters is yummy!

My mommy bought Wikki Stix at the toy store. They are easy to hold so I don't drop them. They look like waxed, reusable, bendable pipe cleaners. I use them to practice making letter shapes, number shapes, and geometric shapes. That's fun!

Two years ago, I learned to match numbers 1, 2, and 3. Last year I learned to match numbers 1 through 6, and this year I can match numbers 1 through 9. [14] I match and say the names of quantities to six. I can match dots cards one to nine, [18] match nine colors, [9] and 13 geometric shapes. [15]

> *Making the matching cards will be easier if you do them all at the same time.*
>
> **Five sets of each:**
> *Numbers (1-9)*
> *Dots (1-9)*
> *Shapes (13)*
> *Colors (9)*
>
> **Two sets of each:**
> *Letter shapes by family:*
> *a-c-e-o-s, d-b-g-p-q*
> *and h-m-n-r-u*
> *Letters of my name*
>
> Download templates at
> www.readyforkindergarten.org

I am beginning to see these letters, numbers, colors, and shapes everywhere I go. It's easy with the game pieces my parents got from the READY! program. After I can match all the letters, numbers, dots, colors, and shapes, then I learn the other stuff about them, like their name and quantity. [15]

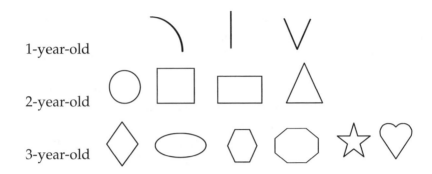

Last year Daddy put three word cards on the refrigerator door. "I," "love," and "butterflies." I learned them easily. In fact, after I knew them well, I put them side-by-side so I could read "I love butterflies." I am learning lots of words of things that I love — "daddy," "ice cream," "books," "crayons," and "baby." You let me choose the objects, involve me in printing the words, and we tape them up together. Then I proudly read them while pointing to the word and the object. Next year you will add 10 more word cards, all of which will be printed in lower case letters one to two inches high. *[13]* This year you made a special sight word and put it by my mommy's picture. For Valentine's Day, I read "I … love … Mommy!" When I say them all together and ask, "Is this reading?" you smile and nod.

Math and Reasoning

I can say, "A pattern is not a pattern unless it repeats itself," and I am getting better and better at finding patterns on my pillowcase, on Grandpa's striped shirt, and even on crosswalks. *[19]*

I can copy and create two-step patterns with the color cards you made me for matching, and have started copying two-step patterns using the number cards. "Can we make two-step patterns with dot cards

Daddy made a big die out of six square note cards, first making dots from one to six in the conventional die pattern and then laying four cards side by side and taping their sides together. You then stood them on their bottom end, and taped the right and left edges together. Then you taped one of the remaining cards to form the top and second to make the bottom. Now you roll the die with me so I can practice recognizing the number of dots that are on top each time.

and shape cards?" I asked yesterday. Singing or chanting three- and four-step sound sequences back to Mommy is a lot faster than making patterns with the color cards.

It's really fun to make sound sequences using a pan and spoon. Mommy taps the pan with her spoon—tap-tap-tap—and I copy her. Then she taps the floor once, then the pan twice. I can do that too! Now it's your turn to copy me. [19]

I love doing my puzzles and have learned to look for clues to put them together, like the straight edges or the colors in the picture. About once a month, Daddy or Mommy plays "Where is the butterfly?" with me. Now that I'm older, there are over thirty different places where the butterfly can go! I know the easy words from last year and I'm learning those for this year too (about, across, after, before, over, into, off, on, and under). You tell me just to repeat the new words after you and soon I will know them. You say that I am using the vocabulary of spatial relationships, whatever that is. [20]

I like the clang that money makes when I sort Daddy or Mommy's loose change by size, from smallest to largest, into muffin tins. I can sort items quickly by color and shape while helping with household chores. Daddy's dark socks in one pile, and his white socks in another. Forks in this slot in the drawer, spoons in this one, and knives in this one. I am beginning to think about why some things belong together in groups but others don't. Daddy asks me questions about how my peas are different from my macaroni and cheese. I can recognize groups of objects to six, like six peas on my spoon. [17]

During snack time, I practice greater than, less than, and equal to. I am doing simple addition and subtraction. Daddy and Mommy play the "take away" game with me. One, two, three M&M's (or raisins). Take one away, and that leaves one, two M&M's. One, two M&M's, add one more and we have one, two, three M&M's. After doing that quite a few delicious times, I can add and subtract numbers to three and sometimes to four without counting. I have to admit that I love math, and the sweet taste it leaves in my mouth. [18]

READY! for Kindergarten

READY! Skills Continuum

	Age Three to Four	Age Four to Five
Reading, Writing, Listening, & Speaking		
Listening to Books	I listen to you read 20 minutes a day to me in short segments. I answer "How" and "What" questions.	I can make up a different plot or ending durning our 20 minute reading time. I can retell a story.
Rhyming	I recite four-five nursery rhymes. I sing/chant ABC and number songs independently.	I recite 6-10 nursery rhymes. I sing/chant ABC and number songs while pointing to letters and numbers.
Hearing Language	I hear my parents speak to me about 30 times an hour.	I hear my parents speak to me about 30 times an hour.
Spoken Words	I understand 3,000-4,000 words. I say four-six word sentences. I accurately repeat sounds I hear in words. I ask and answer questions.	I understand 4,000-5,000 words, speak in complete sentences, and repeat new words correctly.
Visual Matching & Naming		
Colors	I can match and name nine colors; yellow, blue, red, green, black, brown, orange, white, purple.	I can match and name nine colors; yellow, blue, red, green, black, brown, orange, white, purple, grey, pink, magenta.
Letter Shapes	I know and name the letters in my first name (six-seven letters) and I match similar letter shapes: a-c-e-o-s; b-d-g-p-q; m-n-r-u.	I can match and name 12-15 lowercase letters including my first name, and match letters in the shape families: a-c-e-o-s; d-g-p-q; h-m-n-r-u; f-i-j-l-t; k-v-w-x-y-z.
Sounds in Words	I repeat the beginning sounds of words. I clap syllables of names, with help. I make up nonsense rhymes.	I tell words that rhyme; make nonsense rhymes, clap syllables independently, identify the beginning sounds of words.
Letter Sounds	I know the sound of letters in my first name.	I can say the sounds of 12-15 letters.
Number Shapes	I can match number shapes 1 to 9.	I can match number shapes 1 to 12.
Math & Reasoning		
Geometric Shapes	Star Diamond Parallelogram Plus Oval Heart	Cube Sphere Cylinder
Counting	I count by rote (memory) to 10.	I count by rote (memory) to 20.
Patterns	I can extend two-step patterns like; red, blue, red, blue	I can make three-step patterns like; red, yellow, blue, red, yellow, blue.
Social & Emotional Development		
Relating to Others	I play cooperatively with other children and share occasionally.	I settle-in easily to new groups. I play cooperatively with two to more peers.
Attention Span	I complete short tasks through sustained effort.	I can focus on a task for five minutes, even if there are problems or distractions.
Follows Instructions	I remember and follow two-step directions and I undertand basic safety rules.	I can complete three-step directions, and obey rules.
Emotional Well-Being	I show emotional control sometimes, and I am learning not to hurt others.	I talk about feelings of self and others, and show empathy to others.

Social and Emotional

My parents encourage me to play with children my age—in the children's program at church, when we visit my cousin's house, the fitness center, and at the neighborhood park. I am learning to share and get along with other kids. I can take turns and play games in a small group. [21]

I accomplish simple tasks through sustained effort. I easily remember and follow two-step instructions. Mommy starts out with tasks that you know I can do.

"Take your red crayon and draw a circle." "Get your boots and stand by the door." "Please open the drawer and give me the phone book." When you give me three- or four-step instructions and I do not follow them, it is generally because I cannot remember that many actions at once. [23] Generally. ☺ Doing simple household chores helps extend my attention span and persistence. [22]

I understand basic safety rules. In fact, I like to know what the rules and routines are because I want to figure out how my world works. Rules at home are important, too. You are pleased when I help dress myself, put toys away, do my chores, and take responsibility for my bathroom needs. [24]

I am learning to name and appropriately express my emotions. And I am able to guess how someone else is feeling by their face and words and actions. I am learning not to hurt other children and pets. [25] This takes a lot of practice because my feelings are so strong! I can feel an emotion and choose between different behaviors. Your patience, kindness, and example shows me how to handle all my feelings.

When I achieve the age three- to four-year-old targets at 48 months I am generally on course to enter kindergarten in the green band. I am on track to enter kindergarten in the blue band when I achieve them nine months earlier and in the dark-blue band if I achieve them 15 months earlier. Accelerated growth in language, literacy and math skills is more easily attainable at this age although growth may vary by specific sub-skill. A good preschool will help. Vocabulary acquisition, essential for comprehension, is an example of a skill that best grows with a daily dose.

CHAPTER TEN

AGE FOUR TO FIVE

"Extraordinary achievement is less about talent than it is about opportunity."

—Malcolm Gladwell, Author,
Outliers: The Story of Success

I am finally four. In less than a year, I will be holding your hand and reassuring you that I will be okay as we walk into kindergarten. Doesn't it seem like yesterday that you brought me home from the hospital, a helpless little peanut wrapped in a soft blanket? I'm still little and have much to learn, but you have done a terrific job of getting me ready for the big world of school.

You may have noticed that my hand-eye coordination is approaching a pre-Nintendo level. I can place small objects in small openings and talk about places, people, and things that I have seen elsewhere. I can even roll my eyes in a pre-teenage sort of way. Thanks to you, my eyes are working great, tracking with precision and focusing accurately. This year the new eye game is seeing "close up detail" by putting on my pirate patch and looking for little details in my picture books. [1][1] If I cannot see sharply, I may have blurred or double vision. Mommy takes me to a special doctor who can fix it.

You continue to check and protect my hearing, too. My brain takes in information through my eyes and ears so you want them to all work well.

---

[1] Numbers in brackets next to activities correspond to the number in the left-hand column of the age level targets charts.

READY! for Kindergarten

Age Level Targets
Age Four to Five

Reading & Writing

1	Seeing Clearly	My eyes correctly respond to the "H", cross, near-far, field of vision, distant detail, and close-up detail tests.
2	Comprehending Books	During our 20-minute reading time, I can make up a different plot or ending. I can retell a story.
3	Knowing Print Concepts	I know the prior 15 plus (1) letter groups make words; (2) reading moves from left to right and (3) top to bottom; (4) left page is followed by right page; (5) punctuation stops or pauses sentences.
4	Copying-Tracing-Printing	I copy, trace, and/or draw letters, numbers, and two-dimensional shapes.

Listening & Speaking

5	Singing, Chanting, Rhyming	I sing/chant ABC and number songs while pointing to letters and numbers. I recite 6-10 nursery rhymes.
6	Saying Sounds in Words	I identify the beginning sound of words. I say words that rhyme. I clap syllables independently.
7	Hearing Spoken Words	I hear my parents speak to me about 30 times an hour.
8	Developing Verbal Skills	I speak using complete sentences with few inaccuracies. I understand 4,000-5,000 words. I repeat new words correctly.

Visual Matching & Naming

9	Naming Colors	I know 12 colors: red, blue, yellow, green, orange, purple, brown, black, white, gray, pink, light blue.
10	Matching Letter Shapes	I correctly match letters in the shape families: a-c-e-o-s; b-d-g-p-q; h-m-n-r-u; f-i-j-l-t; k-v-w-x-y-z.
11	Naming Letter Shapes	I identify and name 12 -15 lowercase letters, including those in my first name.
12	Saying Letter Sounds	I say the sounds of 12-15 letters, including those in my first name.
13	Recognizing Sight Words	I recognize the meaning of labels on 10 objects in my home.
14	Matching Number Shapes	I match number shapes from 1 to 12.
15	Geometric Shapes	I match and name the prior 13 shapes; I am introduced to three-dimensional shapes: cube, sphere, and cylinder.

Math & Reasoning

16	Counting	I count in order to 20.
17	Sorting Items	I name and sort objects by color, shape, and size. I match items that go together.
18	Adding and Subtracting	I recognize quantities to 10. I accurately use greater than, less than, and equal to. I can do simple addition and subtraction with objects.
19	Making Patterns	I create and repeat 2 to 3-step color patterns, copy 3 to 4-step sound sequences, and play memory games.
20	Spatial Relationships	I know 30 prepositions and do more complex puzzles.

Social & Emotional

21	Relating to Others	I "settle in" to new groups or situations with minimal stress. I play cooperatively with two or more peers.
22	Attention Span	I focus on a task for at least 5 minutes, persisting even if there are problems or distractions.
23	Following Directions	I remember and follow 3-step directions. I obey simple rules.
24	Taking Responsibility	I take care of all my dressing, hygiene, and toileting needs. I help clean up after an activity.
25	Emotional Well-Being	I recognize and manage my own emotions. I show kindness and empathy to others.

> *When I achieve the age four- to five-year-old targets (incoming kindergarten) at 60 months, I will enter kindergarten in the green band. I will enter in the blue band if I achieve them at 52 months, and the dark-blue band if I master them at 44 months.*

This year is important for me. If I start kindergarten ahead, the odds are that I'll stay ahead. However, if I start one, two, or three years behind, it will be really hard for me to catch up, let alone ever reach the top 20% where it will be easiest to qualify for college.

Visual Matching and Naming

We are still practicing skills at my level together, and sometimes I watch you model higher-level skills you want me to acquire next year. My eyes are getting better at recognizing tiny differences between the letters and numbers on the cards you made. When I was a toddler, you wrote the letters two to three inches tall, and now I am practicing with letters that are only one inch high. We are using the same matching techniques that we started using when I was two years old. I sit on Daddy's lap while you hand me a card with the letter "o" on it.

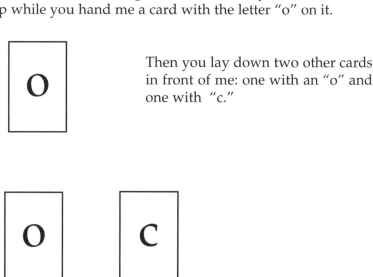

Then you lay down two other cards in front of me: one with an "o" and one with "c."

Daddy asks, "Which of the cards on the table is the same as the one in your hand?"

Sometimes when we are doing an activity that is really easy for me, Daddy makes it trickier by laying down three cards that I am learning with eight other cards from which I have to find matches. The trickiest of all is when the cards are put face down and we turn over two cards at a time to find matches. You call that game *Concentration.*

When I make a match, you say the name of the letter and I repeat it back to you. I can actually say many of the names myself without your help. Last year I learned all the letters and sounds of my first name! This year I have learned five or six more, so I name and know the sounds of 12 to 15 letters. *[11, 12]* When I match letters in look-alike families, I am doing the most difficult matches of all. For instance, the letters a-c-e-o-s look practically the same to me. And b-d-g-p-q are also really, really hard. Learning to match correctly takes lots of time and many,

> **Engaging All of the Senses in Learning Letters**
> - *See and match the shape*
> - *Feel the shape in different textures*
> - *Smell an object that begins with the letter*
> - *Model the shape with my body*
> - *Hear the letter sound*
> - *Taste the shape made with food*
> - *Trace the shape with my finger*

many repetitions. Mommy and Daddy are happy when I get it right, but never scold or get impatient when I make a mistake.

You have made a poster with letters and numbers that hangs by the kitchen counter. By the first day of school, I will easily match, name, and say 12-15 alphabet letters and their sounds, as well as print my first name *[12]*. This means I will not spend my kindergarten year bewildered. I will spend it doing more of the same: connecting names and sounds to the rest of the alphabet letters and connecting names and quantities to more numbers.

That is how I learn best—lots of repetition in a loving, fun environment. Letting me draw and trace letters and shapes is another way to embed them in my brain. You draw them on a piece of paper, and slide it into my tablet of tracing paper for me to copy. I also draw in the sand in our yard, with crayons on paper, and with soap in the bath. Mommy is finding ways to engage as many of my senses as possible. She even cuts some letters out of sandpaper.

Listening and Speaking

These achievements are just a continuation of the learning activities we have been doing together each day since I was born. You talk to me 30 times an hour, explaining what we are doing, asking me questions, listening, repeating or commenting on what I say, and enjoying our chitchat. [7] My vocabulary gets bigger every week. I am using my pre-wired brain to retain the sounds of words and their meanings, as well as their relationships and connections to all of my other words. At night at dinner time we play "high point of my day." I get to remember and think about my day, and practice speaking fluently and in complete sentences using many of the 5,000 words I know. These are three more school readiness skills you tell me: speaking fluently, speaking in complete sentences and understanding 5,000 words. [8]

> "The amount of words heard by children before kindergarten varies by millions. In the same class, some students have heard 45 million words, others 26 million, and others just 13 million words."
> Drs. Betty Hart and Todd R. Risley
> *Meaningful Differences (1995)*

I can accurately repeat almost every word you say. In fact, that is how I am learning some of my really fun, enormous words like "indubitably" and "microscopic."

You have trained my hearing to notice the tiny sounds in words. I can now repeat ending sounds in words (which I learned at age two to three), and beginning sounds in words (at age three to four). I can tell you the first sound of most words, say individual sounds in words like s-a-t, and clap out the syllables in familiar words. We play *Sack of Sounds* where Daddy puts a dozen small things in a lunch bag, like a spoon, brush, and pencil. We take turns reaching into the bag and saying the first sound of the object when we pull it out. [6]

I already memorized the ABC song [5] and numbers to 20 in order. [16] This makes it easier as I learn to point at the letters and the numbers while I say, sing, or chant them in order this year. I like nursery rhymes and say eight rhymes all by myself. [5] Sometimes Mommy and I use props and act out a rhyme while I say it. Last week she put an unlit candle on the kitchen floor and we took turns jumping over it while I said, "Jack Be Nimble." Yesterday at the park my friend and I used my sand pail to be Jack and Jill. When we rolled down the hill we were laughing so hard we couldn't finish the poem. Mommy was laughing too, and she said, "Do it again!" And we did.

Daddy likes rhyming words, too. While he is driving the car he says a word; I repeat it and tell him a word that rhymes. Sometimes I say silly words! Like the time Daddy said, "Monkey," and I said, "Monkey, unckie, funky." Mommy and Daddy got these fun rhyming activities, and lots more, in the kit they ordered at www.readyforkindergarten.org.

Reading and Writing

During the 20 minutes a day we spend reading, I am actively involved. I remember many details about the stories that we have already read. I tell you what will happen next and can even make up a different ending. I am learning to retell the beginning, middle, and end of the story. Mommy helps me by asking, "What happened first? Then what happened? And how did it end?" Daddy is using a sock puppet, who tells the story first, and then I put my hand in the puppet and my puppet tells the story, too. [2]

For three years, I've watched as you occasionally move your finger under the words while you read to me. I've learned that reading goes from left to right, top to bottom, and that the left page is followed by the right page. Now I am learning about punctuation. "Look, a dot without a letter!" Daddy says."That dot tells the reader when to stop, and it is called a period." So now, when Daddy moves his finger under the words while he reads and comes to a period, I say,"Stop."[3]

Seeing a new set of sight words displayed around the house for the fourth year in a row helps me understand that groups of letters make words. I have spent hundreds of hours (a few minutes at a time) learning individual letters and words. What used to be mere squiggles to me are now letters, and groups of letters are what make up words.

I learned five sight words at age three, and 10 this year. I'm happy when Daddy and I make more word cards. We label things I love like my wagon, books, helmet, door, bed, and computer, and things that I do not love, like a can of asparagus. When we say the words on the cards together, I am beginning to understand what it means to read. [13]

I can print (draw) my first name using upper and lowercase letters! Mommy knows how to make all my letters correctly because she got a chart at www.readyforkindergarten.org. I am using a cool pencil grip that can be purchased anywhere that sells school supplies. Mommy puts it on my pencil to help my fingers hold the narrow pencil securely and in the right way. It looks like a pencil eraser but it has a hole in it and the pencil slips through the middle. [4]

In addition to my name, I can draw numbers from 1 to 5 and some basic geometric shapes. [15] My learning comes in layers. The first layer is just matching two shapes that look alike. The next layer is naming and understanding what the shapes mean, like sounds they make or numbers they stand for. Soon I am saying them in a sentence, and printing and drawing them. The next layer is when I add or combine things that I learned separately all together.

Sometimes I use a Q-tip or cotton swab and shaving cream to make letters on a cookie sheet. Daddy draws big letters and numbers and shapes on the driveway with chalk, and I walk on those lines like a tightrope. Later I paint over them with a big brush and bucket of water. [4]

Mommy and I make our own books. You fold two sheets of paper in half, staple them together and presto! I have a book with blank pages to fill. I make up an interesting story with a beginning, middle, and end. It may be about our family camping trip or our day at the zoo or an adventure with a super hero and princess. You suggest I use some of our sight words, and I think that's a great idea. I tell you the story and you print a sentence on the bottom of each page. I draw the pictures, decide on a title, and write my name as author on the front. Grandma will love it when I give her my book. [3]

Math and Reasoning

When I was little, I learned to count to five by rote. Last year I learned to count by rote to 10. This year I am learning to count to 20. Rote counting just means memorizing the sounds in order. Singing makes this easy. I really don't have to know the number shapes or the quantities all the way to 20, just the names. [16] Counting to 20 is important if you want to play *Hide-and-Seek* with your friends. It's also useful when I help my mommy at the grocery store. "Please count the cans as you put them on the counter," Mommy says when we check out. Later we count 20 steps as we walk to our car.

When I was little, I learned to match dots (quantities) to three, and last year to five. This year I am matching dots to 10. [18] One game we play is with our matching cards. We line up the dot cards and then we

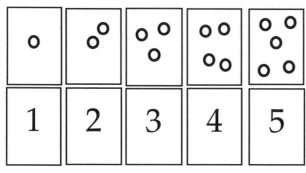

put the correct number cards just below them.

I know many basic math skills. I can sort items by color, shape, and size. [17] I create two- to three-step color patterns, and copy three- to four-step sound sequences. Daddy says, "Can you copy my sounds?" He stomps his foot, claps his hands, and clicks his tongue. I say, "Watch me," and I do it just like he did. [19] I know most of the prepositions, play increasingly complex memory games with cards, and assemble more difficult puzzles. [20]

Mommy and Daddy and I play our matching game using the cards with shapes on them. Here's the big news: not only can I match all those shapes but I know their names, too — like octagon, diamond or rhombus, pentagon, and oval or ellipse. My uncle was surprised when I said the shape names, and Daddy told him it's easiest for me to learn correct vocabulary right from the start. We look for shapes when we go on walks or shopping, and we see lots of them. They're everywhere! [15]

I can do simple addition and subtraction since I learned to count backwards! Give me a number, any number (up to 10), and I can correctly add one or two more to it, or take away one or two from it. Correctly. Generally. Daddy helps me. At first we did it by counting M&M candies (or raisins). One, two M&Ms in a row. Add one more M&M and that makes three. One, two, three M&M's. If we take one away, we have one, two left. I take the big number and

count forward one or two. Or I take the big number and count back one or two and this is simple addition and subtraction. Learning to count backwards out loud helps me when I am subtracting. [18]

I am beginning to problem solve. When I struggle to open my McDonald's Happy Meal, you say I can do it. You have talked me through opening it before.

"What opens, the top or the sides?" you ask.

"So now what do you do first? Put your hands on each side. Push together, pull one side toward you, and push one hand away from you, and then pull apart," you say.

If I do not adjust positively and quickly to school after the first few months, I am four times less likely to be reading by the end of the year, whatever my skills on entry.

Dr. Jeni Riley [2]

Daddy is also big on thinking and problem solving, like discussing who should do which chores and how to sequence our family activities and schedules. Mommy and Daddy help me reason through alternatives and make choices. You say, "If you do this what will happen?" I answer. "Why?" you ask. I get to practice my thinking skills, which reinforces critical brain pathways, making them stronger and faster. Doing puzzles sharpens my reasoning abilities while we are playing together. You are amazed that I can do big floor puzzles and puzzles with 50 pieces.

I am learning to take information I discovered in one place and apply it in other places. I am seeing quantities around me. I move my peas into dot patterns. I know that people who work are workers and people who run are runners and those who drive are drivers. I am learning how language works. When I make these connections, Mommy is very excited. I get kisses and hugs, and I feel very proud so I try very hard to do it again.

Social and Emotional

Daddy tells me I will do best in kindergarten if I have learned to "settle in" to new groups or situations easily.[2] Getting use to my preschool, playing and sometimes sleeping over with my cousins and friends, and spending time at other activities for children (like the children's museum and library story time), all help me learn to be comfortable with groups of kids. You kind of hover in the background at first, so I can see you if I need you. Then you say good-bye and I am fine. [21]

I can now focus easily on a task for at least five minutes. Over the years, this skill is rooted in our reading time, our activities like visual

---

[2] "Children who do not adjust to school are four times less likely to be able to read by the end of their first year in school." Jeni Riley, *The Teaching of Reading: The Development of Literacy in the Early Years of School* (London: Paul Chapman Publishing, 1996), 5.

matching, puzzles, and my daily chores. These routines will transition nicely into the expectations of kindergarten. *[22]*

My experience with three-step patterns will help me to remember and follow three-step instructions in school. "Please close your books, stand up and push in your chair." I am learning to stand patiently in line, to take turns most of the time, and to follow simple rules as well. *[23]*

When problems occur, you help me by giving suggestions. I respond well to redirection. When I tell you that I won't share my favorite toy car, you rarely demand that I do. Instead, you redirect. "Well, the car is nice," you say, "but with your backhoe you could pick up all these blocks and put them in your truck. Then Jason could drive the truck. Or Jason could drive the car and you could follow him to the building site where you'll dump the blocks." I like this idea. I say, "Here is the car Jason. I'll get the truck."

I really want to make and keep friends, so it's good when you guide me on how my friends feel and ways to be kind to them. A little redirection eliminates most of the confrontations, which I am just gaining the social skills to handle. But I know there are clear expectations in our family about safety (like hitting, biting, or throwing things), sharing toys, doing my part of the chores, and getting along. I experience immediate consequences when redirection doesn't work. Sometimes I get a time out. Then we talk about what happened and I say, "I'm sorry." I know that even when you don't like my behavior you still love me very much.

I am beginning to recognize my feelings and am getting better at managing them. Daddy and I say, "Mirror, mirror on the wall, who is happiest of us all?" We compare our happy faces. Then we try hungry faces, then sad and mad and surprised faces. Sometimes Daddy remembers a time when I had a strong emotion. We make faces to match the feeling and talk about it. *[25]* I mostly watch the both of you. That is how I learn to be positive and caring and respectful. I learn to do what you do.

READY! Skills Continuum

	Age Four to Five	End of Kindergarten-One Year Ahead
Reading, Writing, Listening, & Speaking		
Listening to Books	I can make up a different plot or ending durning our 20 minute reading time. I can retell a story.	I read with you 20 minutes a day. I make-up alternative plot/endings
Rhyming	I recite 6-10 nursery rhymes. I sing/chant ABC and number songs while pointing to letters and numbers.	
Hearing Language	I hear my parents speak to me about 30 times an hour.	I hear my parents speak to me about 30 times an hour.
Spoken Words	I understand 4,000-5,000 words, speak in complete sentences, and repeat new words correctly.	I understand 5,000-6,000 words. I use words to explain ideas.
Visual Matching & Naming		
Colors	I can match and name nine colors; yellow, blue, red, green, black, brown, orange, white, purple, grey, pink, magenta.	I recognize 12 colors and shades/tints.
Letter Shapes	I can match and name 12-15 lowercase letters including my first name, and match letters in the shape families: a-c-e-o-s; d-g-p-q; h-m-n-r-u; f-i-j-l-t; k-v-w-x-y-z.	I can name all upper and lower case letters. I can distinguish between letters in a word.
Sounds in Words	I tell words that rhyme; make nonsense rhymes, clap syllables independently, identify the beginning sounds of words.	I begin to blend sounds to read and write. I match pictures with intitial letter sound.
Letter Sounds	I can say the sounds of 12-15 letters.	I can say all the letter sounds including vowels.
Number Shapes	I can match number shapes 1 to 9.	I can match number shapes 1 to 30.
Math & Reasoning		
Geometric Shapes	Cube Sphere Cylinder	I know the prior 13 shapes along with the three-dimensional shapes, cube, sphere, and cylinder.
Counting	I count by rote (memory) to 20.	I count by rote (memory) to 100.
Patterns	I can make three-step patterns like; red, yellow, blue, red, yellow, blue.	I repeat 4-step pattern/sound sequences and play memory games.
Social & Emotional Development		
Relating to Others	I settle-in easily to new groups. I play cooperatively with two to more peers.	I paticipate positively in group activities and I share, help and cooperate.
Attention Span	I can focus on a task for five minutes, even if there are problems or distractions.	I work independetly for 10-15 minutes.
Follows Instructions	I can complete three-step directions, and obey rules.	I complete 4-step directions, and obey rules.
Emotional Well-Being	I talk about feelings of self and others, and show empathy to others.	I talk about feelings of self and others, and show empathy to others.

End of Kindergarten

Reading & Writing, Listening & Speaking

1	Seeing Clearly	I have good vision without glasses or I have corrected vision with glasses.
2	Letter Recognition	I identify all 26 upper and lower case letters and their sounds. I can sound out (blend) simple three letter sound combinations using a consonant, vowel, and consonant (like c-a-t and m-a-t).
3	Phonemic Awareness	I can match and isolate the beginning, ending, and middle sounds of words. I can blend phoneme sounds to make words.
4	Accuracy /Fluency	I can read 50 to 100 sight words.
6	Comprehension	I can identify the setting and characters of a story. I continue to learn more about setting and characters and begin to learn about story elements, such as, problem, solution, and theme. In books, I begin to use the headings and physical features such as table of contents, charts, and graphs to understand and locate information. I dictate a short original story with a beginning, middle and end.
7	Over-all Reading	I can read a simple 200 word selection fluently and with few errors.
8	Developing Verbal Skills	I speak using fewer inaccuracies. My sentences are becoming more complex and my vocabulary had increased to about 5,000 - 6,000 words.
9	Copying-Tracing-Printing	I identify and print 50 familiar words and create 3-sentence stories with some punctuation.

Math & Reasoning

10	Place Value	I count to 30. I am beginning to understand the concept of 12 as 10 plus some ones.
11	Estimating and Rounding	I estimate and round numbers under 20.
12	Read and Write Numbers	I can write the numbers and their number names to 20, (i.e., 5 and five, 10 and ten).
13	Ordering and Comparing	I know which number is more (i.e., 3 or 7). I can order numbers to 30. I can determine equal and unequal parts.
14	Patterns	I identify, extend, and produce AB, ABC, AAB, ABB, AABB patterns, and 5-step sound sequences. I distinguish between two and three dimensional figures. I can identify and draw 16 basic geometric shapes. I am starting to count by 2s, 5s, and 10s.
15	Adding	I know different ways to make numbers from 1-9. I can make a 4 with a 2 and a 2 or 3+1. I can make a 7 with 3 and a 4 or a 5 and a 2. I can make numbers using cubes, counters, and tiles.
16	Subtracting	I am beginning to do simple one digit subtraction (takeaway) using blocks and counting backwards.
17	Application/ Vocabulary	I can correctly choose morning, afternoon, evening, know the days of the week, and months, and understand today, yesterday, and tomorrow.

Social & Emotional

18	Relating to Others	I work independently and finish my tasks on time.
19	Attention Span	I pay attention to a single task for about 10-15 minutes before losing interest.
20	Following Directions	I remember and follow four-step instructions.
21	Taking Responsibility	I understand rules and expectations. I solve some problems and contribute to group accomplishments.
22	Emotional Well-Being	I know who I am and what I can do. I am more likely to use words than physical aggression. I enjoy cooperating with peers. I understand basic manners including sharing and taking turns.

I'm glad I am able to take care of all my own bathroom needs, including wiping, re-dressing, and washing my hands. I cover my mouth and nose with my arm or a tissue when I cough or sneeze. I can tie my own shoes, and put on or take off my coat and hang it on a hook. This is one less thing for my teacher to do, Mommy tells me. She says I need to learn these skills at home before starting school because it will help me to fit into the larger group of kindergarten children. [24]

While playing cooperatively and comfortably will help me fit into my kindergarten group, what will really help is that I am at or above grade level with most of my skills. When we learn alphabet letters in class, I will know what the teacher is talking about. When the teacher asks questions about what we have read, I will have good answers. I will actually know some of the stuff! When we talk about numbers, I will already add and subtract a little. When 60-80% of us leave kindergarten reading a 190-word selection, I will be one of those students.

If I have mastered *entering first grade skills* by the time I enroll in kindergarten, I will be one year ahead. I will be in about the 60th to 80th percentile range — the blue band. That means that I probably mastered most of the grade-level kindergarten skills about 10 months earlier.

If I have mastered *entering second grade skills* by the time I enroll in kindergarten, I will be two years ahead. I will be in about the 80th to 99th percentile range—the dark-blue band. That means that I probably mastered most of the grade-level kindergarten skills 15 to 18 months earlier, depending on the exact date of my birthday and if I enter kindergarten as a five- or a six-year-old.

As Mommy and Daddy may see, I can have really solid skills in one area like language and literacy and be fairly weak in a different area like math or social interaction because my mastery of these grade-level skills may occur in an uneven fashion.

At some point you may ask, independent of my literacy and math ability, whether I am ready to start kindergarten. Obviously, the month of my birthday affects the decision. Public school

End of First Grade

Reading & Writing, Listening & Speaking

1	Seeing Clearly	I have good vision without glasses or I have corrected vision with glasses.
2	Letter Recognition	I identify all 26 upper and lower case letters and their sounds, (same).
3	Phonemic Awareness	I can delete initial and final phonemes in words and also the initial blend phoneme in words.I can do initial, final and middle phoneme substitution in words.
4	Accuracy /Fluency	I can read between 50-60 words per minute with about 90% accuracy.
6	Comprehension	I can identify narrative and expository text. I can retell a narative story with a beginning, middle, and end. I will include the main idea,the problem, and several details in the correct order. I continue to learn more about setting, characters, the problem, the outcome, and the theme. In an expository text, I can state the main idea and include several facts. I continue to use titles, headings, charts, graphs to locate information and main ideas.
7	Over-all Reading	I read simple picture books with about 15-25 short and easy- to- sound-out words a page.
8	Developing Verbal Skills	I speak using fewer inaccuracies. My sentences are becoming more complex and my vocabulary had increased to about 7,000 - 8,000 words.
9	Copying-Tracing-Printing	I identify and print 50 familiar words and create 3-sentence stories with some punctuation.

Math & Reasoning

10	Place Value	I count by ones to 100. I understand two digit numbers as some tens and some ones.
11	Estimating and Rounding	I estimate and round numbers under 30.
12	Read and Write Numbers	I can write the numbers and their number names to 20, (i.e., 5 and five, 10 and ten).
13	Ordering and Comparing	I can tell that a number like 11 is (greater than >, less than <, or equal to =) another number like 3 for numbers to 100. I can use number lines to order numbers.
14	Patterns	I can create two-step figure patterns (like circle, square, circle, square) and three-step patterns (like circle, circle, square, circle, circle, square). I know what comes next in a pattern of 6, 8, 10, _. I can count by 2s, 5s, 10s, and count by even and odd numbers.
15	Adding	I can make numbers from 1 - 12 in different ways. I can add one digit numbers (like $1 + 4 = \_$; $6 + 6 = \_$); two digit numbers (like $19 + 15 = \_$; $31 + 51 + 16 = \_$). I can add by counting forward 1, 2, or 3, add by using doubles, and add by using number lines.
16	Subtracting	I can do simple one digit subtraction (like $5 - 4 = \_$; $6 - 1 = \_$; $12 - 4 = \_$; $6 - 6 =$). I can use a number line to subtract, count back by 1, 2, or 3 to subtract, and use doubles to subtract.
17	Application/ Vocabulary	I can order morning, afternoon, and evening, write time by the hour, half hour, and hour and half. I understand even and odd numbers, patterns, and the concept of greater than, less than, and equal to.

districts have a cut-off for kindergarten enrollment based on my birth date. The cut-off is usually sometime in late August or early September. This means that if I am a July-August baby, I will be barely five (60 months old) when I enter kindergarten. For some children, especially if I am a socially immature boy (less of a problem for girls) with late spring and summer birthdays, delaying kindergarten for a year may be the most strategic decision you can make for me. When I start behind in any category, whether socially, athletically, emotionally, or in simple brain development, I have another obstacle to surmount.

If I am an October baby, I will still be five years old when I start kindergarten, but actually I will be almost six. I will be 71 months old. Not only will I be a year more mature than my fellow classmates, but I have the chance to move up easily almost another band before I start kindergarten if you are working regularly with me.[3]

Offsetting this advantage is the pressure working mothers endure from keeping their child at home or in childcare for yet one more year. Child care considerations alone may cause you to enroll me early.

Remember that the reading and math targets are much softer at these early ages than they are in later years. That is, the relationship between my mastery of them and my relative percentile to other children is less exact and more an approximation than it will be in higher grades.

---

[3] Although the 10 or 11 month difference seems almost invisible, it may have a huge impact. In the Canadian Junior Hockey League, with an eligibility cutoff for age-class hockey of January 1, "in any elite group of hockey players —the very best of the best— 40 percent of the players will have been born between January and March, 30 percent between April and June, 20 percent between July and September, and 10 percent between October and December." Malcolm Gladwell, *Outliers* (New York: Little, Brown and Company 2008), 22.

CHAPTER ELEVEN

ACCELERATED READING AND MATH

"Imagine what our educational system could look like if half of our children entered kindergarten reading and doing simple math by the end of the next decade?"

—Lynn Fielding,
Author

If you are serious about the possibility of extraordinary achievement for me, then you should buy two books by Glenn and Janet Doman:
* *How to Teach Your Baby to Read*, and
* *How to Teach Your Baby Math.*[1]

* * * *

Here's how I might explain it to you if I could. Can you teach me to read while I am a baby? Can you teach me basic math? I think so. Here is the basic approach used by the Domans.

You know that I can recognize Grandma when she comes. No neurologist can actually explain how my brain does this but here's what I think. I take a picture of Grandma's face, and store it in my brain. I connect it to the concept "Grandma," together with her happy sounds and cooing. Next time I see her, I take another digital image and simultaneously compare. Yes, it's Grandma! This is the Doman learning process when I am one, two, and three.

---

[1] This chapter briefly summarizes, with their permission, some of Glenn and Janet Doman's key program. The Doman's program, if it appeals to you, is a powerful way to accelerate your child's reading and math ability. Doman materials are available at <u>www.gentlerevolution.com</u>.

**Mommy and Daddy Prepare for Step 1
(reading single words):**

1. Buy white poster board and a ½" red felt-tipped marker.
2. Cut 200 cards that are 6" by 22" each from white poster board.
3. Print 15 special cards of the 15 most familiar and enjoyable words around me including the names of my siblings, relatives, pets, favorite foods, objects in the house, and favorite activities. The letters should be 3" tall and ½" thick using the red felt-tipped marker. Put one word per card, in lowercase letters (except for proper nouns).
4. Make additional cards using words from the boxes on the next page in the same way. Extend the list using words from my own world and experience, adding any word that I ask about.
5. Print the word again in the upper left corner on the back of the card. That way you will know what is on the other side while showing me the front.
6. Sort the cards and divide them into sets of five cards each starting with my "top 15 words."

Since "How To Teach Your Baby To Read" has been in print for four decades, thousands of libraries across the U.S. have the book and you can save the cost of buying one.

This is just an overview to introduce you to the program, not to teach it to you. You will really need to read their book if this program looks appealing to you. The nuances of the program are important to its success. So this is what you do to get ready.

Step 1—Single Words

The first week we start with the list of my "top 15 words which you have selected from words I like!" Then we move on to some 200 other single words like *shoe, apple, juice, eyes, hand,* and *cookie.* You use the simple method detailed in the Doman books, and summarized here.

1.   On Monday, you select five word cards from my "top 15" special word list, avoiding consecutive words that begin with the same letter. Then you hold up each card sequentially, about fourteen inches from my eyes, for one second and say with great enthusiasm, "This is mommy." Then you put the next card in front of the first card for one second, saying "This is daddy." You continue this process until you have shown me five cards. It is a five-second activity. Five seconds! I simply watch, listen, and learn. Mommy then does the same cards two more times during the day, at least 15 minutes apart, using the same "deck" of words each time. At the end of each session, you hug me and tell me how good and very bright I am and how very proud of me you are. The whole thing lasts under three minutes. I like it! Things you do that really help me are:
     - You start when I am rested, ready, and in a good mood.
     - You use a corner of a room with almost no distracting furniture, pictures, or toys.
     - You shut off anything that makes a competing sound.
     - You do not ask me to repeat words.
     - You take the cards from the back of the deck, glancing at the upper left corner of the back of each card so as you say the word to me, I have your complete attention.

2.   On Tuesday, you repeat what you did on Monday. In addition, you add a second deck of five new words (also from the top 15 word list) which you also show me three times throughout the day, just like the first set for a total of six sessions. You simply say each word as you show it, without saying "this says…"In addition,

you shuffle each deck so the words appear in a different order each session.

3. On Wednesday through Friday, you repeat the Monday and Tuesday decks and add a new deck of five cards each day. With adding the new decks, we do nine sessions on Wednesday, twelve on Thursday, and fifteen on Friday. We take off Saturday and Sunday although we really don't need to.

4. Starting on the next Monday, Daddy removes or "retires" one of the "old" words after they have been shown for five days. You retire "mommy" on Monday. You retire "daddy" and one card from the second deck on Tuesday. By Friday you are retiring one card from each deck *and* each time he retires a card, he adds a new one so we are always using five decks with five words each. Writing the starting date of each word on the back of the card (in pencil) makes it easy to figure out when to remove it.

5. When you see that I am ready (focused, engaged, enjoying the game), you add a fourth and fifth deck of words so I am seeing five sets of five words each day (25 words), with five new words a day. We go through the 200 words in nine to twelve weeks.

6. You do not bore me by reviewing. You do not create tension by testing me. Mommy approaches each session with lots of joy; you smile and give me nice hugs. These are the rules, you say.

Steps 2, 3, and 4—Multiple Words

Step 2 extends the process to two words (couplets), then simple three word sentences (step 3), then more complicated sentences (step 4).

So this is the basic process. It is somewhat difficult to gauge exactly where I am because I do not like being tested.

The Doman program extends to math as well. I have a window where I can "see and learn" quantities. You can recognize quantities to 4, or if they are lined up like dice, perhaps to six. But I can go all the way to 40, and 50 and even 100. I can learn to see and recognize them at a glance. The trick is I have to do it when I am young because big people cannot do it, you tell me. Once I can recognize the quantity of dots, naming them, and adding them, and subtracting them is a simple extension.

Reading One or Two Years Ahead

If I enter kindergarten one year ahead (blue band) or two years ahead (dark-blue band) I will be reading easy books and doing simple arithmetic. So why not try to teach me to read easy books and do simple arithmetic as soon as I am capable and interested? You can start with the powerful three-step process that I use to recognize grandma and other faces.

Again, this is just an overview to introduce you to the program, not to teach it to you. You will really need to buy their books if this method looks appealing to you.

> *"If I can see quantities at a glance, addition and subtraction is almost like face recognition for me before kindergarten, and I am still just a normal kid with parents who still love me, why wouldn't I want this for me? I'll tell you what I want. I want it all – if I can read at age two or three, the world opens for me."*

Institutes of the Achievement of Human Potential

The Institutes of the Achievement of Human Potential were founded in 1955 by Glenn Doman to specialize in children with brain injuries.

Glenn Doman

In early 1964, the mother of a four-year-old brain-injured patient not only taught the child to read but was able to convince the attending physician at The Institutes that this child, with less than normal brain function, was reading. During the next decade, Glenn Doman developed a program to extending this training so parents could to teach reading to normal children. In the early eighties, Doman successfully extended these processes to math.

Once generalized, the processes were quickly applied to a whole series of early learning activities including physical development, playing instruments, and learning vast amounts of information.

A small portion of the medical community, responding to what might be characterized as over-selling the results of the new technology, pigeon-holed it as a "patterning process" in the 1970s. However, the dramatic results achieved by the Institutes with brain-injured and normal children received increasingly wide-spread attention. From 1998 to 2008, some 1,141 of the 1,156 brain-injured children (99%), whose parents attended the on-campus program in Wyndmoor, Pennsylvania (near Philadelphia) were taught to read for the first time. *How To Teach Your Baby To Read* is currently published in 24 languages worldwide.

The dramatic results raises the policy question whether part of the billions of federal dollars spent of early childhood programs since the '60s would have been better spent on this program.

Glenn's daughter, Janet, was raised in The Institutes and, by the age of nine, was actively helping out. She later went on to get her degree at the University of Pennsylvania in physical anthropology, is now a specialist in infant education and brain development and the director of The Institutes. She and her father have written numerous books.

Janet Doman

CHAPTER TWELVE

LIVING WITH REGRET

"Sara is off to kindergarten next week," announces Rob. "Bought her some new clothes, a cute little red backpack, pencils, and some rounded-tip scissors. Didn't wait until the last minute like we usually do. Got her ready last night."

All of these things are great, but of course, Sara isn't ready. Sara is starting kindergarten three years behind in language and literacy skills and two years behind in math. In fact, she will be in the lowest 15% of her class. There was nothing that Sara's parents could have done the week before kindergarten to move her from the 15th percentile to the 50th percentile.

"We didn't read much to her, and she didn't go to preschool. But even if she is a little behind, she'll catch up in a year or two," says Julie. As we have seen before, a majority of parents share this mistaken belief expressed by Sara's mom.

It makes sense, given that most parents also (erroneously) think that the top students are maybe six months ahead and the bottom students are only six months behind. So with a little extra work, can't students who are behind catch up? The grim reality is that those who start behind usually stay behind, and they are not just a little behind. They are *years* behind.

"We're very proud of this young lady," continues Rob."Before we know it, we'll be sending her off to the university. Julie and I didn't go, but we are going to make sure Sara goes."

As the preceding chapters describe, predicting at kindergarten who will go to college is fairly difficult. It is much easier to predict who will not go. The statistics are against Sara, notwithstanding the power of her parents' expectations and their obvious willingness to do what they think will help. Sara's chances at birth of attending a university were one in three. But Sara is not the average kindergarten student. She is at the bottom of the class. Her chances are very low.

"Sara's a very determined little girl," Rob continues. "Every year she will make a year of progress. And 13 years from now, she'll graduate and off she'll go to the university."

Sara's determination will serve her well. But even with this determination, if she makes only one year of growth each year, she will read three years behind every year: three years behind throughout elementary school, and three years behind in middle and high school.

With this determination, she will make progress in math as well. However, even if she gains extra three years of growth and moves from the 15th to the 50th percentile by the beginning of 10th grade, her math scores will only match what her 90th percentile friends achieved in sixth grade.

Without grade-level reading skills, Sara will struggle in history, science, geography, current events, and social studies as well. Without grade-level math, Sara will struggle with biology, chemistry, and physics. In all likelihood, she will fail classes and lose credit. Falling behind in cumulative earned credits is a high predictor of those who drop out.

Given the impact of starting points at kindergarten, where do you want your child to begin?

Even if she graduates from high school on time, when she enrolls in a community college, she will likely spend her first year paying college tuition, but taking remedial classes that earn her no college credit.

All parents yearn to smooth the way for their children, removing the stumbling blocks and impediments and providing any advantages they can. At some point, Sara's mom and dad may finally realize that they could have done a lot to stack the cards in favor of Sara. They could have read to her 20 minutes a day from birth, talked with her continually to build her language skills, and spent another five to ten minutes a day with fun learning activities that would have quietly and effectively wired Sara's brain for school readiness.

When Rob and Julie realize how easily they could have prepared Sara for kindergarten and how hard it will be for her to overcome her starting point, it will be difficult for them not to be filled with regret.

For the most part, you and every parent like you, with a little effort, basically can choose what level of literacy, language, and math-related skills your child will have when he or she begins kindergarten.

Given the impact of starting points at kindergarten, where have you chosen to start your child?

Additional copies of Extraordinary Parents *are available by using the order form in Appendix A at page 228, online at www.readingfoundation.org, or www.newfoundationpress.com, and at your local bookstore. Questions? Call (509) 551-3226*

EXTRAORDINARY PARENTS:

FROM KINDERGARTEN TO COLLEGE

Good, bad, or indifferent, the birth-to-kindergarten years are now over. The years ahead deal with your child's initial kindergarten starting points and focus on staying the course with her for the next twelve years. These years involve the issues of continued and satisfying high-academic performance. However, you may not have been aware of these issues until your child was already in the green or yellow bands or lower. These years could require extraordinary effort for catch-up growth as well. Extraordinary effort for extraordinary results. That is pretty well what X-moms and dads do.

Part Two explores obtaining and maintaining good information about where your child is, knowing the math and reading targets that indicate whether he is at grade level, one or two years ahead or behind, helping him figure out what he wants to do when he grows up, and planning how to pay for it.

If you are a second- or third-generation college graduate in your family, then the essential K-12 patterns to keep post-secondary education squarely in your child's future may already be a integral part of your family culture. But if you have only high school experience, you may need to approach the task of adding successful K-12 patterns consciously and purposefully to your family customs and traditions. These expectations, skills, and attitudes will be critical to your child's success.

That is what these chapters are about: helping you to make the right decisions as your child goes through elementary, middle, and high school so that she is prepared for and can afford the post-secondary education that is optimal for her.

If you are a young parent, in the midst of all of the activities of birth to five, you may be feeling deep discouragement. The next chapters may seem premature and may not merit now the careful attention of the previous chapters. I suggest that a quick overview now will give you a sense of the lay of the land and avoid some surprises later.

Alternatively, you may already have elementary and middle school aged children. Is it too late?

The answer is that early is always better than later because the time to catch up is more limited the older your child is. The process, however, is the same. Create a clear line of sight from where your child is to where he needs to go. The trajectory of growth may need to be steeper. The amount of time spent each day may need to be increased. Your child's commitment to the process may need to be deepened. But assuring that your child makes a one to one and one-half year growth each year starting now will yield a better result than handing off that responsibility to your school system and hoping for a good outcome.

In addition, I suggest that you read Chapter 20 fairly carefully as well. It deals with financing post-secondary education, an activity best started while your child is an infant. You simply cannot start saving too early.

Once again, grandparents can play a powerful role in the lives of their grandchildren as can other relatives, and child care providers and should read themselves into passages where I refer to moms, dads, and parents.

At an average adult reading speed of about 300 words a minute, including sidebars, comment boxes, and footnotes, and spending three minutes on each figure or table, you can read Part Two in 3 hours, 30 minutes.

CHAPTER THIRTEEN

ENTERING KINDERGARTEN: WHERE IS MY CHILD?

"It is common to find within a kindergarten classroom a five-year range in children's literacy-related skills and functioning."

—Dr. Jeni Riley,
University of London

Let's assume that it's August and you've been buying crayons, T-shirts, and pants for your five-year-old. You know that he could enter kindergarten at one of six different language and literacy levels, each about a year apart. Before you read this book, you probably hoped that your child would "get a good start" in kindergarten.

Now your questions are: Where is my child? Ahead? Behind? Which band? How can I tell if the twenty minutes a day I have spent reading to my child from birth and the time I have spent on the activities designed to help him reach the age-level targets have paid off?

Even if your child is entering kindergarten without this conscientious and purposeful preparation, the questions are the same. Where is my child? Ahead? Behind? Which band?

Finding and using this information is your job as a parent. In a system where starting points so strongly predict subsequent achievement, you'll be surprised to learn that national percentile data for your child before the end of second or third grade are rarely available and almost never available to you at the beginning of kindergarten when dramatic growth is easiest.

Even when the information is available, you may well encounter reluctance from the institution when you ask for it. If it's good news, some school officials believe that parents may use the information to "push" their child too hard. If it is bad news, officials worry that parents may blame the school for their child's low performance (which you shouldn't) and then pressure the school to create catch-up growth for your child (which you should).

Parents must shoulder the responsibility when their child starts kindergarten below grade level. While elementary schools must assume responsibility for annual growth for all students and have programs in place that work to catch up those who are behind, parents must help.

This website will provide information about additional kindergarten and first grade assessments as they become available for the next decade:

www.newfoundationpress.com

The right-hand box lists ways for you to get some idea of where your child is, if not by a national percentile, at least in terms of skills by years above or below grade level. Movement of students within and between bands and percentiles is more fluid from kindergarten through third grade than after third grade. After third grade, students are less likely to move up or down as much or as far than in the school years before third grade.

Ideally, multiple safety nets would catch students whose beginning scores fall below the norm. School officials may assure parents that prompt diagnosis, immediate intervention, and effective remediation will give every child an adequate education. Some day that ideal may be true. But it does not describe the current reality in American schools. *Your child needs you and needs your intervention.* The sobering fact is that children who start behind or fall behind because of low skill levels seldom catch up without vision and effort by their parents.

Determining the achievement band of your elementary school child is a matter of synthesizing clusters of information. Consider creating a chart to organize all of the available information about your child's

Ways to Tell Where Your Child Starts and Ends Each Year

1. National percentiles give essential skill-ranking information about your child. If you live in one of the 2,500 districts the Northwest Evaluation Association assesses, your school district can provide this information. The NWEA percentiles reflect the six bands.

2. You may also get percentile data from third-party vendors licensed by NWEA who offer services to individual parents. A list of those vendors appears at www.newfoundationpress.com and will be updated annually for the next decade.

3. If your district uses any assessment that gives your child national percentile ranking, you can use those percentiles to determine band equivalents as well. Names of those assessments also appear at www.newfoundationpress.com.

4. For reading, an increasing number of school and public libraries use a Lexile number to rank books according to difficulty. You can use the conversion chart in Chapter 16 to approximate your child's achievement level from her Lexile number.

5. For math, you can use the math targets in Chapter 10 and the 50th percentile math curriculum summaries in Appendix D. The targets and the math curriculum summaries will give you a sense of "a year ahead, two years ahead" or "a year, two or three behind," although they do not provide a national percentile ranking.

growth—national percentiles, state testing results, observations from her teacher, and the quarterly report card. The data generally form a cluster of data points in close proximity to each other.

You should give the most weight to the NWEA percentiles when they are available, then to national percentiles from other assessments, then to the raw

> *A professional-grade 14"x 24" chart to organize and track your child's academic achievements K-12 can be purchased at www.newfoundationpress.com.*

scores from proficiency levels on state tests, and least weight of all to classroom grades which are most easily biased.

Why Elementary Class Grades Should Be Considered Last

During the golden elementary years where improvement can occur most easily and when parents need the data the most, school districts do not provide it to you. Almost every kindergarten teacher does some kind of intake assessment of each new incoming student. Yet uniformity or consistency in what they test is unusual, and district-wide tests are uncommon. State-wide incoming kindergarten tests are still more rare. Virtually no early grade assessments besides NWEA are nationally normed. What little data are available is rarely shared with parents.

In kindergarten, first, and second grade, report cards in public schools generally give pluses (+), minuses (-) and checks (✓). They rarely give letter grades. Schools have found (correctly) that poor grades tend to discourage students who are already struggling. But after eliminating letter grades, school leaders have not found an effective way to encourage students who are excelling.

However, many states have started administering standardized tests at the second grade, an encouraging practice that provides early, increasingly specific data to educators and parents about how individual children are doing.

Once letter grades are given—say, in the third or fourth grade—another problem arises. Suppose you are a teacher and have a student who starts the year in the 90th percentile. You probably do not know she is in the 90th percentile. What you know is that she is ahead. Suppose the student does almost no work and falls an entire grade level from the 90th to the 70th percentile. Again, if you don't have a national percentile ranking assessment or scoring system that charts this backward slippage, you probably realize that she has made only a little progress, but she is still one of the top 10 students in a class of 30. As the teacher, you could give her anything from an A or B (indicating her achievement level compared with the other students) to a D or an F (communicating that she is not trying and is failing to progress). Which grade do you give her? How do you explain your grading policy to her parents?

Suppose then, in the same class, you also have a student who starts the year in the 30th percentile but finishes in the 50th percentile, equivalent to making two years of growth in a single year. This is a year of annual growth plus a year of catch-up growth. You could give him an A for effort and growth (and many teachers do) or a C indicating his actual achievement level compared to the rest of the class (and again, many teachers do). This is why classroom grades are uneven indicators of national achievement levels. As parents, you need more precise information.

Starting Behind

While your child may be ahead, there is also the distinct possibility that he may be behind as well. Some elementary schools offer a "transition" grade for struggling students either between kindergarten and first grade or first and second grades. This is an approach with a long history of getting students up to grade level that would otherwise spend most of their K-12 experience behind and often failing. If your child is struggling early, a transition grade is an excellent opportunity if it is available.

Northwest Evaluation Association Data

Chapter 2 presents average growth data in reading for two million students in elementary, middle, and high school from districts all over the United States using data from the Northwest Evaluation Association (NWEA). The Northwest Evaluation Association tests in 2,500 of the 13,862 school districts nationwide. This chapter encourages the use of national percentiles to measure learning, which the NWEA provides.

One of the most powerful benefits of NWEA assessments is their accuracy, not only for the 20% of students at grade level, but also for the 40% of students who are above grade level and the 40% of students who are below. Traditional reading tests, including your state tests, usually consist of 50 questions, about 35 of which are centered at grade level. While the reason for this concentration is obvious, it leaves only seven or eight questions to identify where in the one- to two-year range above grade level 40% of students are, and another seven or eight questions to place the 40% of students who are one, two, and three years below grade level. Standard tests give the least accurate information about the lowest 40% and highest 40% of students.

NWEA assessments are computerized and internet-based. They automatically adjust for difficulty depending on the student's response. Within five or six questions, NWEA locates your student's general reading level. The remaining 42 questions concentrate on sub-skills (like accuracy, fluency phonemic awareness, and comprehension) within that level. NWEA assessments are among the most accurate in the United States.

A second strength of NWEA assessment is the power of its reporting platform. It uses an equal interval scale that has remained constant over the last 30 years. It is like a measuring tape where the intervals between the feet and inches remain constant over time. If you had taken the NWEA reading test as a third grader, you and your daughter could compare scores and get valid results. The longitudinal accuracy is immensely important in measuring growth.

Another use of the scale is to translate scores to grade level equivalents. Most parents find it useful and easy to understand that their child is two years above grade level if he is reading at the 90th percentile or a year below grade level if he is reading at the 30th percentile. While standardized weights and measures have been common in virtually every industry for over a century, stable interval measurement scales are still cutting-edge technology in education.

A third strength of NWEA data is the sheer size of its database. Its student data are based not on thousands or tens of thousands but on two million student scores. Its norming sample sizes are 33% to 56% larger than those used for the National Assessment of Educational Performance (NAEP), the largest federally mandated testing program in the United States. The size of the database and the accuracy of the testing make NWEA data highly reliable.

NWEA data are obviously very powerful in pinpointing your child's progress, and obviously you want to have access to the most accurate information possible about your child as she transitions out of your primary care and into kindergarten at a public or private elementary school. But other sources are also available. (See the list "Ways to Tell Where Your Child Starts," pg. 125).

CHAPTER FOURTEEN

ELEMENTARY SCHOOL: ANNUAL GROWTH VS, CATCH-UP GROWTH

"You no longer have to deliver your child to the K-12 system and quietly resign yourself to whatever the eventual outcome may be."
— Carl VanHoff, Community Relations,
Nuclear Power Industry

If you have been successful to this point, your child has finished kindergarten in or near the dark-blue achievement band. Now you need to assure that he makes annual growth during first grade and each year thereafter.

Did My Child Make Annual Growth This Year?

Annual growth is a simple concept. It is an average year of learning in a given subject area. Your child makes annual growth when she makes the same amount of growth as other students nationwide in the same grade level. She maintains her place in the pack. She neither moves ahead of her peers nor falls behind. She stays at the same national percentile. National percentiles help you determine whether your child is gaining or losing ground.

Annual growth works like this. Each year at each grade level, the 3.7 million students in U.S. K-12 schools take reading and math. Their starting and ending achievement levels can be determined with proper measurements.

The difference between their beginning achievement and ending achievement is their individual growth for the year. The "average" growth at each percentile is the average of the thousands of students at each percentile.

If your child is reading at the 70th percentile nationally at the beginning of the year and makes annual growth, she will score at the 70th percentile at the end of the year. In relationship to her peers, she will maintain her relative position. This means that she stays in the mid-part of the blue band.

If your child makes less than annual growth in reading, he will slip downward in his reading band. If your child makes no growth during a year in reading, he will slip down an entire band.

Small movements (two or three percentiles) on the same test or four percentiles between different tests are generally attributed to normal measurement variation (standard error) and are not significant.

Without national percentiles to verify growth, your child probably makes annual growth if she is:

- Getting pluses (+'s) or A's and B's.
- Doing challenging homework each night.
- Scoring at or above the same point that she scored in the previous year's state tests.
- Attending school with few absences.

Assuring that your child makes annual growth is a never-ending process that starts at kindergarten and continues through twelfth grade. If you were successful in creating dark-blue performance during the five years between his birth to his entrance into kindergarten, your primary concern is maintaining his position or, in other words, achieving annual growth.

As you might suspect, it is easier for individual classrooms and school districts to create *annual growth* for most students than it is to create both *annual growth* for most students **and** *additional catch-up growth for those who are behind*. However, there are wide differences between school districts in creating consistent annual growth in reading and math in elementary and middle schools. Figure 14.1 shows this variance among the 2,500 NWEA school districts.

Here's the way to use Figure 14.1. When you know the percentage of students who make annual growth in reading or math in your school, you can compare it to other schools by selecting the subject (reading or math) and the grade. Then run your finger down until you reach the percent. For example, if you know that 58% of students in your school made annual growth from spring of second grade to spring of third grade, run your finger down column 2 until you get to 58%, then move to the left to find your child's school. You see that your school is in the top 60 percent of schools in creating annual growth in reading at second grade.

(1)	(2)	(3)	(4)	(5)	(6)	(7)
Where Your School Ranks in Creating Annual Growth						
		Reading			Math	
	2-3	3-4	4-5	2-3	3-4	4-5
1	18	27	22	13	18	16
5	31	34	33	23	25	26
10	36	38	37	30	32	32
20	42	44	43	37	38	39
30	47	48	47	42	44	43
40	51	52	50	46	48	48
50	54	54	50	50	52	52
60	58	57	56	54	56	56
70	61	60	60	59	60	60
80	65	65	63	65	65	64
90	70	69	68	72	72	71
95	75	72	72	78	77	75
99	83	80	81	87	84	84

Percentile Ranking of School

Figure 14.1 Where your school ranks in creating annual growth.[1]

You may be very surprised to see that some (20%) of schools create a year of math growth or more for only 37-39% of their students during elementary school. Is one of these elementary schools your child's school? This is why parents must continually nudge their local schools toward higher levels of academic proficiency. This is why PTAs should look beyond fundraising and playground equipment to what matters most to parents.

---

[1] John Cronin and Branin Bowe, "Study of Growth Index Performance by School," NWEA research report (2007), 9,15.

Can Students Move Between Bands?

Figures 14.2 and 14.3 show how much students move between bands from the end of third grade to the end of eighth grade in reading and math. Suppose that your daughter is with 100 other students in the dark-blue band at the end of third grade.

Put your finger on the dark-blue square just under column (1). This number represents her and the other 100 students in her band at third grade. Then slide your finger down past the arrow to the dark-blue band just below the arrow. This number represents the 67 of those 100 students who will still be performing in the dark-blue band at the end of eighth grade. Now move your finger down another row. Twenty-eight of the 100 students will be in the blue band. Each succeeding box shows the number of students of the original 100 blue band students in that band at eighth grade. Notice that 95 of the 100 students will be in the top two bands five years later.

Now go over to column six. By repeating the same exercise you can see that of the 100 students who started in the red (lowest) band in third grade, one student actually makes it, against the odds, to the blue band and one student makes it into the green band.

The good news is the hope this should create. Movement is possible. Dramatic gains can occur. Students can make five years of normal growth plus five years of catch-up growth in reading in five years. It does not occur with a good week or month's worth of work. It is on-going effort that must continue throughout the rest of your child's educational career. Significant sustained effort by extraordinary parents and their student occurs.

The bad news is the persistent power of early achievement levels. Most (70-80%) students stay in their initial band, move up a band, or move down a band. For example, go over to the yellow band in the middle of Figure 14.2 at column (3). Then run your finger down to the green band in eighth grade. Of the 100 students who started in the green band, 33 are still there. There are 24 just above in the blue band and 30 in the yellow band just below. That is, 87 of the 100 students are at the same band, one above or one below the band they started in. This is true of the dark-blue band (95%), blue band (78%), green band (87%), and orange band as well (94%).

Did My Child Make the Necessary Catch-up Growth?

Where 100 3rd graders in each reading band end up at 8th graders						
	(1)	(2)	(3)	(4)	(5)	(6)
3rd graders by band	100	100	100	100	100	100
	⬇	⬇	⬇	⬇	⬇	⬇
Number of students in each performance band at 8th grade	67	23	7	2	0	0
	28	35	24	10	1	1
	10	28	33	22	6	2
	4	15	30	35	12	4
	2	9	19	37	22	11
	2	4	8	28	32	26

Figure 14.2 Reading. Tracking 100 3rd grade students in each performance band into their resulting performance bands at the end of 8th grade.[2]

Where 100 3rd graders in each math band end up at 8th graders						
	(1)	(2)	(3)	(4)	(5)	(6)
3rd graders by band	100	100	100	100	100	100
	⬇	⬇	⬇	⬇	⬇	⬇
Number of students in each performance band at 8th grade	80	16	4	1	0	0
	37	37	20	5	1	0
	16	31	32	16	4	1
	5	17	33	31	11	3
	2	6	19	36	26	11
	1	3	6	24	27	40

Figure 14.3 Math. Tracking 100 3rd grade students in each performance band into their resulting performance bands at the end of 8th grade.[2]

---

[2] This chart was derived from copyrighted data provided by NWEA from 7,520 students whose reading scores and 8,842 students who's math scores were available during both at the end of third grade and the end of eighth grade in reading and math. © 2009 Northwest Evaluation Association. By its nature, these data exclude the transient populations who are not around five years later to register an eighth grade score. Their frequent moving often decreases the amount of time these students are in school by up to 20 days a year. See Appendix B for a longer description of the methodology of these figures. Elimination of the transient population creates a slight distortion in the data by overstating the percentages in the upper bands and understating the percentages in the lower bands. The degree of distortion can be seen when each column is totaled.

Despite your efforts, your child may not have started kindergarten in the dark-blue or blue band and may need to grow an extra year or two to be on grade level—maybe even an extra three years. How can you make this happen?

First, a short reminder. The easiest way for you to assure that your child is in one of the blue bands is to invest purposeful, conscientious effort from birth to five. It is easier on you as the parent, easier on your child, and probably less expensive. You will see why shortly.

The Part That Will Be Easier

If your child is achieving below your state's standard, you will get a lot of help to catch him up. For the first time in the history of public education, America's 50,000 elementary schools (including your child's) are focused on catching up the 40% of children who are behind. Catch-up growth is built into the structure of the current educational reform legislation.

When states set a standard and measure individual school performance by the percentage of students above or below that standard, the structure of the reporting mechanism creates extraordinary pressure to raise academic performance of students below the state standard. If school reform achieves only one objective, it should be this: *We should catch most students up to a standard close to grade level in reading and math during elementary school.*

If your child is below state standards, your elementary school will have a menu of services and activities to create a year and a half to three years of reading and math growth each year. In all likelihood, your school will be recruiting your help in this endeavor. Because of the immense federal and state pressure on schools to bring increasing numbers of students up to state minimum standards, getting your child up to state standards is the part that is easy.

Increasing the number of minutes spent on direct instruction is one of the obvious and common sense ways to catch kids up. Students who are behind do not learn faster than students who are ahead. They need more time. Targeted Accelerated Growth (p. 139) explains one implementation of this strategy.

The Dead Zone—the Part That Will Be Harder

You can begin to understand the hard part by looking at Figures 14.4 and 14.5, which show state standards in reading and math in twenty-six states. You can see that some states set their minimum

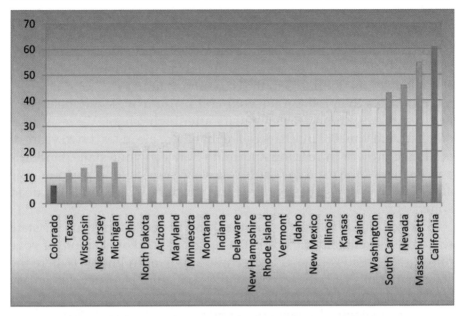

Figure 14.4 Reading: Check at which percentile and in which band your state or a neighboring state has set its third-grade reading standard.[3]

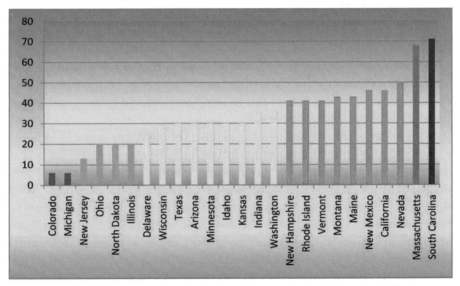

Figure 14.5 Math: Check at which percentile your state or a neighboring state has set its third-grade math standard.[3]

[3] Where 26 states have set their reading standards and 25 states have set their standards for eighth grade based on NWEA comparative data retrieved from http://www.edexcellence.net/doc/TheProficiency illusion.pdf. on June 18, 2009.

standards in the orange band (10-20th percentile), most in the yellow band (20-40th percentile), a few in the green band (40-60th percentile), and fewer still in the blue band (60-80th). Understandably, none of the states has set its standards in the dark-blue band.

But here's the problem for your child. You may desperately want her to enroll in a four-year university after high school. Yet regardless of what state you live in, chances are that there are at least two years of academic growth in reading and math between your state standards and the dark-blue band in which you want your child to perform. The area between your state standards and the dark-blue band is the dead zone.

Growth in addition to the annual growth needed to reach the state standards is generally called "catch-up growth." For example, if your third-grader reads at the 21st percentile and lives in Illinois (where the state standard is set at the 35th percentile, see Figure 14.4), her elementary school will want her to make annual growth each year so that she keeps up. Her school will also want her to make an additional 14% of growth (almost another year's worth of growth), to move from the 21st percentile to the 35th percentile. In this case, catch-up growth constitutes that distance between the 20th and the 34th percentiles.

Once your daughter has made this growth, she's in the 34th percentile (middle of the yellow band). Her teacher is satisfied. Her school is satisfied. Your state is satisfied. But you want her to achieve in the 80th percentile (bottom of the dark-blue band). You may be the only one in this relationship who wants her to keep on "catching up"— catching-up to her college-bound peers.

But what is this growth called in your elementary school? What is growth above your state standards to the 80th percentile called? It is just random growth. It is a "good thing," but it is not something that your local elementary school is designed to make happen. Your daughter's 90-minute reading block will not be lengthened to create it. Special reading teachers will not use their limited time with pull-out sessions to assure it. The cut-off points on the tests used to determine where students are in relation to state standards (cut scores) will not be raised to reflect students in the blue bands.

When you want your child to move up to the dark-blue performance level, there are no public schools goals or public school objectives that define this kind of accelerated growth as "required" or "needed" or "necessary" growth. It's merely a family goal, a personal target, and an extra aspiration.

Calculating Catch-Up Growth

Mindy's little sister Celia is starting third grade when her parents realize that she is reading at the 40th percentile—the bottom of the green band. Mindy's mom and dad would like to see her reading at least at the bottom of the dark-blue band (80th percentile) by the time she starts middle school.

If this growth is spread equally over third, fourth, and fifth grades, Celia will need to make three years of normal growth plus two extra years of catch-up growth. She will need to make a year of annual growth each year plus two-thirds of a year of catch-up growth to move up through the green band and blue band in three years. Her targets would be:

End of third grade	52nd percentile
End of 4th grade	66th percentile
End of 5th grade	80th percentile

Celia's accelerated growth will probably require the normal 90 minutes of classroom instructional time plus an additional 60 minutes (two-thirds of 90 minutes) per day of direct instruction each day at school. Because the extra 60 minutes of classroom instruction is not likely to be available, she may need 60 minutes of private tutoring plus additional practice at home.

When you push for accelerated growth through the dead zone, be prepared to hear confusion and even resentment from your educational system. "Your child is just fine," they'll say, or "You are pushing her too hard," or "You have unrealistic expectations." Don't waste your energy blaming the teachers, administrators, or the system. You have to *use* the system.

Given time to think about the problem, most elementary principals would say something like this:

I agree with your goals for your child. It's exactly what I want for my own kids. It's hard to argue with the odds of university enrollment.

The problem is, I have 22 classroom teachers, five specialists, and 500 students. Our day-to-day school structure of selected curriculum, minutes of classroom instruction per subject, and ever-increasing teacher

instructional skill is barely designed to produce annual growth for all students and to catch up students who are behind.

The legislators who fund us are very clear about bringing the bottom end students up to state standard. We spend all of our extra resources on those students. They're our first priority. We have spent the last ten years trying to figure out how to restructure school curriculum, time, and resources to help them catch up. We spend about twice as much on the lowest 40% as we do on the upper 60%. We are not positioned to move your daughter and the many, many others like her to the dark-blue band with our current resources. It's not a job mandated by any legislation, and it's not funded by anything other than common sense and intelligent aspirations for your child. I wish you luck.

Students in the red band do not learn faster than students at state standards. They need more instructional time if they are going to catch up. Likewise, students in the yellow and green bands do not learn faster than students in the dark-blue band. Rarely does a student navigate across the dead zone without increased instructional time, expert teaching and effective curriculum.

What are Your Best Shots for Catching Your Child Up to the College-Bound?

1. Maximize your child's in-school learning. Expect A's. Support him outside of the school day so he can achieve them.
2. Read aloud to your child. Induce him to read an extra hour or two a day. Provide incentives to lure him into reading on his own and to try new, more difficult books. Find and surround him with the books that sing to him or feed his passion. Keep track of and celebrate the amount of time spent reading. Talk about what you read as a family.
3. Hire an outside tutor. Make it clear what the targets are and what the required growth needs to be. Consider Sylvan although be aware that instructional quality may differ from location to location.
4. Watch what the tutors do. Learn how to teach or at least support the teaching of the four sub-set skills of elementary reading: accuracy, fluency, phonemic awareness, and comprehension.
5. As you learn which university may best serve your child's interests, increase his motivation by connecting him to it. Learn the fight song. Attend its sporting events, plays, and concerts. Buy the sweatshirts and baseball hats. Wander with him around its library, gymnasiums, and concert halls. Hang a poster in his room.

Targeted Accelerated Growth

In Kennewick, Washington, educators have found that they can create two and three years of reading growth in a single year by a four-step process called the Targeted Accelerated Growth Loop, or "TAG."

- We begin with 120 minutes of excellent eyeball-to-eyeball reading instruction for all students in morning reading blocks, 60 minutes of which is ability-grouped and which stresses systematic phonics.
- For students who are behind, our elementary schools use diagnostic tests to determine which sub-skills our students lack. (The sub-skills include accuracy, fluency, comprehension, and phonological awareness or the ability to hear the difference in word sounds.)
- We then increase the amount of direct eyeball-to-eyeball instructional time in proportion to how far the child is behind. This additional instruction ranges from ten to sixty minutes for a total of 130-180 minutes a day.
- We use the additional time to teach to the deficient sub-skill, rather than re-teaching the same material that that whole class learned in the morning.
- We retest to assure that adequate catch-up growth (in that particular sub-skill) actually occurred. If it has not, the adults adjust what they do in the instructional process.

For your student to make two years of growth in a single year, he must grow at 200% the rate of normal reading growth. The first 100% comes from normal instruction and time. Improved instruction during the current year can account for another 10% of this growth. Improved curriculum may account for another 10-20% (although in the first year of a new curriculum, it may not add that much). The remaining 70% of growth must come from increased instructional time.

Catch-up growth is so difficult to achieve that it can be the product only of quality of instruction in great quantity. This is why instructional time must be often doubled or even tripled, especially in elementary school, to catch a child up. That's where you as a parent can reinforce the learning that is happening at school.

Longer Shots

6. Join your local PTA or PTO. Urge your building's leadership to read *Annual Growth for All Children, Catch-Up Growth For Those Who Are Behind* (available in Appendix A at page 227) and being used by thousands of elementary schools nationwide. Convince your elementary school to extend the process by which students make more-than-annual growth to include students above the state standard.

> One Saturday when I was in fourth grade, my parents took my sisters and me to our elementary school, explaining how long we would each be there as we moved through the grades. Then we went to a middle school, where we would go after fifth grade, learned that it was three years long and which neighbor kids and babysitters were going there now. Then we did the same for our high school.
>
> A few months later, we drove a little out of our way to walk across the campus of a major university and its gigantic library. Mom told us that we would all be going to a university like this, that we would first get a four- year degree, then a master's degree and finally a doctorate degree. Dad pointed out that his sister had a doctor of English literature. At that point I wanted to know if she had a stethoscope and why she didn't wear a white coat like the other doctors we knew.

7. NWEA has a report that allows reading and math growth targets to be set individually. If your district uses NWEA testing, you may ask that your child's targets be set for accelerated (150-200% of normal) growth and work with your child's teachers to achieve it.

8. Ascertain whether certain teachers would be a more appropriate "match" for your child given these goals. Request these teachers.

9. Consider moving into a neighborhood where the elementary school assessment scores are consistently improving and/or high. Chances are that this school would have higher expectations for your child and probably a better learning environment.

This chapter is only 12 pages long. Like other chapters it has, of necessity, omitted many other valuable elementary school perspectives that are important for your child including co-curricular activities, health and fitness, and expanded social skills. It has only one goal: your child's preparation for post-secondary education.

CHAPTER FIFTEEN

GIFTED AND TALENTED

"I really had a lot of dreams when I was a kid, and I think a great deal of that grew out of the fact that I had a chance to read a lot."

—Bill Gates

When parents of children with normal IQs accelerate their academic growth between birth and age five, the achievement of these children often rivals students with higher IQs who have not experienced accelerated academic growth. As you push for higher performance for your child, it is easy to mistake those increased abilities for increased IQ.

"If my child is performing in the dark-blue band," you might ask, "won't she automatically qualify for my district's gifted program?" Probably not. Most districts with more than 3,000 students offer an accelerated program for their very brightest students. These programs differ widely from state to state as well as within each state, and often have local designations like GATE (gifted and talented education) TAG (talented and gifted), the Odyssey program, and the Challenge program. Gifted programs generally start in the second or third grade, try to enroll the top 2 or 3% of students, and have a fixed number of available seats that increase or decrease in increments of 20-25 students (add a class, subtract a class).

In a district of 13,000 students, for example, there are about 1,000 students per grade level (13,000 divided by 12.5 grades equals 1,040 students). Two percent of 1,040 students is 21 students or roughly a single class. In a district of 4,000, a class of 20 students in each grade will include the top 6% of students.

Intelligence Quotient (IQ): The Basics

1. The theory of IQ is that human ability to process language and math concepts can be measured and that the measured ability varies across a continuum. IQ is analogous to the concept of a computer processor or hard-drive speed. Some individuals process information very quickly. Others process the same information more slowly. The analogy is not perfect. There are some dense, complex concepts that those with lower IQ's will never process.

2. Language and math ability are measured separately.

3. High, normal, and low IQs are distributed across the general population in a manner that forms a bell curve. Scores are scaled around 100 which is the average. Of the entire population:
   - One-sixth score below 84.
   - One-third score between 85 and 100.
   - One-third score between 100 and 116.
   - One-sixth score above 116. Included in those who score above 116 are the top 3% percent who score above 133 and the top 2% who score above 140.

4. Before one of the major college admission tests, the SAT, was revised in 1992, a score of 1235 was basically equivalent to an IQ score of 140, or the beginning levels of genius.

5. IQ is rarely a barrier in schooling or employment except at the extremes where extraordinary intellect (150+) is required to deal with complex matters or where diminished mental capacity (less than 75-85) may preclude a university experience.

6. Higher IQ, while creating an initial and ongoing advantage, is only a single factor. The path to higher achievement always includes increased time on task, repetition, motivation, work ethic, and common sense.

7. In the classroom or on a job, a difference of four points in IQ is virtually undetectable.

8. Public schools refer to high-capacity and low-capacity students. Except for placement in the gifted program or special education, however, assessment for IQ in public schools is rare.

Districts select students for these gifted programs on the basis of IQ, teacher recommendations, standardized test scores, and other local standards. Your child's accelerated achievement may help your child almost everywhere except here.

Gifted and talented classes create a homogeneous (similar) group of fast learners and high achievers, saving vast amounts of instructional time. Unlike in normal classes, these gifted students are not fidgeting with impatience because they understood the new concepts on Monday or Tuesday but must wait for the other half of the class who will master the concepts on Thursday or Friday. This is a fairly typical result when

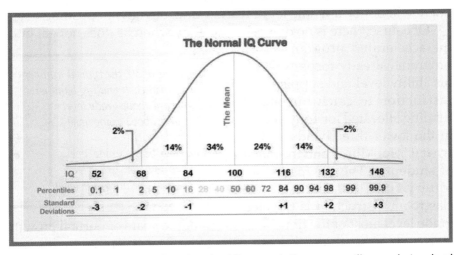

Figure 15.1 The IQ Curve showing the IQ, cumulative percentiles and standard deviations of those scores.

there is a five-year span in reading achievement and an initial four-year span in math achievement in one classroom.

There is huge downside for students like Mindy who may be in the 90th percentile but who do not qualify for their school district's gifted program. With an IQ of 130 or so, she is likely to miss the cut-off for the program. Instead of spending the next eight years being pushed in an accelerated class, she will spend them coasting.

Each year she and Tony will be part of the elementary school lottery. In this lottery, students in each grade are divided into three groups: the high, medium, and low performers. The high-performing students are equally divided among teachers at each grade level, then the medium performers are divided, then the low performers are divided.

Each teacher gets equal numbers of students at each general performance level.

Educators have their reasons for this division into proficiency levels that the lottery creates, but the result is that for Mindy and the 40% of students in the blue and dark-blue bands, and for Tony and the 40% of students in the red, orange, and yellow bands, most of the instruction for most of the day is either below or above where it would do them the most good.

This generally means that Mindy will be in classes where she reads and does math two years above the average student in her classes and three to four years above another 40% percent of students in her classes. There will not be a whole lot of teacher time devoted to pushing her.

Of course, there is no downside for Tony when he does not get into the accelerated program. Normal programs already focus well above his ability level and supplement his instruction to catch him up. The funding allocated for Tony and those in the lower three bands is double what it is for Mindy and the majority of students.[1] The downside of the lottery for Tony is that normal classroom instruction is targeted at grade level most of the time, which is a couple years of normal growth above where he needs his instruction to be. The exception to this is if elementary teachers combine classes to regroup their lower performing students together during reading or math.

In a class of 30, the typical number of students at each reading band is:

Two years above grade level	6
One year above grade level	6
At grade level	6
One year below grade level	6
Two years below grade level	3
Three years below grade level	3

Why the Focus on Reading and Math?

The rationale for this incessant drum roll for reading and math should be apparent. Reading is the language of all academic content areas including math. Math, in turn, is the language of science. These two disciplines are the access points for virtually all other content area.

Reading is the fundamental academic skill your child will use from elementary school through high school, college, and during her post-graduate studies, if any. Public K-12 schools deliver 85% of their curriculum

---

[1] Lynn Fielding, Nancy Kerr, and Paul Rosier, *Delivering on the Promise*, (Kennewick, WA: New Foundation Press, 2004), 191, Table 17.3. The highest 2% receive only a minor increase in funding (above that for most students) in the form of small amounts allocated for elementary gifted programs and smaller class size in high school honors, Advanced Placement (AP), and International Baccalaureate (IB) classes.

through reading, whether it's by textbooks, whiteboards, handouts, computer screens, or class notes. Virtually every academic subject (excluding P.E., welding, shop, and art) requires high levels of reading proficiency. That is why they are the two foundational skills measured by college entrance tests as well as IQ tests. Early acquisition, for early failure to acquire these skills follow students throughout their schooling.

(1)	(1)	(2)	(3)	(4)	(5)	(6)	(7)
		Longitudinal Correlations Between Reading Scores					
		End of Grade					
		3*	4	5	6	7	8
(a)	3*	1.00	0.80	0.76	0.74	0.72	0.69
(b)	4		1.00	0.78	0.76	0.74	0.71
(d)	5			1.00	0.77	0.75	0.72
(d)	6				1.00	0.78	0.75
(e)	7					1.00	0.77
(f)	8						1.00

Figure 15.2 Reading scores in early grades predict subsequent math scores.[2]

You can see the staying power of starting points in Figure 15.2. Place your finger at third grade at row (a) and move it horizontally to the right to column (3). Third grade reading scores correlate perfectly with 3rd grade scores, (1.0), correlate very high (.80) with their fourth grade scores (column 4) and correlated to decreasing but still high degree with scores through 8th grade (.69). Reading scores at third grade are very high predictors of subsequent reading scores.

The correlations between early and later math achievement is even higher. In Figure 15.3 on the next page, place your finger on third grade at row (a), column (3). Third grade math scores correlate perfectly with 3rd grade scores, (1.0), correlate very high (.80) with their fourth grade scores (column 4) and correlated to decreasing but still high degree with scores through 8th grade (.69). Math scores at third grade are very high predictors of subsequent math scores.

The same is true for math scores. This is another way to make the same observation that students tend to stay in or near the band in which they start.

[2] Data for Figures 15.2, 15.3 and 15.4 provided by NWEA (© 2009 Northwest Evaluation Association) with matched students in each cell varying from a low of 15,756 to a high of 22,184 depending on the grade or year. *Data for end of grade three are actually from the beginning of grade four.

		Longitudinal Correlations Between Math Scores					
		End of Grade					
		3*	4	5	6	7	8
(a)	3*	1.00	0.82	0.79	0.78	0.77	0.75
(b)	4		1.00	0.83	0.81	0.80	0.78
(d)	5			1.00	0.84	0.83	0.82
(d)	6				1.00	0.87	0.85
(e)	7					1.00	0.88
(f)	8						1.00

(End of Grade shown on left axis)

Figure 15.3 Math scores in early grades predict subsequent math scores.[2]

You can predict your child's subsequent math scores from reading scores and reading scores from math scores almost the same accurately. Figure 15.4 shows the high degree of correlation of spring achievement starting highest at third grade (.70) and decreasing through eight grade but never falling below .59 between any grade.

		Cross-Subject Correlations Between Reading and Math					
		Grade in Reading					
		3	4	5	6	7	8
(a)	3*	0.70	0.67	0.65	0.64	0.64	0.62
(b)	4	0.68	0.71	0.67	0.66	0.66	0.64
(d)	5	0.65	0.67	0.70	0.68	0.68	0.66
(d)	6	0.64	0.65	0.67	0.70	0.69	0.68
(e)	7	0.62	0.64	0.65	0.68	0.72	0.69
(f)	8	0.59	0.61	0.63	0.65	0.68	0.70

(Grade in Math shown on left axis)

Figure 15.4 Reading scores accurately predict math scores and vice versus.[2]

Reading is critical in math acquisition. There are far more words than numbers in even simple math books. Inability to read will begin to limit math acquisition as early as second grade. Each year thereafter, the math textbooks grow thicker, the vocabulary more extensive, and the explanations more complex with many of today's 3rd-10th grade math books exceeding 700 pages. In short, a major key to your child's starting and staying in the dark-blue band (even in math) is dark-blue band language and literacy proficiency.

CHAPTER SIXTEEN

DARK-BLUE TARGETS FOR GRADES TWO TO EIGHT

"I have always considered educating my kids as one of my primary jobs as a parent. The public schools are there to help me do my job."

—Dave Bond, Superintendent,
Kennewick, WA , School District

This chapter will help you use reading and math curriculum or other reading and math material to determine where your child is and the targets you should set for your child. These techniques do not have the accuracy of national percentiles developed by teams of assessment experts. They do have a common sense approach to these same issues however. They extend your ability to see your child's national percentile, not as an isolated number, but in the context of real reading and math material within your child's competency level.

Reading

More school and public libraries are using a Lexile number to rank books according to their reading difficulty. Your librarian should be able to provide you with these numbers. Alternatively, you may find them yourself by going to www.lexile.com and clicking on "search for books," then "Lexile book data base," and typing in the name of the book. By tracking the Lexile number of the material your child is comfortable reading into the achievement bands, you can get additional information about your child's reading level.

Run your finger down the left hand side of Figure 16.1 until you reach your child's grade level. Then go across horizontally until you find the Lexile range where your child is reading.

For example, suppose your daughter is reading *Junie B. Jones and the Mushy Gushy Valentine* which has a Lexile score of 340L You can determine the reading band of your child with this book by going down the left hand side of Figure 16.1 until you get to her grade level (which we will assume to be second grade) and then moving across until you reach 340L which you can see is well into the blue band. If she reads it easily, she is probably above 340L, and if she struggles, this may be a good indication of her current upper limit.

Suppose she is reading *Romona the Brave* as a fourth grader. Again, you move down the left hand column of Figure 16.1 to fourth grade, then move horizontally across until you reach 820 which is the Lexile score you may have looked up at www.lexile.com. As a fourth grader, she is creeping into the dark-blue band.

Suppose your son is reading *Harry Potter and the Sorcerer's Stone* with a Lexile of 880L. For fourth graders, this book is dark-blue band level (which you can see by tracing across at fourth grade until you get to 880L), blue band for fifth graders, green band for sixth graders, and yellow band for eight graders.

A word of practical advice. Instead of using just a single Lexile from a single book, use the Lexile scores from at least five or six books. This gives you a range of values. And pay more attention to the Lexile of books which are at the upper range of his reading ability. These will give you a better idea of his ability than the Lexile scores of easier books which your child is just reading for fun (and which you should also encourage).

Lexiles will also give you better information if you use them consistently over time. When you track these books every couple

Convert Your Child's Lexile Scores to Reading Bands						
Percentiles	5	15	30	50	70	90
Grade 2			40	200	375	560
Grade 3		160	320	460	595	760
Grade 4	85	320	500	625	740	900
Grade 5	225	460	625	760	860	1020
Grade 6	320	560	720	840	955	1120
Grade 7	375	625	775	920	1030	1180
Grade 8	445	700	840	970	1100	1240
Grade 9	500	740	900	1030	1135	1245
Grade 10	580	805	955	1020	1150	1330

Figure 16.1 Converting Lexile scores to bands at each grade level. The Lexile number represents the mid-point of the achievement band.

months over a four- or five-year period, you should see an upper and lower range in values emerge that move upward over time.

Math

Appendix D lists the math curriculum your child should master by the end of each grade if she is at grade level. Each year provides a list of concepts and a scattering of examples. You can help by making sure your child is conversant with the vocabulary. She is generally in the dark-blue band if she achieves these skills two years early, in the blue band if she achieves them a year early, and in the green band if she achieves those skill at the end of her normal grade level. The same boxes can also be used to describe yellow and orange band skills if students achieve those same skills one year later or two years later, respectively. You should bookmark Appendix D. It's an important reference.

It is easy to understand the five-year math span as students begin to take substantially different math classes in high school and even in middle school. It is intriguing that there is such a large range in ability in elementary school when virtually all students are studying from the same or very similar textbooks.

Dark-blue band students take Algebra I as eighth graders and geometry as ninth graders. They take math each year of high school and are taking at least calculus (with A's or A-'s) by their senior year.

Students in the top 10% may be accelerated even faster. They may finish Algebra I as seventh graders and geometry as eighth graders. Generally they will finish calculus with A's or B's their junior year.

Figure 16.2 shows that the range between the bands in math at the beginning of second grade is three quarters of a year, a total of four years overall. Unlike reading, however, where the range between the bands remains constant, the math bands begin to visibly diverge after second grade. The distance in skill level among the students in different bands also begins to widen. By the beginning of fourth grade, the top four bands are one year of normal growth apart. By the beginning of tenth grade, the dark-blue band is 2¼ years ahead of the blue band, 3¾ years ahead of the yellow band and 5¾ years ahead of the orange band.

Said another way, at the beginning of tenth grade, the blue band students achieve a RIT score of 247. Students in the dark-blue band achieve this same score (247) during the latter part of their seventh grade, 2¼ years earlier. You can imagine the competitive advantage dark-blue band students enjoy when they take the college entrance exams and how those years of extra math growth translate into higher ACT and SAT scores. Conversely, imagine your child competing against these dark-blue band students if she is a yellow band student (3½ years behind) or an orange band student (4½ years behind).

It is easy to understand why the ACT research shows that the level of academic achievement that students attain by eighth grade is a greater predictor of their college and career readiness than what happens academically in high school.[1]

---

[1] From ACT, Inc. The Forgotten Middle. Retrieved on March 23, 2009, from http://www.act.org/research/policymakers/pdf/ForgottenMiddle.pdf.

A Simple Exercise

You can see that green band students are about 3½ years behind dark-blue math students by 10th grade with a simple exercise. Notice that the green-band students score 238 at the beginning of their 10th grade year (see green arrow on the right-hand margin). By placing your finger on 238 at the end of the arrow and following it horizontally to the left along the dotted line, you can see that it crosses the dark-blue line during sixth grade. Dark-blue students score 238 during their sixth grade or 3½ years earlier.

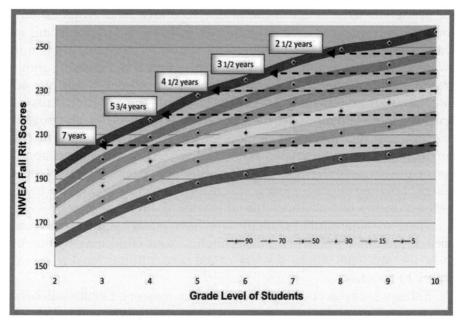

Figure 16.2 Math achievement by band from the beginning of second grade through beginning of 10th grade. Derived from NWEA data.[2]

---

[2] Dark-blue band students achieve the math scores during seventh grade that blue band students achieve in tenth-grade—in other words, 2¼ years earlier. Dark-blue band students achieve the scores of tenth-grade yellow-band students during sixth grade (3½ years earlier). Dark-blue band students achieve the scores of tenth-grade, orange-band students in fifth grade (4½ years earlier), and achieve the scores of the red-orange and red band students in fourth grade and third grade respectively. The left hand scale or y-axis is the substantially equal interval NWEA RIT scale. (In RIT scores, each point of growth along the interval is equal to every other point of growth and runs vertically across grades. This scale is unlike percentile or rank order scales that compare fourth graders only to other fourth graders. NWEA has used the RIT scale for over thirty years.)

Students' differing ability to master curriculum—the academic skills and concepts— ultimately determines their achievement band. In math, it is mastery of discrete areas of arithmetic, algebra, geometry, trigonometry, statistics, and calculus, generally taught in a fairly rigid sequence. Interconnections between the areas are vital. These concepts are extended into a host of applications. In elementary school these applications include time, quantities, and things we call story problems. By high school and college, the extensions are into chemistry, biology, engineering and actuarial science.

With reading, the lines between the areas are less clear. Mastery of the academic skills is about the ability to understand an increasing complex and nuanced syntax, grammar and vocabulary. Learning to read begins with mastery of letter and sound recognition, phonemic awareness, accuracy and fluency. By fourth grade it is increasing about grammar and vocabulary. By middle and high school, it has moved into increasingly specialized vocabulary and the parallel skills of speaking more and more clearly and writing with precision and power.

Tests are measurement devices of your child's mastery of the curriculum and the associated skills. Test scores are messengers about your child's mastery. High achieving student are generally good "test takers" but they are never just good "test takers." It is impossible to do well in Algebra or Calculus without mastering those subjects.

There are a handful of students who have mastered the underlying curriculum but do poorly on assessments. Your child may be one of those few students whose mastery of the curriculum is masked by inability to take tests.

Either way, keep your eye on curriculum mastery. Lexiles will help you track your child's mastery in reading. Appendix D will help with math.

CHAPTER SEVENTEEN

MIDDLE SCHOOL: ANNUAL GROWTH, CATCH-UP GROWTH

"When students spend two to four hours a day video gaming starting in elementary and middle school, continuing through high school and persisting as it hollows out their lives in their mid-twenties, gaming has all the elements of an addiction."

—Dave Powell, Author and
ecclesiastical leader

If you successfully started your child in the dark-blue band at kindergarten and have successfully assured annual growth each year in elementary school, then he is still in the dark-blue band in reading and math. You need to continue what you did throughout elementary school:

1. Identify your child's performance band each year.
2. Assure annual growth in reading and math.
3. Assure catch-up growth if needed.

And add the following four items. Your child needs to:

4. Learn Algebra I by seventh or eighth grade.
5. Learn to memorize using mnemonics.
6. Begin to learn to speed read.
7. Begin to learn how to think critically.

1. Performance Band

Locating your student's achievement band is much the same as it was in elementary school. Use all available information. Look for clusters of data.

Tests providing national percentile rankings are still your best source of information because your student's national percentile will track directly into the bands in reading and math. Part of the power of the national percentile rankings is how easily you can see the impact of initial starting points. It is also easy to make reasonable projections of your student's academic performance in the future. Once you realize that your student's academic outcomes can be accurately predicted, you can take responsibility for those outcomes and begin to make critical mid-course adjustments.

State accountability test scores, like a high jump, measure the percentage of students, including yours, who score above and below the state bar. But these tests rarely tell where the bar was set in relationship to national percentiles. Many states set their bar in the orange band (somewhere between the 20th and the 39th percentile), which is a year below grade level and three years below dark-blue band performance. Figures 17.1 and 17.2 show where twenty-six states have set their reading and math standards for the seventh or eighth grade.

Your state assessment provides a total score that might help. Let's say the assessment score range is 0 to 800, for example, and the target bar is set at 400. You have determined (possibly from Figures 17.1 and 17.2) that this target is at the thirtieth percentile. You can estimate/ approximate that each percentile above the bar has a 5.7 point range. (The 400 points above the bar divided by the 70 percentiles above the bar equals 5.7 points per percentile.) To be in the top 20 percent in your state, your student should score above 685 (5.7 points x 20 percentiles equals 114 points. 800 minus 114 equals 685.)

Classroom grades continue to provide the same mixed-message information. An A or B in an advanced math class, where your student is competing with the top 10 or 20% of the students in that grade, is good news. It is assurance of annual growth. However, it provides no hard information about catch-up growth. High grades in remedial and ELL (English Language Learners) classes measure growth relative to orange- and red-band populations. These grades are clearly deceptive measures of growth, because the reference group is struggling and two or three years below grade level. Often, students in these classes get A's throughout middle school only to be academically slaughtered (D's and

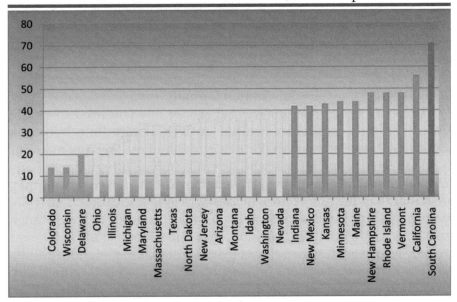

Figure 17.1 Reading: Check at which percentile and in which band your state or a neighboring state has set its eighth-grade reading standard.[1]

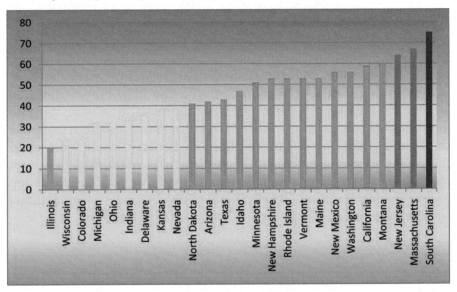

Figure 17.2 Math: Check at which percentile and in which band your state or a neighboring state has set its eighth-grade math standard.[1]

[1] Where 26 states have set their reading standards and 25 states have set their math standards for eighth grade based on NWEA comparative data retrieved from http://www.edexcellence.net/doc/TheProficiency illusion.pdf. on June 18, 2009. The Texas reading and the Texas, New Jersey, and California math standards are from their seventh-grade data as eighth-grade data are not available.

F's) in high school when they take classes with green and blue-band students.

2. Annual Growth

After you determine where your student is, you need to assure annual growth each year. Annual growth at middle school is a somewhat dicey proposition. Rates of growth in reading and math for U.S. students, compared to sixth-, seventh-, and eighth-grade students in other first world countries, have flattened out.[2] Even worse, they are flatter than the rate of growth in U.S. *elementary* schools. Thirty-six to thirty-eight percent of students in the lowest quartile (red and orange bands), who are three years behind, make no growth at all.[3]

Twenty years ago, America converted most of its junior highs to middle schools. The middle school philosophy of many schools, admittedly oversimplified here, is that middle-school students are captive to their raging hormones. Because of their diminished capacity to make significant academic growth, these students are better served by minimizing core subjects, exploring a rich offering of electives, and expanding their social skills instead.

Although this attitude has little to recommend it, such an approach creates an opportunity if your student has labored through elementary school to make more than annual growth but hasn't yet made the jump into the college-bound blue bands. If you can help him continue to grow at his elementary school rate, he can make up a year. With no more effort than you have applied by assuring (and insisting) that your child run at the same rate as he did in elementary school, your child can move up many places in the reading and math pack. Without capitalizing on this opportunity to move ahead, your student may keep pace with his peers but will be actually falling behind his international counterparts.

---

[2] What appears to be a surge in the scores of students from other countries at middle school is actually due to a flattening or slowing in the rate of growth in U.S. middle school students. "The mathematics and science performance of the United States relative to this group of [17] nations was lower for eighth-graders in 1999 than it was for fourth-graders four years earlier, in 1995." National Center of Education Statistics, U.S. Department of Education, *Pursuing Excellence: Comparisons of International Mathematics and Science Achievement from a U.S. Perspective*, 1995 and 1999, NCES 2001-028, (Washington, DC: U.S. Government Printing Office, 2000), Figures 18-19. See also Cheri Pierson Yecke, *Mayhem in the Middle* (Thomas B. Fordham Institute, 2005) www.americanexperiment.org/uploaded/files/yecke091405.pdf retrieved on June 23, 2009.

[3] Lynn Fielding, Nancy Kerr, and Paul Rosier, *Delivering on the Promise* (Kennewick, WA: New Foundation Press, 2004), 191, Table 17.3.

3. Catch-Up Growth

The dead zone continues in middle school. There is a legislative mandate to move middle school students who are below the state standard up to the standard, and concerned teachers and administrators take it seriously. But just as in elementary school, there is no legislative mandate to move students who are at or above state standards to the dark-blue band.

A young middle school teacher recently shared his experiences of teaching in heterogeneously grouped classes, meaning that they are not grouped by skill level. In each class, there is a five- to six-year range in achievement levels between the students.

"You know," he said, "I generally start a new math unit on Monday, which is the way the textbook is designed. On Monday, 20% of the class understands the new concepts [dark-blue band]. They are ready to move on. On Tuesday, another 20% of the class gets it and they are ready to move on [blue band]. These two groups are what we call the high cap kids—our high capacity students.

"On Wednesday, another 20% of my class masters the unit's concepts [green band].

"By Thursday, the next 20% get it [yellow band]. Of course, my Monday and Tuesday kids are alternatively going out of their head with boredom, going crazy, or begging to move on.

"By Friday, the last 20% of my class gets it. These and the Thursday kids are what we call the low cap kids [orange and red bands]. On the following Monday, we move on to a new unit and repeat the cycle.

"This system works well for the lower end kids," the teacher said, "but it's a hell of a waste of time for the top end kids."

4. Algebra I

Mastering Algebra I in middle school allows your student to take geometry as a freshman, Algebra II as a sophomore, trigonometry/pre-calculus as a junior, and calculus or statistics as a senior. This sequence typically represents the math schedule for blue and the bottom half of dark-blue band AP and IB math class schedule. The top 10% are taking Algebra I as seventh graders and geometry as eight graders.

> *One of my daughter's middle school friends had recently moved to Kennewick from India. I found out that she and a few other eighth grade students were going to a nearby high school one period a day to take honors geometry.*
>
> *"So I guess when you are really good, we let you leave Desert Hills Middle School, and we bus you to Kamiakin High," I said.*
>
> *"Something like that, yes," she said.*
>
> *"Leaving middle school, an elite band of scholars on wheels. You must love it," I suggested.*
>
> *"Not really," she said.*
>
> *"Oh?" I said, adroitly leading my witness.*
>
> *"I'm taking the class with my sister," she said. "She's in the sixth grade and is doing better than I am."*

Middle school resistance to algebra was fierce fifteen years ago when little (25%) time was spent introducing new concepts, and most (75%) of math instruction time was spent on review.[4] Such an approach is disastrous for your student. Three years of wheel-spinning in math means, on the individual level, that algebra, with its flood of new concepts, will come as a nasty shock to your middle-school graduate as a freshman in high school. On the national level, it means a precipitous drop in U.S. student standing in international math scores.

If your student's middle school does not offer algebra, she will probably drop about a band in math. If this is unacceptable, you should consider hiring a tutor. If your child is successful with algebra, then she should begin with geometry in high school.

---

[4] Gilbert A. Valverde and William H. Schmidt. "Reforming U.S. Middle School Education." *Issues in Science and Technology Online.* Winter 1997. Retrieved January 14, 2009, from http:// www.issues.org/14.2/schmid.htm. "… Both Germany and Japan teach algebra to all of their eighth grade students, although the level of rigor may differ by track. In contrast, in the U.S. a heavy focus on algebra is usually reserved for students in the higher track, and few U.S. eighth graders in any track study much geometry." U.S. Department of Education. National Center for Education Statistics, *Pursuing Excellence: A Study of U.S. Eighth-Grade Mathematics and Science Teaching, Learning, Curriculum, and Achievement in International Context – Initial Findings from the Third International Mathematics and Science Study.* 60, 38, NCES 97-198, November 1996. Retrieved January 14, 2009, from http://nces.ed.gov/pubs97/97198.pdf.

5. Mnemonics

The transfer of the massive frameworks of math, science, and social studies to each student involves a lot of raw memorization. Mnemonics (pronounced new-mon-niks) is the simple technique of associating a list of words, numbers, or concepts that your child needs to learn with a series of mental "hooks" (like rooms in your house, songs or phrases,

---

Books on Mnemonics
- *Super Memory – Super Students* by Harry Lorayne
- *Every Good Boy Deserves Fudge: Book of Mnemonic Devices* by Rod L. Evans
- *The Memory Book: The Classic Guide to Improving Your Memory at Work, at School, and at Play* by Harry Lorayne and Jerry Lucas

Websites on Mnemonics
- MindTools.com, then search for mnemonics
- Web-Us.com   http://brain.web-us.com/memory/mnemonic_techniques.htm

---

acronyms, mental images, or auditory sounds-a-likes) that she knows. She will be able to memorize a list of 25 items in about three to five minutes using this technique.

Many blue-path students have already figured out on their own some of these memorization techniques including the increased retention that comes from studying material immediately prior to going to sleep.

6. Speed Reading

Instead of your child being assigned a single history book, visualize her being assigned five, a frequent occurrence as her education advances. Learning to double reading speed will cut four hours of reading down to two hours. This make a big difference the further she goes in her education.

Reading speed is controlled primarily by eye movement. Watch your child's pupils while she reads. You will see the pupils jerk and stop seven to ten times on each line, usually once for each word. She can learn to read at 500 words a minute merely by training her eye to stop only three times per line and "see" two to three words at each stop.

She can practice expanding her focus by drawing three lines down the pages of this book as markers for her eyes to stop three times per line. She could also practice by running her finger down the center of a newspaper column. The column has four to five words per line and this exercise forces her eyes to see three to four words at a time. Ten to twelve hours of practice will do wonders for her reading speed.

Like mnemonics, the sky is the limit. With the proper training, the eye can be trained to see whole paragraphs at a time, reading a novel as fast as your student can turn pages. Even a modest goal of doubling reading speed will result in your student remembering the first part of the chapter better because less time has elapsed between when he starts and when he finishes.

You may want to read parts of this book aloud with me in sixth and seventh grades. Start with chapters 1 and 2. Then skip the birth-to-five stuff and start again in Part Two.

7. Thinking

Your child may experience his curriculum as the middle wagon in a wagon train. He follows the wagon ahead, rolling over unending hills, but never really sees where he or anyone else is going or notices how many drop out along the way. It's time to climb a tall mountain with him, allowing him to see where he has been and where he is going in the next seven to eleven years.

The beginning of sixth grade is not too soon for your student to understand that every student in the world is trying to master the same ancient math concepts. In fact, students across the globe learn the concepts in generally the same order as well–arithmetic (addition, subtraction), multiplication, division, then algebra and geometry, later trigonometry, calculus, and statistics. The earliest evidence of simple arithmetic is found in central Africa in about 18,000 B.C. Algebra has been traced back to third-century Greece and seventh-century Persia.

Geometry was first developed in the Indus Valley and Babylonia around 3000 B.C., and the beginnings of trigonometry are generally

Books on Speed Reading
- *Remember Everything You Read* by Frank
- *The Complete Idiot's Guide to Speed Reading* by Beale and Mullan
- *Power Reading* by Ostrov
- *Breakthrough Rapid Reading* by Kump

Speed Reading Software
- Speed Reader X   www.speedreaderx.com
- Speed Reading Secrets   www.speedreadingsecrets.com
- The Reader's Edge   www.readfaster.com/tre.asp

Websites on Speed Reading
- Speed Reading Test Online
  www.readingsoft.com/index.html#results
- MindTools website
  www.mindtools.com/speedrd.html
- How to Learn Speed Reading
  www.wikihow.com/Learn-Speed-Reading
- TurboReads website   www.turboread.com/read_checks.htm

linked to the Greeks in the second-century B.C. Sir Isaac Newton and Gottfried Wilhelm Leibniz share credit for the development of calculus. Statistics was first practiced by Blaise Pascal and Pierre de Fermat of France in the seventeenth century.

It is not too soon for her to realize that she should know the history of the United States from pre-Revolutionary War up through the recent past. She should also understand that when she has learned U.S. history, she has only grasped a 300-year history for one country. Surveying the basics of biology, chemistry, and physics and learning to read and write in English help her process the difference between mastering basic uniform content and learning to think using the content.

Thinking is the ability to foresee the consequence of action. Thinking is the ability to remember, compare, contrast, and synthesize more than one (often many) different views of a problem, marshalling the most relevant facts to optimize a solution or to persuade someone to accept a conclusion. Learning to think is much more difficult for your child than mastering specific subjects. Consider involving your child in contexts where the primary point of the exercise is thinking—activities in which the thinking process is critiqued, "graded," and celebrated for improving.

Willingness to allow your child to fail *and* face the consequences of her decision is an important aspect of learning to think, and a lesson more inexpensively learned in middle school than in college.

However, good parents, willing to allow their child to take the consequences from poor decisions, do not allow their younger children to wander on to busy streets, or allow them to become addicted to alcohol, drugs, or extensive video gaming. The thinking component of video gaming is very tiny and the dexterity developed with the joy stick transfers to very few professions outside surgery and flying military drones.

The gaming addiction is less of a physical dependency than it is a psychological one, a black hole for your child's discretionary hours, robbing time that could be better used in social development, physical growth, and learning to think. It is an addiction that can extend beyond high school. Many twenty-something's, even thirty-something's are content to live in their parents' homes, work for minimum wages, and forego a normal social life so they can devote themselves to gaming.

> Extensive video gaming is a silent trap for the unwary parents. It is a black hole for the discretionary hours usually spent in social development, physical growth, deepening thinking skills, and attachment to real world goals.

Middle school is a good time to make sure that your child does not get sucked into what initially looks like a healthy fascination with computers and turns out to be slow-moving quicksand. Like excessive TV viewing, it is just another thing that you may need to limit or ration (and stoically face all the teenage angst and drama 😟 that this may entail).

CHAPTER EIGHTEEN

SHARING THE JOURNEY

"In the final analysis it is not what you do for your children but what you have taught them to do for themselves that will make them successful human beings."

—Ann Landers

The middle school and junior high are quirky years. Your child is getting A's on her test but cannot remember to turn in homework which was completely done the night before. Go figure. We were novices, perhaps beginner parents like you. Our kids survived and prospered. Yours will too.

At some point, however, you have got to get the kid pulling on the oars with you. If this is just your project, you'll be like the parents of so many young promising athletes who just hang it up, tired of doing it for someone else. Transferring the vision to him is critical in elementary and middle school years, more so in high school, and absolutely essential in college.

Up to this point, each chapter has presented age-specific activities and goals related to your child's education. Now I am going to pause for a reality check. The reality is that kids, families, cultures, communities, and opportunities are all uniquely different and wonderful! Allow me to reflect on my experiences as a father of four.

Connecting our children to the things that sing most deeply to them is one of my wife Wendy's many parenting gifts. When children connect with what they love, they flourish and spend an exuberant amount of time with it. When they connect, they experience sweet success, they work hard, and they savor the joy of self-actualization and the payoff

---

[1] Jared got admitted to the School of International Business at University of Washington, dropped out after one quarter (dealt with his parents), worked for the Children's Reading Foundation for a year, started a real estate business, finished up a degree in education at Central Washington State University, taught middle school for a year, returned to buying and selling real estate, and now makes more than his tax-attorney dad.

from preparation. The momentum carries over into other areas of their lives. Your child may not live for math, but if something else is singing in his life, it makes math way more tolerable in short doses.

For our son, the connection was to technology, especially computers. As a sixth grader, he spent fifteen hours a day working on a bulletin board (an early type of website), falling asleep at night with a massive C++ programming manual on his chest.[1]

For our oldest daughter, it was art and drawing. She would spend three to four hours at a stretch with her paints and colored pencils protesting that she was really a basketball player and would be going out to practice in "just a few minutes."[2]

For her younger sister, Autumn, it was horses. This daughter would get up at 5:00 a.m. on Saturdays, rush through her chores, pack a lunch, and head off 200 yards down the street where we kept her horse, not returning until dark.[3]

Wouldn't Be Seen Dead in Public With Parents

When Sonnet, our oldest daughter, turned 14, she wanted to go out for dinner with the family for her birthday. It conflicted with a time I had agreed to help my carpenter, an unemployed psychologist from California, stand up a heavy interior wall for an office remodel job.

"A 14 year old? Dinner with the family? You must be kidding!" he said. When I came back the next day, he still wouldn't let go of it. After he had hit it another 10 times, I finally said, "Look, it was her birthday. It was her favorite place. It was no big thing. You're a bright guy. Why do you think this was a big deal?"

"I must know 50 parents with kids this age in California," he said. "Not one of those kids would be seen dead with their parents in public."

I was still thinking about his comment when we took our girls to Seattle to play at a competitive soccer tournament that weekend—drove them over, fed them, got them to bed early, cheered them and their teammates with other soccer parents as they won some and lost some, fed them again, did it again Sunday morning, and then drove them home. It started to make sense.

---

[2] Sonnet finished a degree at Western Washington University in English Literature, worked as a tour guide in Alaska for two years, and is in the middle of a two-year nursing program at Bates Technical Institute in Tacoma, Washington.

[3] Autumn went through college on a basketball scholarship, spent a spring in Ireland, sold her horse to finance a summer in Uganda, and is now getting deeper in debt working on a master's degree in International Peace and Conflict at the University of Bradford, England. She is currently following her dreams, loving it—and has no idea what she will do when she grows up.

Sports, band, these extra and co-curricular activities seem to be the royal road. In the '60s, our parents took us camping but increasingly this generation of parents spends time with their kids at basketball tournaments and band competitions. We are their transportation and fans and food tickets away from home. Not such a big difference from when we are at home. Students in band and orchestra, as well as those in AAU basketball, soccer, Little League baseball and a host of other youth sports, participate with competitive, physically disciplined students who consistently have high grades and good relationships with their parents. We just kind of lucked into the rhythm of sports with our kids.

Going Through a Phase

Wendy never did figure out the one single thing that resonated with Shalom, our youngest.[4] But by the time she hit her teenage years, we were way more pro-active and were having a lot more fun parenting.

The night before Shalom started middle school, I said, "I probably shouldn't but I am going to let you in on a secret."

"I already know about sex, Dad," she said.

"It's not that, Lome. It's bigger. No one ever talks about it."

"Yes?" she said.

"You are now a teenager. ThirTEEN. And when you turn thirteen, everything that your Mom and I do is going to start embarrassing you. Really embarrassing you. The way we talk, our jokes, the way we laugh, the clothes that we wear, when your school board father asks your friends what they are going to be when they grow up. You are going to feel deep, deep shame about us."

"It's already happening," she said.

"Yup," I said, "but this is the way we have been for many years. Do you know why it didn't bother you a couple years ago?"

"No. Why?" she said.

"Because you weren't a teenager. But now you're going through this phase. It's going to last anywhere from three to seven years. Maybe more. But when we do something that embarrasses you, you can tell us."

"But you aren't going to change?"

"Nope. Well maybe. A little. Mostly we're just going to remind you that you are going through a phase. You will just have to endure."

---

[4] Shalom survived her middle school years with us, did well in high school and college, and is finishing a Doctorate in physical therapy at the University of Las Vegas.

"That's it?" she said.

"We could get you a T-shirt, 'I am going through a phase.'"

"That won't be necessary Dad."

If your child wants to run in the blue pack, it will still be work. It is just easier to do things she wants to do than do things she doesn't. It just won't feel as hard. The lesson from birth to five is still applicable. It's got to be fun. High expectations require high support, and high results are more likely if the journey (as well as the end) is one of high enjoyment.

And finally, there comes a time when the race is no longer an external race for external, extrinsic rewards. It is no longer about the grade, or the score, or the regard of the teachers and parents. There is a time when the race is internal. The real competition is your child's previous best. The results are what he wants for his life. It is a good seed to plant in elementary school. It can grow in the middle school years. It often blossoms in high school. It is truly extraordinary coaching to create this breakthrough with your runner.

Sailing by the Ash Breeze

In an older time of wooden masts and canvas sails, sailors were often becalmed when their ships drifted into stretches of sea devoid of wind or breeze. The ships could sit for weeks in these zones, sails drooping, riding up and down on the endless waves. Many sat until the wind came up or a storm blew them out of the zone. Some sat until the food and water ran out and the crew died.

Crews in other ships hooked a stout rope on to a long boat with ten to twelve men at the oars, pulling the 150- to 300-ton ship across the sea. They pulled the becalmed ship, an inch at a time, day after day and night after night, out of the becalmed zone.

And the wooden oars? They were made from a kind of wood called white ash. Sailors called it "sailing by the ash breeze."

It is far easier for your child to sail into a four-year university with the wind at his back, carried by momentum inherent from dark-blue band achievement. Yet over the years, students of every age, with less than stellar high school careers or aptitudes have found ways to enter and complete degrees at four-year universities. Almost any student, with iron determination, can move himself forward. It's not as easy as moving by a powerful wind, but it can be done. They sail by the ash breeze.

CHAPTER NINETEEN

THE MIDDLE SCHOOL WORK BOOK FOR COLLEGE

"What we call fate does not come to us from the outside: it goes forth from within."

—Rainer Maria Rilke

It is almost never too early for you to sit down with your blue-band child and ask, "What do you want to be when you grow up?" Introducing your child to this discussion at sixth grade before he knows more than you ☺ is a really good time. It is a good time to start to identify career clusters he has an interest in, to start an annual dry run of the college admission and testing process, and to explore alternatives to four-year universities.

Clusters of Interest

Your child's tested preferences, even in middle school, are highly predictive of her occupational preferences after high school. Taking the Kuder Preference Test (www.kuder.com) is the simplest, fastest, and least expensive way to identify possible career clusters. The test matches your child's interests with those of other people who enjoy working in their particular occupation. Kuder provides three online tests for $19.95

with results linked to sixteen career clusters. It can be taken as early as sixth grade and can be updated at no additional charge for the rest of your child's life. You can use it as an adult as well. It's a heck of a deal.

Kuder is a practical way to help your child connect to highly compatible career interests while sharing your own ambitions for your child. At sixth grade, the discussion should be a soft and tentative one, as you help your child to find his own way.

After you know your child's areas of high interest, the next step is to mesh these interest areas with her academic strengths. You then can start to help her explore some of the resulting occupations, including spending time talking with and job-shadowing adults in similar jobs.

The U.S. Department of Labor operates an excellent website at www.bls.gov/oco/. It lists some 700 different job types (summarized in Appendix F), describes the duties of each job, its required training, the number of jobs nationwide, whether the numbers employed in this type of job are increasing or decreasing, hourly and annual earnings, and similar or related jobs. It's a gold mine of career data for your child.

There is no perfect method of matching what a student loves with what she does best. Or even what she does best with what she at least likes. Still, spending seven years patiently exploring occupations in middle and high school using the Kuder data is preferable to exploring during an additional year or two of college at $17,000+ a pop. A lot of drifting thirty-year-olds may have been better served if their parents had started this dialogue far earlier.

College Admission

The "Common Application" at www.commonapp.org provides a generic application now used by over 300 universities including Stanford and Yale. Helping your child complete this application (but, of course, not submitting it) once a year starting in sixth grade will help both of you see where that application can be strengthened.

Most universities determine admission using multiple factors to paint a picture of your student. Each university is fairly clear about the specific factors it uses, although each generally looks at ACT or SAT scores, GPA, the rigor of the completed classes, class standing, an admissions essay, extracurricular participation and community service. Creating diversity in the student population by race and geographic origin, with some deference to generous alumni parents, are also factors in some decisions.

Most of the same data captured by college entrance scores, GPA, and class standing have already been captured by your child's reading and math achievement bands. Tracking academic proficiency by these national percentiles from kindergarten gives you a preview of what to expect.

Quality of writing is one of the consistent predictors of good thinking and an identifier of students who will do well in college. That said, however, the ease with which a professional or other adult can write (or "edit") an essay on a student's behalf tends to undermine the utility of essays in the admissions process and has led to the addition of a writing component on both the ACT and SAT. Appendix E provides an example essay.

Universities often look for leadership skills and experience, community service activities, and other achievements outside the academic area in their admission process. An obvious surge in reported service or leadership just as an application is being filled out, however, is less compelling than continuous community service, class leadership, music, drama, sports, debate, and writing activities that start in middle school.

College Entrance Testing

Although there is a minor trend away from requiring entrance assessments, most four-year universities still require certain levels of ACT/SAT scores as a condition of enrollment while community colleges usually require another test called the ASSET or Compass test. In community colleges, the scores are used less to determine admission than to determine placement—which classes your child has enough skill to take. For instance, these scores are used to determine the number of remedial math and English classes your student must take, if any, pay for, and successfully pass before he starts taking college level courses and getting credit for them.

The best predictor of your son's seventh grade national percentile scores, provided he continues to make annual growth, is his sixth grade national reading and math scores. Your best predictor of his eighth grade scores is his seventh grade scores, provided he makes annual growth. This means that, if your sixth grader is in the top 10% nationally and stays in the top 10% nationally by making annual growth each year, there is a very high probability that he will score close to a 1300 on the SAT and 29 on the ACT. If your child's current performance band equates to a college entrance scores acceptable to your local university, your child is on track.

Figure 19.1 shows the data from the ACT and SAT Concordance Tables jointly developed by these testing companies which show ACT and SAT score equivalencies for 2006 in columns 3 and 6 , taking into account the differences in the tests.[1]

Students in the Early Grades

Move your finger down the center of the chart (columns 4 and 5) until you reach your child's current performance band color.   Then move your finger to the left (column 3) to find her projected ACT score as a senior. Move your finger to the right (to column 6) to find her projected SAT score. You can refine your projection a little by determining whether your child is in the upper or lower part of her band and looking for the corresponding ACT or SAT score. If there is a difference between her reading and math band, you may want to average those achievement levels.

The range of probable college entrance scores for your child moves higher or lower only to the extent that she makes more than annual growth or less than annual growth during earlier years.

This chart is placed here instead of in the high school chapter because of the common sense suggestion repeatedly made throughout this book: Students generally start and stay near the same percentile bands in their 3.7 million student cohort. *If your child is not currently in the national percentile corresponding to the range of ACT/SAT scores that he needs in order to enroll in a four-year university, now is the time for you to take corrective action.* My heart aches when a kid ends up in the yellow band with limited postsecondary opportunities because no one knew, or thought about it, or cared very much about changing his level of academic proficiency. Even now you can make a difference.

Many parents took the ACT or SAT a single time. Today it makes sense to take it annually starting in the eighth grade, showing up with the juniors and seniors at the testing center, and forking over the $45

---

[1] In 2008, 1,421,941 college-bound seniors took the ACT, and 1,518,853 took the SAT, a total of 2,940,794. There are 3,752,000 students in each age-level cohort (Chapter 2), a fairly high 78% of the cohort, even after allowing for duplicate test takers when you consider that only 70% actually graduate. Assuming that this 78% can be roughly mapped on the top 80% (dark-blue band 20%, blue band 20%, green band 20% and yellow band 20%) the result is Figure 19.1. The psychometricians for ACT and SAT tests developed concordance tables which show approximate equivalences for their scores for 2006. The tables also show corresponding percentiles of students for each score, which differs between the tests. Retrieved June 1, 2009 from www.act.org/news/ data/08/pdf/National2008.pdf and from http://professionals. collegeboard.com/ profdownload/ act-sat-concordance-tables.pdf.

| (1) ACT | (2) ACT | (3) ACT | (4) | (5) | (6) SAT | (7) SAT | (8) SAT |
2006 College Bound Seniors	Percentile Ranking	Scores	Performance Band Equivalence		Scores	Percentile Ranking	2006 College Bound Seniors
216	100	36			1600	99	1,130
1,806	100	35			1560	99	2,969
4,249	100	34			1510	99	2,934
6,964	99	33	90th to 99th	90th to 99th	1460	98	17,860
10,772	99	32			1420	97	19,233
15,971	98	31			1380	95	26,474
22,719	97	30			1340	96	34,460
28,186	95	29			1300	90	45,220
37,436	92	28			1260	86	55,379
45,731	89	27		80-89th	1220	82	67,213
54,941	86	26			1190	78	57,697
64,245	81	25	80-89th		1150	72	84,991
73,260	76	24			1110	66	94,640
80,292	70	23		60-79th	1040	54	102,587
87,327	63	22			1030	52	107,407
93,787	56	21	60-79th		990	45	110,509
94,252	48	20			950	38	108,991
90,986	40	19		40-59	910	31	105,439
87,955	33	18	40-59		870	24	97,912
79,507	25	17			830	19	87,726
70,020	19	16			790	14	74,214
56,562	13	15			740	9	73,461
43,340	8	14	27-39th	27-39th	690	6	52,531
30,052	5	13			640	3	34,890
16,945	2	12			590	2	22,604
6,422	1	11			530	1	15,852
2,512	>1	1-10			400	>1	10,530
1,206,455							1,514,853

Figure 19.1 The ACT/SAT equivalents of the Percentile Bands.[2]

[2] Columns 3 and 6 shows ACT and SAT equivalency scores, columns 2 and 7 show the percent of college bound seniors with that score, columns 1 and 8 show the number of actual students at the score, and columns 4 and 5 show performance band equivalence taking into account low-performing students or high school drop outs who do not take the test.

for either the ACT or SAT. Here are some reasons:

- Practice improves scores, especially for those who take increasingly challenging curriculum and for those who have more room to improve. Taking tests is a skill. If two students have the same amount of knowledge but only one of them is skilled at multiple choice answers and understands the relative risk of guessing and getting it wrong or leaving the answer blank, that student has quite an advantage. Minimizing test-taking errors, getting used to question types, and learning how to pace yourself on time-limited tests are also skills.

- Taking this test annually refocuses your child on his goal. It maximizes your student's chances of doing his best on the single assessment that will have more impact on college placement than almost all of his other test scores combined. Eighth graders in the dark-blue band should score (400-450) on reading and (400-450) on math for a total of 800-900 on the SAT, 13 in English and 17 in math of the ACT.

- The scores give you advance information about whether tutoring makes sense, whether starting early on ACT/SAT preparation programs makes sense, or whether your student is still pretty well on track. Test prep courses generally cost between $250 and $850 and improve ACT scores up to four points and SAT scores up to 75 points with the more improvement among low end than high end performers.

- The PSAT (Preliminary SAT) helps universities identify the nation's 5,000 top high school juniors so they can initiate early recruiting with lucrative scholarship offers. Unless your student is in the top ½ of 1% of the college bound, he is probably better off practicing the SAT or ACT than taking the PSAT.

- The ACT provides two other tests that provide equivalent senior ACT scores for eighth graders (Explore®) and tenth graders (Plan®). The ACT also provides early systematic career planning and educational support.

- The SAT also is developing similar tests which provide early prediction of SAT college entrance scores.

Alternatives to Four-Year Universities

The social contract of the 1960s was that the more education you had, the better off economically you would be. The contract has changed. The social contract of the 21st century is that the more *skillful*

ACT College Readiness Benchmarks

The ACT has provided benchmark scores at eighth grade with EXPLORE®, and with PLAN® at tenth grade which are normed with the ACT at twelfth grade. These benchmarks represent the level of achievement required for students to have a high probability of success in selected credit-bearing, first-year college courses.

Test	EXPLORE®	PLAN®	ACT®
English	13	15	18
Mathematics	17	19	22
Reading	15	17	21
Science	20	21	24

The ACT research shows that the level of academic achievement that students attain by eighth grade is a better predictor of their college and career readiness by the time they graduate from high school than anything that happens academically in high school.

your child is, the better off economically she will be. This is why one in six college (17%) graduates earn less than the average for high school graduates. These graduates tend to be younger so as they get more experience, the number drops, but it only drops to one in seven (14%). Yet in some occupations, like service, farming, transporation, machine operators, laborers, and administrative support, more that 40 percent of workers with a bachelor's degree earns less that than the average high school graduate in the same occupation.[3] Skill matters.

This is why sheet metal workers (one-year training) start out at $20 an hour or $40,000 a year. Highly competitive one- and two-year programs will often get you jobs that pay as well or better than those jobs that you can get coming out of less competitive four-year programs.

Entry-level pay for radiologists and dental hygienists with a two-year degree is $45,000. Crane operators at sea ports with strong unions may make $120,000 a year while working four days a week. Your child should consider his or her possibilities for strong union-based employment as well.

---

[3] *TED: The Editor's Desk*, United States Department of Labor, Bureau of Labor Statistics. Retrieved August 21, 2009, from http://stats.bls.gov/opub/ted/1998/Oct/wk4/art05.htm.

Those who are self-employed and operate small businesses may have a better chance to become wealthy than those who work for traditional wages. Family businesses offer an entrance into that world. The downside is that the self-employed initially work massive amounts of hours and often risk losing all of their prior earnings.

It may make sense to consider these one- and two-year programs, unique union apprenticeships, and owner-operator opportunities when trying to find the best educational and occupational fit for your child. Chapter 23 explores alternatives to four-year universities in greater depth.

A Modest Proposal

And so here is a suggestion for parents: It seems only fair to let capable students who are flirting with low-achievement levels to start earning money in middle school in the kinds of physical, repetitious tasks they may spend the rest of their lives doing should they choose low-skill coursework and less-than-ambitious educational goals. It introduces them to the lifetime of jobs that lies ahead of them, especially during the years when their education is still free and choices can be more easily reversed. It gives them the experience to make a truly informed decision.

Many professionals, especially those who made their own way through substantial adversity, tell of spending a good portion of their youth doing tedious, repetitious work and resolving to do whatever it took to prepare for and have a different life.

"My dad had a little egg ranch when I grew up," Paul said. "Almost all of those small operations are gone now, but back then there was lot of physical work involving loading feed, filling cages with birds, and cleaning up droppings. Always there was the sorting of the eggs. Every day the eggs would come along on a tiny three-inch-wide conveyor belt. Under a halogen light, I could see and remove eggs with cracks and defects in the shells that would spoil or break at the store. I stood there endlessly it seemed. It was where I learned patience and my work ethic. It was sorting eggs where I dreamed of what I would do with my life, and it was there I vowed it would not be sorting eggs."
—Paul Sampson

CHAPTER TWENTY

FINANCING POST SECONDARY EDUCATION

"Planning is bringing the future into the present so that you can do something about it now."

—Alan Lakeini, Author
*How to Get Control of
Your Time and Your Life*

The earlier you start saving for your child's postsecondary education, the better. Dark-blue and blue band parents are generally extraordinary long-term planners. While others are figuring out how to buy a jet-ski, blue band parents are updating their projected investment accumulations to fund their child's college tuition.

Current costs of a four-year state university education including food, lodging, transportation, health care, tuition, fees, and books are about $17,500 a year or $70,000 for four years. Private university costs are more than twice (2.4 times) that.

There are many ways parents can choose to plan and pay for their child's postsecondary education. What works well for one family may not suit another family's situation, values, or resources. If you are parents with plentiful resources, paying for four or five years at a university may be part of an easily affordable lifestyle where money is really not a constraint. If so, you can skip this chapter. On the other hand, you may be parents for whom the university costs are at or even beyond the limits of your financial means. You may be somewhere in between. You may consider paying only 75% of the cost, or some other percentage. What is essential is developing a plan, communicating it clearly to your children, and consistently implementing it.

Splitting Costs, Saving Money

If $70,000+ will be a stretch, you may want to consider splitting the costs of postsecondary education with your child. Requiring your child to match some portion of your contribution to his own education may be a reasonable option, especially if you have more than one child. Figure 20.1 shows how splitting costs with your child may move these funding requirements into the realm of possibility. A $70,000 bill becomes more manageable at $35,000 each.

Figure 20.2 shows that, if your child spends the first two years at a community college (while continuing to live at home), earns an AA., and transfers to a four-year university for the last two years, the overall bill can be cut by about $23,000 from $70,000 to $46,000. These savings come mostly from reduced tuition, housing, and food.

Further savings can come by clarifying your child's interests early (see Chapter 19). Changing majors multiple times often results in an extra year or more of college. Career exploration starting in middle school may avoid the extra $17,650 that each additional year brings.

There are additional benefits to splitting costs with your child. Splitting costs engages your child in her own educational goals. It encourages her to work to earn money at an early age, developing a thrift and savings mentality before she leaves high school. It creates a bank account for her money to go into instead of the cash registers at the mall. She will not be doing it for you. She will be doing it for herself.

It encourages frugality. Your child (probably) has little problem frittering away your money. However, when it is partially his money also, he is more likely to insist on getting full value for what he has exchanged his time and sweat for.

In addition, a student who is paying for at least a portion of her own college is more likely to apply for scholarships, to work and save money during the summers, to take college credit classes offered in high school, and to choose a less expensive college. She is more likely to look for discount textbooks and live an overall less expensive lifestyle throughout college. She's also less likely to delay her graduation date by casually rotating through multiple majors. The process teaches responsible spending in middle school, a full seven years before she is out on her own.

Four Year State University Costs

	Annual	Total	Parent Portion	Student Portion
Tuition	$10,000	40,000	$20,000	20,000
Books, fees, and supplies	750	3,000	1,500	1,500
Housing	4,000	16,000	8,000	8,000
Food and incidentals	2,000	8,000	4,000	4,000
Transportation and Insurance	500	2,000	1,000	1,000
Health Insurance	400	1,600	800	800
	$17,650	70,600	$35,300	35,300

Figure 20.1 Four-year state university costs.

Year one and two at a community/technical college

	Annual	Total	Parent Portion	Student Portion
Tuition	$4,500	9,000	$4,500	4,500
Books, fees, and supplies	750	1,500	750	750
Housing	0	0	0	0
Food and incidentals	0	0	0	0
Transportation and Insurance	500	1,000	500	500
Health Insurance	400	800	400	400
Year two subtotal	6,150	12,300	6,150	6,150

Followed by year three and four at a 4-year university

	Annual	Total	Parent Portion	Student Portion
Tuition	$10,000	20,000	$10,000	10,000
Books, fees, and supplies	750	1,500	750	750
Housing	4000	8,000	4,000	4,000
Food and incidentals	2,000	4,000	2,000	2,000
Transportation and Insurance	500	1,000	500	500
Health Insurance	400	800	400	400
Year three and four subtotal	17,650	35,300	17,650	17,650
Over-all total	$23,800	47,600	$23,800	23,800

Figure 20.2 Attending community and four-year universities.

www.newfoundationpress.com provides up-to-date costs for current and future projected expenses based on when your child starts college.

Cost Splitting

Here is a formula you can modify to fit your family. You (as parents) and your child each agree to pay one-half of the following:

- Current in-state tuition
- Books and fees
- Housing
- Food
- School supplies
- Allowance for spending money
- Medical insurance
- Non-covered medical expenses
- Transportation at school
- Transportation to school and home

Consider paying half of car insurance at the premium level where she has no traffic tickets. Consider paying for her cell phone on a family plan to keep in touch. Consider using scholarships and grants to reduce both the parent and student sides equally. Or, perhaps, grant and scholarship monies that she finds and applies for could be applied only to her side, another motivation for her.

Set up the accounting and reimbursement process in advance. Require receipts or cancelled checks for reimbursement or credit.

Student loans are available from a variety of sources. If either party struggles to pay their half, student loans can help with short-term cash flow problems although such loans are not without their own problems as Chapter 23 will explore.

Credit card companies prey on college students, knowing that most parents will bail their freshman out up to $5,000-$8,000 at least once before considering bankruptcy for their student. Part of your agreement with your student should stipulate either no credit cards or regular credit monitoring.

Grandparents and others can be enlisted to contribute to the child's college fund each year, providing opportunities to encourage their grandchild, giving gifts with lasting value, and creating an extended ownership in their grandchild's use of that money. As the account grows, a network of adult expectations also grows around him. The ongoing discussion about the long-term benefits of education reinforces the importance of today's homework.

Other Ways to Decrease College Costs

In many states, qualifying juniors and seniors can earn credit at the local community college in programs called "early start" and "running start." Some of these students manage to graduate from high school and from community college in the same month, saving themselves and their parents about $20,000.

Other big ticket savings can result from completing high school Advanced Placement (AP) and International Baccalaureate (IB) classes and doing well enough on the third party testing to get college credit. AP scores are graded on a five-point scale (1-5), and students are not required to have taken the corresponding AP course in order to take the exam. IB exams are scored on a seven-point scale (1-7). Every university and college has its own policies and procedures (all subject to change) for awarding credits to AP and IB students. You should research and obtain these policies in writing before making decisions based on them. Advanced Placement and International Baccalaureate offer a much more rigorous curriculum than traditional high schools or community colleges, and also make your student more attractive to universities.

CLEP testing (College-Level Examination Program) is another popular and generally effective way to save money and time in completing a college degree. Although acceptance policies vary widely, several thousand accredited colleges and universities recognize CLEP scores toward degree completion. CLEP exams allow your student to "test out of" courses in which she has already acquired college-level knowledge or proficiency. The two-hour, computer-based exams are offered in 34 different subject areas. Exams are scored between 20 and 80 points and cost approximately $90 to take. In many cases, students who earn a satisfactory score (generally 50 or more, but this requirement also varies widely) on a particular CLEP exam can receive 3-12 credits in that subject area. Some colleges do not grant course credit for CLEP scores but do allow students with satisfactory scores to opt out of required introductory courses in favor of more challenging courses.

With inflation, both tuition and living expenses will certainly escalate by the time your child or grandchild gets to college. Tuition costs have increased at 8% per year and normal living expenses have increased at 3% per year for the last several decades. States that offer a tuition freeze for those who pay in now (for some unspecified student in the future) provide a hedge against increases in excess of normal inflation.

Scholarships, Loans, and More

Scholarships, federal aid programs, internships, and loans are ways to pay for an undergraduate program. Application for aid is usually based on academic achievement, demonstrated financial need, or both.

Academic achievement. One of the advantages of dark-blue academic performance is the increased probability that universities will compete for your student by making offers of decreased tuition, free books, and/or housing. Like college sports where recruiting the best available athletes is a crucial step to a highly competitive program, recruiting the smartest and highest performing graduating high school seniors is essential for universities to maintain their reputation for academic excellence.

Average students. Scholarships are also available for students without a high GPA or high college entrance tests scores but with demonstrated excellence in non-academic areas like athletic or artistic merit, community service, extracurricular activities, or other non-academic disciplines. These scholarships are fewer in number and competitive, as the winners are students who best reflect the goals of the scholarship sponsor.

Over $3 billion in scholarships are awarded each year by universities, foundations, businesses, and the U.S. military. A quick run through a couple of websites will give you a feel of the scope of what is available.

http://apps.collegeboard.com/cbsearch_ss/welcome.jspmize
www.coca-colascholars.org/cokeWeb/index.jsp
www.finaid.org/scholarships/

Beware of paying $10 to $35 in upfront fees to scholarship-finding agencies. You will probably be contributing to what amounts to a $100 million a year scam operation.

Practice in writing scholarship applications in middle school with your student will heighten awareness for both of you about what the criteria are, giving your student time to adjust. It will give him a clear advantage over those starting the process in their senior year.

Developing Frugality

I was the first of three children, had just finished eighth grade at a parochial school, and was headed off into a suburban, upper–middle-class, college-focused high school. I desperately wanted to fit in, or at least not stick out. My solution was to start with some $300 designer jeans and go up from there. My dad grunted and gasped, but I kept up the campaign.

I had him. He could either say "yes" and be my hero on a white horse or say "no" and be the awful dad who didn't love me, his wonderful daughter and destroy my life.

One evening in early August, he sat me down at the kitchen table and said, "I understand that you want some new clothes for school." Finally!

Dad then put $500 cash on the table and slid it across to me. "This is for you, so you can buy some clothes."

As my eyes got bigger and my imagination started dancing, he continued.

"You can go to the mall a block away and buy anything you want. If you want those jeans, go ahead and get them. Get that top too. You can probably do that a couple of times, and you'll look pretty sharp for Monday and Tuesday. Then the rest of the week you can wear what's in the closet. Or, you can shop around, and see what kind of deals you can find. Get anything you want. I just want to see what you've purchased when you're done." Seemed fair enough.

"Oh, there's one more thing," he said. "No more clothes money until Christmas."

The shopping excursions lasted for four days. As you can guess, when it was over, I showed Mom and Dad many, many outfits, all of which looked great. The jeans with the fancy label were nowhere to be found.

In four days, I got a new wardrobe, but more importantly, I learned how to deal with limited resources, something that set a new tone for my high school, college, and life beyond.

Many students enroll in a four-year university or two-year community college only to drop out. If this is a fifty-fifty possibility for your child, you should jointly explore specific one- or two-year programs that end in a marketable degree or certificate.

Some technical degrees in the computer or health service fields described in the previous chapter provide entry-level skills for jobs that start at $40,000. This means that, with an investment of $6,200 each, your blue-band child could qualify for these competitive programs and achieve nearly the equivalent earning power of the average college graduate, if the right programs are available in your community. (This cost estimate assumes that your student can continue to live at home.)

Penetrating the Bubble with Real World Financing

A bubble surrounds your child and protects him from most of the real world, especially the one of finance. It is always a shock when large amounts of reality break through. Here are some numbers relating to that reality if your child finances half of his education.

1. Savings and gifts from birth at $500 a year
    21 years x $500 = $10,500

2. Summer work from age sixteen for the junior
    and senior summers, and the three summers
    during college. 5 x $2,000 = $10,000

3. Student loans $14,700

Obviously, interest on savings, increases in college costs, and projected increases in summer work wages make these numbers mere estimates, but they point to reasonable alternatives which may not be obvious at the outset.

Setting Goals

One of the best ways to achieve the long-term goal of preparing your child to enroll in a four-year university is to establish intermediate goals at the beginning of kindergarten, the end of elementary school (fifth grade), the end of middle school (eighth grade), and the end of high school. These intermediate goals logically ramp backwards from academic achievement levels necessary for college admission at twelfth grade to corresponding achievement levels at eighth grade, fifth grade, and kindergarten. Successful goals are measurable, written down, and regularly reviewed.

Once you define intermediate goals, you should set annual goals that stair-step to the *next* intermediate goal. For example, if your goal is that your child start kindergarten in the 90th percentile, then your annual goals define what you need to achieve each year (in specific measurable terms) until the start of kindergarten.

Once you set annual goals, you establish goals for this month and this week that are necessary for achieving *this year's* goal. These goals should also be written in a permanent notebook and evaluated regularly. Consider spending a half-hour to an hour a month in the planning and evaluation process *in addition* to the time it takes to execute your plan. If you did not attend college, consider finding someone who has put children through college or graduated himself to coach you with the planning and evaluation process.

Tell your friends what you intend to do. After you do, you will become a magnet for knowledgeable people with useful information to help you.

CHAPTER TWENTY ONE

HIGH SCHOOL: ANNUAL GROWTH, CATCH-UP GROWTH

"Life is not about finding yourself. Life is about creating yourself."
—Bernard Shaw

In high school, staying in the dark-blue band involves three tasks for your child:

- Taking a strong college-preparatory menu of classes which high school counselors are well aware of and will help you and your student with.
- Learning to think critically and write fluently, clearly, and persuasively.
- Applying for university admission smoothly and on time.

The final page of this chapter is a checklist.

Year by Band		Math	English	Science
Dark Blue	Freshman	H. Geometry	Pre-AP English I	Pre-AP Chemistry
	Sophomore	H. Algebra II	Pre-AP English II	Pre-AP Biology
	Junior	H. Trig/Stats	AP English III	AP Chemistry
	Senior	H. Calculus	AP English IV	AP Biology
Blue	Freshman	H. Algebra I	English I	Pre-AP Chemistry
	Sophomore	H. Geometry	English II	Pre-AP Biology
	Junior	H. Algebra II	English III	Pre-AP Physics
	Senior	H. Trig/Stats	English IV	AP Biology
Green	Freshman	Algebra I	English I	Biology
	Sophomore	Geometry	English II	Chemistry
	Junior	Algebra II	English III	
	Senior		English Elective	
Yellow	Freshman	Basic Math	Basic English I	Biology
	Sophomore	Algebra I	Basic English II	Science 1-2
	Junior	Geometry	Basic English III	
	Senior	Algebra II	English Elective	
Red & Orange	Freshman	Basic Math	Basic English I + Reading	Biology
	Sophomore	Algebra I	Basic English II + Reading II	Science 1-2
	Junior	Algebra I	Basic English III + Reading	
	Senior		Basic English IV + Study Skills	

Figure 21.1. High school course work by achievement bands.

1. The High School Class Schedule

You, together with your high-schooler, are now knowledgeable about and skilled in the practices you employed during elementary and middle school years. By now, your student should be an enthusiastic participant. These necessary practices are:

- Knowing your student's national percentile starting points at the beginning of each school year.
- Assuring annual growth in reading and math.

In high school, the focus for these practices is embedded in your student's four-year class schedule. Figure 21.1 presents the essential core of a typical four-year high school schedule arranged by achievement bands with the orange and red bands collapsed together. That is, the matrix tells you not only which subjects need to be taken but when—depending on which color band your student occupies.

On the surface, each of these band matrices looks a lot alike: English, math, and science—with social studies, world language, and electives not included here. But beneath the sound-alike topics in the specific class offerings are buried the two-years-ahead/three-years-behind achievement ranges. Math is a good example.

Math. In Figure 21.1, the dark-blue band students take geometry as freshmen, Algebra II as sophomores, trigonometry/statistics as juniors, and calculus as seniors. The top half of the dark-blue band generally shifts one year ahead of this schedule while the blue track trails behind by a year. The green band lags two years behind the dark-blue band, and the classes shift to the non-honors track. The yellow band is shifted three years behind this schedule. The orange/red band is basic math, often starting out at two-digit addition. Virtually no one starting high school with basic math gets beyond Algebra I. In smaller high schools with limited offerings, sometimes only math classes in the blue and green bands are offered. In that case, your student should consider distance learning or correspondence classes.

English. Dark-blue band students will generally take four years of the most rigorous English courses available. If AP or IB tests are offered, your student should take them at the end of the year and may score high enough to earn college credit. Blue students generally take similar courses but often choose less rigorous courses as juniors and seniors, such as "English for College" or "Advanced Communication" over honor courses. Green band students take standard English courses as freshman and sophomores. As juniors and seniors, they either continue with a standard track or opt for English electives such as journalism, creative writing, mythology, or debate. Yellow, orange, and red band students take basic English and often receive some extra attention in the form of reading "pull-outs" or mandatory enrollment in Reading Lab or Learning Lab.

Science. Most school districts require only two years of science for students to graduate. As you might expect, blue band students take three to four years of the most rigorous science courses offered by their school. For example, dark-blue students take *pre*-IB/AP biology as freshman, honors/IB/AP chemistry as sophomores, then honors/IB/AP biology as juniors, and honors/IB/AP chemistry as seniors. Blue students typically also take *pre*-IB/AP biology and or *pre*-IB/AP chemistry as sophomores. As juniors, they opt for honors physics, honors biology, or honors chemistry but then skip science as seniors unless they are particularly interested in science. Green band students take biology and chemistry but generally stop there unless it is a favorite subject. Yellow, orange, and red band students generally choose the two easiest science courses that will allow them to graduate, which are

---

Senior Writing Goals

Your blue-band high school senior should be able:
- To produce complex, analytic, persuasive arguments that will stand up to scrutiny in academic contexts.
- To read, analyze, and synthesize complex texts and purposefully incorporate multiple kinds of evidence to generate and support his writing.
- To demonstrate an awareness of the strategies writers use in different writing contexts.
- To develop flexible strategies for revising, editing, and proofreading his writing.

Figure 21.2 Course writing goals for University of Washington English 131, 2008, a freshman level course.

Evaluate this Statement

"Events on the frontier between 1763 and 1788 and the development of government policies in response to them were more significant for the development of the United States than the events that took place in the settled areas of the eastern seaboard between 1763 and 1788." Adapted from William O. Kellogg, *Barron's AP United States History, 8th Edition* (New York: Barron's, 2008), 222.

Figure 21.3 Writing to high-level questions.

usually biology and an elective science. Some schools offer "integrated," basic, or physical science options for low-level students.

You can again see why grades are a deceptive communicator of student progress. Four different freshman students may be in four different math classes—basic math, Algebra I, honors Algebra I, or honors geometry and all bring home A's. There is nothing on their report cards that will even hint to their parents of the nearly seven-year spread in their math abilities.

2. Thinking Critically and Writing Better

In the academic contexts of high school and college, *learning to think better also means learning to write better.* College is about working with ideas and concepts. The rigor and quality of expression for ideas is akin to true craftsmanship in the trades.

One activity that will pay huge dividends is identifying the top writing teachers in your student's high school. Make sure she enrolls in the classes of English teachers who consistently develop excellent writers. Your student needs to learn to think critically and write well.

Students who consistently get B's, C's or D's on papers do so because they do not know how to write A papers. Writing 12-14 B or C papers in a quarter will teach them how to create a volume of mediocre work but it will never teach them the skills they lack to write A papers.

Thinking critically and writing well involve cycles of writing, thoughtful criticism, editing, and rewriting until the paper moves from being adequate (a C paper) to being excellent (an A paper). In middle school one or two rewrites were often enough. In high school, you should search out teachers for your student who require as many rewrites as it takes to get it right. While the concept of spending fifteen hours on a two-page paper may strike parents who have never done it as bizarre, it will take at least two years of this kind of effort for your child to learn the high-level forms of exploring, elaborating and integrating ideas, as she synthesizes, criticizes, revises and finalizes her report. It is nearly identical to the patience and skill required for true craftsmanship in shaping wood or steel, wiring a panel, or laying out circuit boards.

Accompanying this skill will be the purposeful analysis of excellent writing, so that your student can respond knowledgeably and with pleasure to good writing, clear thinking, and outstanding argumentation by others *and* can identify the qualities that produce these effects.

An example of the kind of essay question your student should be able to answer (in a timed-test setting) specific to the course of study appears in Figure 21.3. The kind and quality of answer he should be able to generate appears in Appendix E.

3. The College Admission and Test Process

A third to a half of high school freshman and sophomores are surprised to learn that they have to actually apply to get into college. They didn't have to apply to get into elementary school, they just showed up at middle school and high school. Why should college be any different? All postsecondary education is different. You have to apply. You have to get accepted. The more competitive the university, community college or trade school program, the higher the chance that you may not get accepted.

Filling out the application. You and your student are now reaping the rewards of exploring his interests and annually filling out (but not sending in) the standard college application since sixth grade, as suggested in Chapter 19. The application should show balanced strengths, the test scores should be in the expected range, and best of all, he will send applications to institutions whose departmental strengths match his interests and abilities. You have optimized his chances by starting early and practicing annually, especially if the universities he applies to accept fewer than 50% of their applicants.

Course requirements. As a condition of entrance, virtually all universities require students to complete a minimum number of years in different subject areas. Most universities require:

English	4 years
Math	3 years (4 recommended)
Science	2 years (many universities moving to 3)
World language	2 years
Social studies	3 years

You must get the actual requirements of your student's target university and match them against your student's high school offerings. Universities change their requirements from time to time, so stay current. Call the university if there is any question about whether it will accept particular classes and document these "rulings" in writing. Parents are shocked when their target university rejects a "fun" high school English class, with the result that their student no longer has the classes that make him eligible for admission.

Deadlines. The window during which most universities accept most student applications opens in September of your child's senior year and closes in December or mid-January. Early application (usually November) and early decision are also an option. The College Board suggests: "Your child should apply under an early decision or early action plan only if he is very sure of the college he wants to attend . . .

---

[1] www.collegeboard.com/parents/apply/college-applications/21342.html

[but not] if he plans to weigh offers and financial aid packages from several colleges later in the spring. Also, your child shouldn't apply early if it is advantageous to have more senior year work to show a college."[1]

Scholarships. The mere fact that you have created a family culture around academic achievement means that you are likely to know two or three times more about the available scholarships than other parents who start midway through their child's junior year. Writing practice applications for these scholarships starting at sixth grade can be a highly effective and lucrative—perhaps even critical strategy, especially if family finances are tight.

For better or worse, the kindergarten through high school years are now over. Watching a child walk at high school graduation is an experience only 70% of U.S. parents get. Your child has completed the second part of his training and education, a fairly homogeneous and similar experience to most high school students despite the range in potential achievement between the bands.

Your child is the sum of your collective decisions – mostly yours in the early years, increasingly hers as she moves through the high school and post high school years. Her current set of opportunities now depends on her strengths and weaknesses, her skill levels, her available finances, her work ethic and personality, her sub-culture, and her passions. Increasingly, her opportunities also depend on the global economic market. Now real depth and diversity will occur as postsecondary training, education, and job opportunities begins.

The four final chapters explore moving into the job market with or without additional intervening education or training. About 41% of American jobs are held by workers with a "high school or less" level of training (Chapter 22). Another 31% of jobs are held by workers who have completed "some college," either at a two-year community college, trade school, or four-year university (Chapter 23). Another 28% of the jobs are held by persons with "college or more" (Chapter 24). The chapters describe each of these major post-secondary opportunities. The final chapter (Chapter 25) summarizes the Maxims or essential points of this book.

Student High School Checklist

1. Maintain 85th to 90th national percentile achievement (or higher) in reading and math.
2. Commit to a realistic and rigorous program to assure annual growth (and catch-up growth where needed).
3. Four years of math and science is optimal but not always required. In any event, math should most certainly be taken the junior year to be "fresh" for the ACT, and SAT, and the senor year for the COMPASS, or ASSET tests.
4. Complete college-required high school coursework.
5. Continue taking the ACT or SAT annually.
6. Learn mnemonics and speed reading.
7. Re-take the Kuder preference test annually or at least every other year, discuss the results, and spend time with those employed in the areas of greatest interest.
8. Continue filling out the college application each year.
9. Resist buying a car if it interferes with either your (or your student's) ability to fund his share of the planned saving for postsecondary education.
10. Be proactive about building your student's staying power and sense of responsibility to prevent dropping out of high school and college.
11. Visit the colleges with your child early. Apply well before your university's cut-off deadline to avoid last-minute panic or rushed work.

Parent High School Checklist

12. Celebrate all the successes of your child. It will help assure that your high consistent expectations are less likely to be confused with "not good enough" messages.
13. Remember to move occasionally from the ground level perspective to the views at 10,000 and 50,000 feet. See his successes today from that of ten years from now. See his efforts from the day he gets married or graduates from college or when he comes to see his aging parent in an assisted living facility.

CHAPTER TWENTY TWO

CHOOSING HIGH SCHOOL OR LESS

"As you become more clear about who you really are, you'll be better able to decide what is best for you – the first time around."
—Oprah Winfrey

The U.S. Department of Labor tracks 150.6 million U.S. jobs by three educational categories: "high school or less," "some college," and "college completion or more." This chapter deals with the training and employment opportunities of "high school or less."

You probably do not expect your child to end her formal education after earning her high school diploma. You certainly are not expecting her to drop out of high school. In all likelihood, the information in this chapter is merely cautionary. Yet it may also be information that you want your child to consider when the going gets tough.

At birth, your child has almost the same chance of dropping out of high school as of enrolling in a university. Approximately 28-30% of students drop out during high school: 1.4 million students *a year*.

Some students drop out for non-academic reasons. Boredom or burn-out among capable students lead to failing to do or turn in homework, followed by non-attendance, then acting out and finding a group of peers who are doing the same. Other reasons include addiction to alcohol and other drugs, addiction to video games that consume two to four hours a day, pregnancy, criminal activity, and untreated depression. A few drop out because they are struggling to survive economically, are homeless, and/or work to support their siblings.

Notwithstanding these non-academic factors, poor reading and poor math skills generally factor heavily into who will drop out and who will not. Figure 22.1 shows high school students who drop out by reading band (solid white line) and math band (dashed white line). By following the solid white line, you can see that about 12% of students reading in each of the top three bands drop out (dark-blue 11%, blue 12%, green 13%), doubling in the yellow band (23%) and nearly doubling again in the orange and red bands (42%).

The drop out rate by math achievement is more pronounced. By following the dashed white line, you can see that only a handful of dark-blue math students drop out (1.6%). That rate then doubles or triples at each band (blue 4%, green 12%, yellow 28%) until reaching the lowest quartile where 54% of the orange/red band students leave without graduating.

While your child is still at risk of dropping out in the dark-blue band, her odds of doing so are nothing like the odds facing students with yellow, orange, and red band skills in reading and math. The odds for most of these lowest performing students were initially established by starting behind in kindergarten and become less likely to change with each passing year.

Spending the elementary, middle, and high school years in the red and orange bands creates an intellectual death spiral for many students. "I read one to three years below grade levels" leads to "I am behind in math, science, and social studies as well." Faced with daily proof of one's inadequacy in nearly every class leads to avoidance —"I will come to school late, I will leave early, and I will skip as often as possible" — and detachment — "I don't care, I will act out, I will hang out with others like me."

In the early 1970s, Dee Norman Lloyd conducted research showing that students most likely to drop out could be predicted with a high degree of accuracy as early as sixth grade. In a 1978 follow up study, Lloyd found that he could predict at students' third grade 75% of those who would graduate and 70% of those who would drop out of high school, primarily from their reading and language skills, almost as accurately as he could in sixth grade.[1] The six-year range in starting points, as well as the difficulty of moving from one band to another without significant intervention (described in prior chapters), explain many of the reasons why.

---

[1] See Dee Norman Lloyd, "Prediction of School Failure from Third Grade Data," *Educational and Psychological Measurement* 38 (1978): 1193-1200. "As the last of the primary grades, the third grade is the point at which basic reading skills have been taught (and hopefully learned), as well as the grade in which it has been estimated that 50% of future achievement patterns have been set." Predictive factors other than reading include IQ, retention, and GPA.

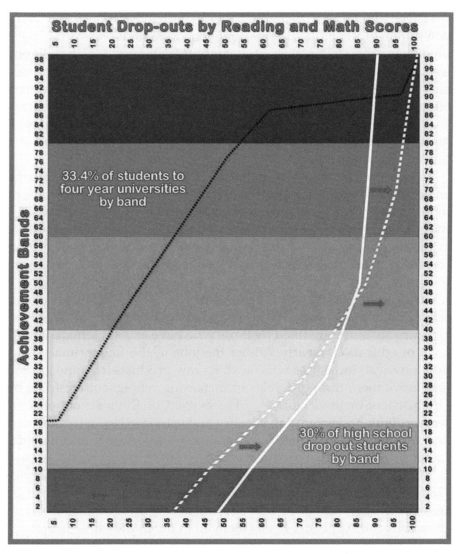

Figure 22.1 High school drop-outs by percentile bands.[2]

---

[2] The dropout rate by band for reading and math is based on the reading and math WASL scores of 40,459 confirmed dropouts in Washington State from 2004-05 to 2007-08. The 30% national dropout rate used can be established fairly easily by going to the U.S Department of Education's Common Core Data (www.nces.ed.gov/ccd/bat/) selecting *basic* on the first screen and selecting the appropriate years, *eighth grade* and *high school diplomas* on the second screen, *all states* on the third screen, and downloading the results as an Excel file. True national anchors of dropouts by performance bands are impossible to find.

Given the academic disparity between the bands, it is also easy to see why failure to accumulate normal high school credits is one of the highest predictors of non-completers. Students with reading and math skills one to three years below grade level are most likely to struggle in classes and either withdraw or fail. After multiple failures, they realize they will not have the credits to graduate in four years, five and sometimes six years, and so they drop out. What is surprising is the number of high school students who actually attend all four years and are still unable to graduate.

It is not uncommon to find that 10-15% of those who make it to the end of their senior year have insufficient credits to graduate. Some of these students just barely miss getting to the wire by a class or credit or two. Many however, lack almost a whole year of credits, are really academic juniors in standing, and it has been obvious since their freshman and sophomore year that they were not going to graduate in four years.

The good news is there is plenty of work for students with high school diplomas or less. Sixty-two million (41%) of the 150.6 million U.S. jobs are currently filled by those who have a "high school or less" level of education. Nearly 70% of the jobs in the four primary (and very physical) industries which extract raw products from the ground and move them through cycles of increasing refinement are filled by "high school or less" workers. The percent of "high school or less" workers is highest in farming, forestry, and fishing (83%), in construction and extraction (72%), and decreasing in transportation and material moving (69.5%), and in production and manufacturing (69.5%). Almost half of the jobs in installation, maintenance, and repair (56%), in service (58%) and office and administrative support (38%), are also filled by those with high school or less education. Figure 22.2 lists many of these jobs and Appendix F lists them all in much the same format.

These are all honorable and necessary jobs. Cooking, laundry, grounds keeping and janitorial work form part of almost all of our domestic daily lives. Almost all of us do these jobs around our own homes almost every day from the time we are very little to the time we grow old. In addition, these jobs are often the entry level, part-time, and summer jobs for those who are planning to or are attending college as well.

More good news is that training for these workers is generally free, occurs on the job, and usually consists of someone taking a few minutes to demonstrate and then supervise the task.

(1)	(2)	(3)	(4)	(5)	(6)	(7)
Total Positions 2006	HS or Less	**Unskilled** Job Description	$ Hourly Wage by percentile			Median Annual Compensation
			10th	50th	90th	
77,182	88	Pressers, textile, and garment	$7	$9	$12	$18,440
517,358	87	Dishwashers	7	8	10	16,410
603,083	86	Farmworkers and laborers, crop, nursery	7	8	11	17,020
59,451	86	Agricultural equipment operators	7	10	16	21,180
106,843	86	Farmworkers, farm and ranch animals	7	10	15	20,350
65,364	84	Helpers—Brickmasons, blockmasons	9	13	20	26,260
109,060	84	Helpers—Carpenters	8	12	17	24,340
105,340	84	Helpers—Electricians	8	12	17	24,880
24,455	84	Helpers—Painters, paperhangers, plaster	8	11	15	22,300
84,643	84	Helpers—Pipelayers, plumbers, pipefitters	9	12	18	25,350
21,769	84	Helpers—Roofers	8	11	15	22,810
37,564	84	Helpers, construction trades, all other	8	11	18	23,900
833,812	83	Packers and packagers	7	9	14	18,310
122,074	83	Slaughterers and meat packers	8	11	14	22,500
144,228	83	Meat, poultry, and fish cutters and trimmers	8	10	14	21,050
131,352	83	Butchers and meat cutters	8	13	21	27,480
368,216	83	Cleaners of vehicles and equipment	7	9	15	18,680
232,810	82	Sewing machine operators	7	9	14	19,370
541,605	81	Helpers—Production workers	7	10	16	21,090
1,469,519	81	Maids and housekeeping cleaners	7	9	13	18,350
385,988	80	Packaging, filling machine operators, tenders	8	11	19	23,760
238,681	79	Laundry and dry-cleaning workers	7	9	13	18,420
637,034	79	Industrial truck and tractor operators	9	13	21	28,010
1,232,002	79	Construction laborers	8	13	25	27,310
1,220,054	78	Landscaping and groundskeeping workers	8	11	17	22,240
135,970	77	Refuse and recyclable material collectors	8	14	24	29,420
163,379	77	Helpers—Installation, maintenance	7	11	18	22,920
271,745	77	Cutting, punching, and press machine	9	13	20	27,240
629,405	77	Cooks, fast food	6	8	10	16,130
401,027	77	Cooks, institution and cafeteria	7	10	15	21,340
850,343	77	Cooks, restaurant	7	10	15	21,220
195,495	77	Cooks, short order	7	9	13	18,630
462,833	76	Painters, construction and maintenance	10	15	26	32,080
416,276	76	Dining room and cafeteria attendants	6	8	11	16,040
106,426	75	Coating, painting, and spraying operators	9	13	20	27,550
2,386,570	75	Janitors and cleaners	7	10	16	20,800
142,842	75	Mixing and blending machine setters	9	15	23	30,340
182,676	74	Automotive body and related repairers	10	17	29	35,690
105,842	74	Tire repairers and changers	8	11	16	21,880
901,660	74	Food preparation workers	7	9	13	18,150
532,840	73	Counter attendants, cafeteria, coffee shop	7	8	11	16,890

Figure 22.2 Twenty-six million of the 62 million jobs held by persons with a high school level diploma or less sorted in descending percentage. Numbers of available jobs (column 1, far left), the percentage of individuals who hold that job with a high school education or less (column 2), the common job description (column 3), the hourly income for the bottom 10%, the middle 50%, and the top 90% (columns 4-6), and median annual income (column 7).

The bad news is that the jobs are generally repetitious, usually physical, frequently seasonal, and often outside. Being outdoors is an aspect that is often a plus for many of us, but the extremes in outside weather which have incidental impact when we are young, are usually harder on us as we age.

The "high school or less" positions are generally subject to more frequent layoffs, have a higher risk of injury, are among the poorer paid and offer less opportunity for advancement in their industry. Years of experience usually result in a fairly small increase in hourly wages especially in comparison to the impact of experience in jobs requiring "some college" or "college or more."

In the food preparation industry, they are the dishwashers, waitresses, fast food cooks, bartenders, and counter attendants.

In agriculture, they are the tractor drivers, fruit pickers, irrigators, vine pullers, and the sorters and graders on plant produce lines.

In construction, installation, and repair industries, they are the helpers, lifters, and carriers of the tools and materials for those who are the actual craftsmen: the painters, roofers, carpenters, electricians, pipe layers, plumbers, pipe fitters, and brick masons. In the production occupations, they are the laundry workers and dry-cleaners, pressers, sewing machine operators, meat, poultry, and fish cutters and trimmers, and shoe and leather workers.

In the service industry, they are the maids and housekeepers, janitors and cleaners. They are the childcare workers, security guards, landscapers, grounds keepers, maintenance and repair personnel.

In retail and wholesale, they are the freight movers, stock handlers, order fillers, cashiers, receptionists, and information clerks.

In the medical field, they are the nursing aids, orderlies, and attendants. In transportation, they are the light and heavy truck drivers.

The columns to the right (4, 5, 6) show hourly wages paid to the lowest 10%, the average paid worker, and top 10% of workers in this job. For example, the lowest paid dishwashers on the previous page average $7 per hour, and the highest paid ones get $10. This is also true with non-restaurant food servers, waiters and waitresses, and amusement and recreation attendants. Experience makes very little difference

By contrast, there is a very significant range for truck drivers ($8 to $23 per hour), heavy equipment mechanics ($13 to $30), and construction and extraction trade supervisors ($17 to $43).

(1) Total Positions 2006	(2) HS or Less	(3) Unskilled — Job Description	(4) 10th	(5) 50th	(6) 90th	(7) Median Annual Compensation
		$ Hourly Wage by percentile				
156,842	72	Molding, coremaking, and casting setters	8	13	20	26,430
304,906	72	Production workers, all other	8	12	25	25,640
113,107	72	Paper goods machine setters, operators	10	15	23	32,050
149,047	72	Cabinetmakers and bench carpenters	9	13	21	27,970
2,416,034	72	Laborers, freight, stock, material movers	7	11	17	21,900
2,502,891	71	Combined food preparation and serving	6	8	10	15,750
1,274,303	71	Team assemblers	8	12	19	24,630
291,591	71	Assemblers and fabricators, all other	8	13	28	27,910
445,092	71	Driver/sales workers	7	10	21	21,380
1,859,848	71	Truck drivers, heavy and tractor-trailer	11	17	26	36,220
1,051,159	71	Truck drivers, light or delivery services	8	13	23	26,380
149,266	70	Bakers	8	11	17	22,590
213,381	69	Electrical and electronic assemblers	8	13	21	26,540
96,199	68	Service station attendants	7	9	13	18,290
197,594	66	Printing machine operators	9	15	25	31,490
768,974	64	Shipping, receiving, and traffic clerks	8	13	20	26,990
189,234	64	Food servers, nonrestaurant	7	9	14	18,850
1,704,921	63	Stock clerks and order fillers	7	10	16	20,490
3,500,169	63	Cashiers, except gaming	7	8	12	17,160
772,675	62	Automotive service technicians	9	16	28	34,170
168,431	61	Installation, maintenance repair workers	9	16	27	33,010
454,800	61	Bus drivers, school	7	12	18	25,860
198,488	61	Bus drivers, transit and intercity	9	16	25	33,160
771,796	60	Supervisors, construction and extraction	17	27	43	55,950
238,015	59	Parts salespersons	8	14	23	28,130
767,257	59	Personal and home care aides	6	9	12	18,480
1,390,952	58	Maintenance and repair workers, general	9	16	25	32,570
282,237	58	Managers, housekeeping and janitorial	10	16	26	32,850
228,531	57	Taxi drivers and chauffeurs	7	10	16	20,810
787,315	55	Home health aides	7	10	13	20,010
1,447,233	55	Nursing aides, orderlies, and attendants	8	11	16	23,160
476,623	53	Counter and rental clerks	7	10	19	20,070
491,417	53	Inspectors, testers, sorters, samplers, weighers	9	15	25	30,310
699,259	53	Supervisors of production workers	14	23	38	48,670
103,166	53	Ushers, lobby attendants, and ticket takers	6	8	12	16,340
617,452	51	Hairdressers, hairstylists, cosmetologists	7	11	20	22,210
2,360,630	51	Waiters and waitresses	6	8	14	15,850
351,188	51	Restaurant, lounge hostesses	7	8	11	16,790
394,783	50	Telemarketers	7	10	18	21,390
1,388,168	48	Child care workers	7	9	14	18,350
270,869	47	Order clerks	8	13	21	26,920
291,199	46	Amusement and recreation attendants	7	8	12	16,850
1,040,287	46	Security guards	8	11	18	22,570
218,776	44	Hotel, motel, and resort desk clerks	7	9	13	18,950
1,172,666	42	Receptionists and information clerks	8	11	17	23,710

Figure 22.2. Continued

Figure 22.3 shows the categories for five million of the building trade jobs, most of which are also held by workers with a "high school or less" education (see column 2). These jobs pay considerably better than the unskilled jobs in

Figure 22.2. They generally start out $2 to $4 an hour higher (column 4), the average between $16 to $33 an hour (column 5), and top out from $20 to $45 per hour (see column 6).

Again, the issue is primarily training. Unlike the jobs listed in Figure 22.2, most building craft jobs, especially those at the upper end of the pay scale, require substantial classroom training either at community colleges or by union shops plus years of on-the-job training. Safety issues surrounding the operation of multi-million dollar equipment require increasingly skillful operators as well.

Hourly wages drive annual income. Hourly wage times 2,000 hours a year[3] equals annual wage.

---

[3] Eight hours a day times five days a week equals 40 hours a week. Forty hours a week times 50 weeks equals 2,000 hours a year.

(1) Total Positions 2006	(2) HS or Less	(3) The Crafts Job Description	(4) 10th	(5) 50th	(6) 90th	(7) Median Annual Compensation
			\$ Hourly Wage by percentile			
21,830	48	Elevator installers and repairers	$19	$33	$45	$68,000
17,571	75	Boilermakers	16	24	36	50,700
109,730	31	Construction and building inspectors	15	23	36	48,330
5,584	78	Pile-driver operators	14	23	39	47,550
705,015	51	Electricians	13	22	37	44,780
502,201	68	Plumbers, pipefitters, and steamfitters	13	21	36	44,090
158,316	82	Brickmasons and blockmasons	13	21	34	44,070
10,043	71	Continuous mining machine operators	14	21	28	43,860
19,923	77	Rotary drill operators, oil and gas	13	21	32	43,480
4,291	74	Roof bolters, mining	17	21	25	43,270
71,736	68	Structural iron and steel workers	12	20	36	42,130
14,635	61	Rail-track laying operators	13	20	27	42,120
54,312	85	Tapers	12	20	32	42,050
5,333	63	Explosives workers	14	20	29	41,520
188,655	63	Sheet metal workers	11	19	34	39,210
9,750	74	Extraction workers, all other	11	19	32	38,960
79,183	80	Tile and marble setters	11	19	31	38,720
424,152	78	Operating engineers/equipment operators	12	18	32	38,130
30,162	83	Reinforcing iron and rebar workers	11	18	34	37,890
18,784	77	Derrick operators, oil and gas	13	18	27	37,790
1,462,071	73	Carpenters	11	18	32	37,660
23,844	82	Stonemasons	11	18	30	36,950
28,446	80	Insulation workers, mechanical	11	18	33	36,570
185,864	85	Drywall and ceiling tile installers	11	18	30	36,520
61,148	87	Plasterers and stucco masons	11	18	29	36,430
39,497	63	Hazardous materials removal workers	11	17	29	36,330
21,681	78	Earth drillers, except oil and gas	12	17	28	36,310
73,205	80	Carpet installers	10	17	33	36,040
54,992	72	Glaziers	10	17	31	35,230
28,991	80	Floor layers, except carpet, wood, tiles	10	17	31	35,120
9,899	66	Paperhangers	11	17	32	34,580
221,539	86	Cement masons and concrete finishers	11	16	29	33,840
409,024	73	Welders, cutters, solderers, and brazers	10	16	24	32,270
156,284	86	Roofers	10	16	27	33,240
23,774	75	Septic tank \ sewer pipe cleaners	10	16	24	32,740
145,216	69	Highway maintenance workers	10	16	24	32,600
64,255	84	Paving, surfacing, and tamping operators	10	16	26	32,360
462,833	76	Painters, construction and maintenance	10	15	26	32,080
14,319	80	Floor sanders and finishers	10	15	24	31,290
66,590	68	Pipelayers	10	15	26	31,280
32,414	80	Insulation workers, floor, ceiling, and wall	9	15	26	31,280
221,539	86	Cement masons and concrete finishers	11	16	29	33,840

Figure 22.3. Five million building craft jobs, sorted by average annual income (column 7) in descending order.

Choosing an Income Level			
Hourly Wage	Times Hours	Annual Wage	Take Home
$8.00	2,000	$16,000	$13,176
$12.00	2,000	$24,000	$20,640
$16.00	2,000	$32,000	$26,240
$20.00	2,000	$40,000	$31,200
$25.00	2,000	$50,000	$37,000
$40.00	2,000	$80,000	$53,800

The box shows hourly wages time 2,000 hours a year for a total annual wage. After deducting 7.65% for wage taxes (and there are another 2% to 10% of other deductions depending on the jurisdiction and occupation)and another 10% to 26% for state and federal income taxes, the far right column shows annual take-home pay. These amounts may seem large to your middle and high school child, but letting him pay the monthly family bills for a year

will put these amounts in a better perspective.

If your blue band student drops out or stops after completing high school, he will be at a significant advantage over red and orange band students when testing for a GED, testing to get into an apprenticeship, or working to advance in the job market. Like riding a bicycle, reading and math skills may get rusty, but they do not go away.

CHAPTER TWENTY THREE

CHOOSING SOME COLLEGE

Two just-awakened campers watched the rapid approach of an obviously hungry brown bear with increasing alarm. The first camper suddenly dressed and began lacing up his tennis shoes.

"Are you crazy?" the other camper asked. "You can't outrun brown bears — they can run up to 40 miles an hour."

"I don't have to outrun him," said the first camper. "I just have to outrun you."

Between a high school diploma and a four-year college degree is a level of education called "some college." The U.S. Department of Labor estimates that 46 million jobs (31% of all U.S. jobs) are held by persons with "some college."

Workers holding "some college" jobs either:

- Earned a two-year associate's degree from a community or technical college,
- Earned a two-year applied associate's degree from a community or technical college,
- Earned a certificate requiring anywhere from three months to two years from a community college, technical college, vocational institutes, or trade school, or
- Dropped out of a four-year university program or one of the above programs before successfully completing it.

The message of this chapter is this: If the odds are 50-50 or higher that your child may *not* finish a four-year degree, he may be money ahead getting a two-year degree with concentrated skills in a specific area or a specialized certification. He will have a much easier entry into the job market with specific skill training, increased likelihood of higher income, and significantly less debt as he starts his economic work life.

Associate Degrees

There are more than twenty different types of two-year associate degrees, often collectively referred to as AA's: Associate of Arts (AA), Associate of Science (AS), Associate of Technology (AT), etc. You can access the websites of the 1,100 community and technical colleges sorted by state from a single website at www.utexas.edu/world/comcol/state/.

AA degrees more closely track the general requirements of traditional majors at major universities. When your student completes her AA degree, she can generally transfer it intact to an in-state university, which means the four-year university will generally accept all of her credits and she will basically have junior class standing.[1] In contrast, if she transfers early, perhaps only a single credit short of her AA, she might find that the university has arbitrarily denied 20-35% of her credits in the transfer based on non-equivalent course descriptions.

The issue is rarely whether your student has actually mastered the curriculum. Post-secondary education institutions are in the business of exchanging credits for money. The same arbitrary transfer-of-credit denial that occurs between community colleges and four-year institutions may occur when transferring between national and regional trade school programs as well. This is truly an area of "buyer beware."

In the event of early transfer, your daughter may want to explore enrolling in the four-year university without transferring the credits, take the missing courses at the university, transfer those credits back to the community college (thus completing the AA degree), and then transfer the AA degree intact to the university. All the credits the university would have denied to your student based on the transcript analysis (and depending on your state system) may now be allowed to her when she transfers her AA.

Students earn 486,300 associate degrees from community and technical colleges each year. Their completion rate is abysmal, hovering between 14.3% and 17%. Less than 11% receive associates degrees.[2] In other words, relatively few students earn a two-year associate degree.

---

[1] It is important to check regulations of your state as not all states require this inter-school cooperation.

[2] Phillippe and Sullivan, *National Profile of Community Colleges*, 78-79. Data are for the years 2001-2002. See also Laura Horn and Stephanie Nevill, (2006). *Profile of Undergraduates in U.S. Postsecondary Education Institutions: 2003–04: With a Special Analysis of Community College Students* (National Center for Educational Statistics Publication No. 2006-184), retrieved on May 27, 2009, from http://nces.ed.gov/pubsearch/pubsinfo.asp?pubid=2006184, vii Table B, for

Community College Completion Rates

1.	Typical annual enrollment at all community colleges	10,133,874
2.	Less non-degree/non-certificate-seeking attendees (12%)	<u>-1,216,065</u>
3.	Certificate- or degree-seeking students	8,917,809
4.	Full-time two-year equivalent students	4,458,904
5.	Associate degrees awarded annually (11%)	486,293

6. Certificates awarded annually:

Less than one year	133,249
One to two years	94,724
More than two, less than four	<u>8,026</u>
Annual certificates awarded (5%)	235,999

7.	Total AA and certificates awarded annually	722,292
8.	Completion rate as a percentage of degree/certificate-seeking students in a two-year program (line 7/line 4)	16.2%

Figure 23.1. Community college completion of certification and associate degree programs as a percentage of degree/certificate-seeking students assuming a two-year completion rate for all programs.

12% "not committed" and Table 14, p. 33 for 14.3% attaining credential. See footnote 1 Horn and Nevill's work at Table 14, page 33 for the lower 14.3% completion percentage. The 11% associate degrees awarded is calculated by dividing the 486,293 AA's granted by 8,917,809 certificate- or degree-seeking students.

Figure 23.2 shows about five million relatively well-paying jobs held by workers who earned an AA degree and who indicated on the Department of Labor surveys that their associate's degree was their primary source of training. What you should get from this chart is this: whereas the jobs in the "high school or less" have average annual compensation ranging from $15,000 to $30,000, and the building craft jobs annual compensation ranges from $31,000 to $40,000, the annual compensation for these AA jobs are in the $35,000 to $50,000 range (see column 7 on each of the figures). The additional compensation should give your child substantial motivation to navigate his way through the common pitfall of completing an AA.

Your student will initially be required to take a test, like the Compass or ASSET (not the ACT or SAT), which is usually used to determine placement and rarely used to deny admission. If he scores below the locally determined cut-off scores, he will be required to take remedial English, math, or writing classes. That is, a red, orange, yellow, green and sometimes blue band student may have to take remedial classes as a prerequisite to taking college-level coursework. You and he will pay college tuition to take remedial classes on the college campus for which he gets no college credit.

Nationally, 43 out of every 100 incoming community college students are required to take one or more remedial classes. The first year, 34 take remedial math classes, 13 take remedial writing classes, and 13 take remedial reading classes. During the second year, 29 are still taking additional remedial math classes, 13 are taking additional remedial writing classes, and 10 are taking additional remedial reading classes.[3] These additional classes assure that at least 43% of students will not complete two-year programs in two years.

You should plan to avoid this trap. A thoughtful strategy is to have your student take the ASSET as a high school sophomore or junior to get an advanced look at his proficiency levels. Based on that information, he (and you) may save a lot of money if he takes higher levels English and math during his high school junior *and especially math his senior* year to avoid the remediation in college.

This unexpected remediation creates another twist for your student. Under current law, she can qualify for federal grants to attend community colleges for the equivalent of two years. Remediation which

---

[3] Horn and Nevill, *Profile of Undergraduates in U.S. Postsecondary Education Institutions* p. 137, Table 6.2.

extends her program only beyond two years may create an unforeseen funding crisis.

(1) Total Positions 2006	(2) Some College	(3) Associate Degree Job Description	(4) $ Hourly Wage by percentile 10th	(5) 50th	(6) 90th	(7) Median Annual Compensation
2,504,664	43	Registered nurses	$20	$29	$42	$60,010
552,458	44	Computer support specialists	12	20	33	42,400
275,269	49	Legal secretaries	12	19	29	38,810
237,703	43	Paralegals and legal assistants	14	22	34	44,990
196,200	68	Radiology technologists	16	24	34	50,260
170,433	54	Electrical/electronic technicians	15	25	37	52,140
169,742	51	Medical records technicians	9	14	23	29,290
167,017	64	Dental hygienists	20	31	43	64,740
102,406	71	Respiratory therapists	18	24	32	50,070
90,650	54	Civil engineering technicians	12	20	31	42,580
81,824	54	Engineering technicians	15	27	38	56,060
74,915	54	Industrial engineering technician	15	23	38	47,490
71,178	57	Veterinary technicians	9	13	20	27,970
60,296	65	Physical therapist assistants	13	21	29	44,130
47,792	54	Mechanical engineering technician	15	23	35	47,280
45,668	68	Diagnostic sonographers	20	29	39	59,860
45,378	68	Cardiovascular technologists	12	22	34	44,940
37,881	44	Broadcast technicians	8	16	32	32,230
37,645	57	Medical equipment repairers	12	19	32	40,320
28,770	51	Funeral directors	14	24	45	50,370
24,981	86	Occupational therapist assistants	13	22	30	45,050

Figure 23.2 Jobs where an associate's degree is listed as the primary source of training by those holding the job. Numbers of available jobs are listed in descending order (column 1, far left), percent of jobs held by workers with "some college" (column 2), the common job description (column 3), the hourly income for the bottom 10%, the middle 50%, and the top 90% (columns 4-6), and median annual income (column 7).

Applied Associate Degrees

A specialized kind of two-year degree is the *applied* associate degree. In the 1980s and 1990s, community colleges began to seriously compete with trade schools in offering vocational training with extended length and breadth. These programs provide hands-on coursework but less English, math, and social studies than in regular AA programs. The reduced English requirements may have a minor impact on job performance and the eliminated math might never be used. Few jobs utilize math beyond Algebra I. The good news is that  these degrees tend to be tailored for locally available jobs, increasing your child's entry level skills and probability of immediate employability.

The bad news is that your child cannot transfer one of these degrees to a four-year institution. The degrees can be upgraded but only by taking additional English, writing, and math classes with no credit for the additional applied coursework.

Figure 23.3 shows typical community course offerings with tuition, length of training in semesters, and estimated cost of supplies. The particular community college shown in Figure 23.3 offers no three-month certifications (one semester) but does offer multi-level training in most of its programs. A two-semester program or three-quarter program usually takes nine months like the traditional school year. A seven-quarter program (like the medical laboratory technician program shown here) might start in the fall of a given year and run straight for a year and nine months.

Technical colleges and technical institutes provide significantly deeper curriculum offerings than community colleges. One of the best ways to get a sense of the differences is to compare course catalogs. For example:

Technical college course offerings:

Louisiana Technical College www.ltc.edu

Florence Darlington Technical College (SC) www.fdtc.edu

Community college course offerings:

Clark State Community College (OH) www.clarkstate.edu

South Texas College www.southtexascollege.edu

Figure 23.3 Community College Offerings	Quarters	Tuition	Supplies
Accounting Clerk	2	$2,484	$643
Accounting Paraprofessional	4	$4,057	$991
Accounting Specialist	6	$6,251	$891
Administrative Office Management	4	$4,347	$1,100
Applications Developer	4	$4,347	$520
Band Instrument Repair Technology	3	$3,726	$1,000
Basic Machining	4	$4,347	$1,230
Executive Assistant	5	$6,210	$730
Office Support Specialist	4	$4,347	$520
Civil CADD	4	$4,347	$750
Commercial Building Engineering	8	$6,707	$750
Computer Applications	2	$2,484	$552
Computer Network Technology	4	$4,347	$1,100
Computer Numerical Control	2	$2,484	$600
Computer Science	4	$4,347	$520
Construction Management	4	$3,823	$1,000
Construction Trades Preparation	2	$2,132	$235
Cosmetology	4	$6,210	$975
Culinary Arts	6	$8,118	$1,070
Dental Assistant	4	$4,347	$3,059
Early Childhood Careers, Basic	3	$3,105	$300
Early Childhood Careers	6	$7,286	$500
Engineering Design Technology	4	$4,347	$725
Industrial Engineering	6	$6,707	$1,000
Kitchen Major Appliance	4	$4,347	$1,000
Land Surveying/Field Survey	4	$4,347	$850
Laundry Major Appliance	4	$4,223	$1,000
Legal Secretary/Legal Assistant	4	$4,347	$750
Licensed Practical Nurse	4	$4,426	$1,350
Major Appliance & Refrigeration	8	$8,694	$1,200
Massage Therapy Practitioner	3	$3,767	$2,005
Ophthalmic Assistant	4	$4,347	$1,150
Paraeducator/Bilingual Asst	3	$3,726	$376
Pharmacy Technician	4	$4,451	$437
Precision Machining	8	$8,694	$1,430
Professional Baking	4	$4,347	$232
Property Maintenance	1	$1,242	$200
Refrigeration Technology	4	$4,347	$500
Registered Nurse, AA	2	$3,009	$1,150
Surgical Technologist	4	$4,982	$595
Welding, Basic	2	$2,484	$500
Welding	5	$5,589	$1,000

Certification Programs

Certification programs are relatively short, job-specific vocational training programs offered by trade schools, community, and technical colleges. They lead to "Post Secondary Vocational Awards" (PSVAs) that result in entry-level, marketable skills. Figure 23.4 (right) lists jobs where PSVAs were listed as the primary source of training.

Your child could complete some of these programs in as little as three months. Many take a year, and a few require up to two or more years of training. Nationwide, students earn 235,999 of these certificates each year. Some 133,000 are for programs of less than one year, 95,000 are for courses of study lasting one to two years, and 8,000 are for coursework more than two but less than four years long.

In the business field, these programs build basic competency in bookkeeping, accounting, and data entry. In the medical, automotive, computer, crafts, real estate, and hair and beauty areas, these programs either fulfill state-required coursework requirements or prepare your student to take and pass a licensing examination.

The medical field uses certified technicians to draw blood, administer particular screenings, take X-rays, operate diagnostic equipment, or run lab tests. Their job titles frequently include the terms "technician," "licensed practical," or "licensed vocational."

In the legal profession, court reporters must pass tests showing that they have acquired the competence to take rapid verbatim transcripts of depositions and court proceedings.

Beauticians, in most states, acquire skills such as dyeing and cutting hair, performing manicures and pedicures, and applying acrylic nails —functions generally governed by state-required licenses. In the building industry, crafts like electrical, pipefitting, steam fitting, and welding are governed by state regulations, while carpentry, dry walling, and concrete work are controlled primarily by the trade unions, if at all.

Trade schools often specialize in a single cluster of skills like beauty or business, while community and technical colleges provide a broader range of training options. In general, the providers of computer certifications are still major computer companies.

Income of those who earn a certificate is something of a mixed bag. Given the short duration of these programs and the step-up in compensation, certification programs provide a great return on investment for a small amount of additional training and cost beyond a high school diploma. In terms of pay, these positions generally fit

(1) Total Positions 2006	(2) Some College	(3) Certifications — Job Description	(4) 10th	(5) 50th	(6) 90th	(7) Median Annual Compensation
			\$ Hourly Wage by percentile			
1,447,233	37	Nursing aides, orderlies	\$8	\$11	\$16	\$23,160
772,675	34	Automotive service technicians	9	16	28	34,170
748,605	72	Practical/vocational nurses	13	18	25	37,940
617,452	42	Hairdressers, hairstylists	7	11	20	22,210
437,088	38	Preschool teachers	10	15	27	23,130
432,291	37	Real estate sales agents	10	20	51	40,600
409,024	25	Welders, cutters, solderers	10	16	24	32,270
274,876	31	Bus and truck mechanics	12	19	27	38,640
234,841	32	Fitness trainers & instructors	7	13	28	27,680
201,099	68	EMT's and paramedics	9	14	23	28,400
197,993	51	Telecommunications installers	15	26	33	54,070
174,961	53	Office machine repairers	11	18	28	37,100
122,472	57	Aircraft mechanics technicians	15	24	32	49,010
121,256	28	Library technicians	8	13	21	27,680
117,696	49	Massage therapists	8	17	34	34,870
115,522	62	Architectural and civil drafters	13	21	31	43,310
101,167	49	Travel agents	9	14	23	30,130
98,454	59	Medical transcriptionists	11	15	21	31,250
86,197	57	Surgical technologists	13	18	25	37,540
83,523	44	Gaming dealers	6	8	13	15,610
80,226	46	Commercial equipment repair	14	23	32	47,110
79,344	45	Healthcare technologists	11	18	29	36,630
78,340	62	Mechanical drafters	14	22	33	44,740
78,121	31	Manicurists and pedicurists	7	10	16	19,960
70,899	38	Prepress technicians	10	16	26	33,990
62,098	57	Psychiatric technicians	10	14	23	29,670
60,034	34	Barbers	7	11	19	23,510
56,959	44	Installers, security/fire alarm	11	17	27	35,390
52,803	25	Welding machine setters	10	15	24	30,980
52,219	31	Jewelers and precious stone	9	15	26	31,200
39,700	44	Installers, home entertainment	10	15	24	31,260
38,209	31	Skin care specialists	7	13	25	27,190
34,848	62	Electrical & electronics drafters	15	24	37	49,250
31,833	44	Desktop publishers	10	17	27	35,510
27,596	21	Commercial pilots	17	34	68	61,640
26,897	29	Camera operators	10	20	38	41,850
25,474	43	Electric motor repairers	10	16	26	34,130
25,083	57	Dietetic technicians	8	12	19	24,750
24,521	62	Drafters, all other	14	21	35	44,690

Figure 23.4. Jobs where PSVAs were listed as the primary source of training. Numbers of available jobs listed in descending order (column 1, far left) percent of jobs held by workers with "some college" (column 2), the common job description (column 3), the hourly income for the bottom 10%, the middle 50%, and the top 90% (columns 6-8), and median annual income (column 9).

between the unskilled and the crafts although certified jobs requiring higher levels of skill like real estate agent and commercial pilot bring what we have seen elsewhere: higher skill levels, higher pay.

Unlike the educational categories of "high school or less" and "college or more," the "some college" jobs are spread more evenly across the ten industry categories.

- Office and administrative support   44%
- Installation, maintenance, and repair   37%
- Sales and related occupations   32%
- Service occupations   31%
- Management, business, and financial   28%
- Production occupations   25%
- Transportation and material moving   25%
- Construction and extraction   23%
- Farming, fishing, and forestry   12%

Whether your child gets an AA, an Applied AA, or a certificate, he will experience the two-tiered demographics of community college and trade school systems. Because these institutions also serve as our society's second-chance safety net in postsecondary education, they serve a population of students who are often much older, less financially well off, more ethnically diverse, and less likely to complete their programs than the average freshman class at a four-year university.

Many students are over 25 years old (45%), on their own financially (61%), enrolled part time (66%), have delayed enrollment (50%), work full time while enrolled (41%), have dependents (35%), are single parents (17%), or have a GED or no high school diploma (12%). Most (86%) community college students fit into at least one of these at-risk categories, and the average number of risk factors per student is 2.4.[4] Those who complete an AA and transfer to a four-year university face an additional 15-33% decreased likihood of completion compared with direct enrollees, a common sense result given the increased risk factors.[5]

The good news is that those who finished a certificate or an AA degree have invested less and are getting a better return than those who drop out of postsecondary education. They will have a much easier entry into the job market with specific skill training, increased likelihood of higher income, and significantly less debt.

[4] Phillippe and Sullivan, *National Profile of Community Colleges* 52.
[5] M. Alfonso (2006) The impact of community college attendance on baccalaureate attainment. Research in Higher Education, Vol. 47, and E. Pascarella, and P. Terenzini (2005). How college affects students (vol. 2): A third decade of research. San Francisco: Jossey-Bass.

CHAPTER TWENTY-FOUR

GETTING THROUGH YOUR FOUR-YEAR UNIVERSITY

"Choosing an occupation that is projected to have many opportunities can ease your way into employment. But in the end, it takes only one job opening to start a satisfying career."
— Olivia Crosby and Roger Moncarz

Understanding Your Child's Interests

Despite discussions about career choices since middle school, it is still likely that your child will select a career using imperfect information about his interests and abilities, his selected niche, and the future impact of the economy on his chosen industry.

Yet a good decision made on time is better than a great decision made too late to implement it. Ideally, your child has zeroed-in on a couple areas of interest by her freshman year in college. Since the sixth grade, the Kuder interest test has repeatedly updated her interest data. Three years in middle school and four years in high school gave your child an excellent chance to talk with adults who work in her interest areas and observe and job shadow some of them. Few students who wander aimlessly in college took early advantage of testing to pinpoint their high-interest areas and using the middle and high school years to get hands-on experience in those areas.

The next two pages show the number and compensation of common job descriptions sorted in descending order by percentage held by college graduates. This list shows 16.7 million jobs. Categories having fewer than 15,000 jobs were eliminated from this listing.

The 42.9 million jobs (27.9% of the 150.6 million total jobs) which require a four-year degree or more are spread throughout every industry. Yet like jobs requiring a "high school or less" education, the majority of college degree jobs are also concentrated in a few industries.

(1) Total Positions 2006	(4) College or moe	(5) College or More Job Description	(6)	(7)	(8)	(9) Median Annual Compensation
			$ Hourly Wage by percentile			
			10th	50th	90th	
32,740	100	Optometrists	$23	$45	#	$93,800
62,196	100	Veterinarians	21	36	65	75,230
136,323	100	Dentists, general	34	66	#	137,630
87,402	99	Medical scientists	18	31	60	64,200
152,381	99	Clinical and school psychologists	18	30	50	62,210
760,672	99	Lawyers	25	51	#	106,120
15,479	99	Administrative law judges	17	36	65	74,170
27,192	99	Judges and magistrates	15	52	#	107,230
18,137	99	Actuaries	23	41	#	85,690
23,881	98	Physical scientists, all other	21	42	65	87,660
109,677	98	Speech-language pathologists	19	29	46	60,690
52,725	98	Chiropractors	16	32	#	65,890
243,482	97	Pharmacists	35	48	61	100,480
633,292	97	Physicians and surgeons, general	23	45	#	94,540
1,037,547	96	Secondary school teachers	22	32	52	62,980
95,534	96	Vocational education teachers	22	33	50	62,310
16,516	95	Physicists	25	47	#	96,850
20,131	95	Biochemists and biophysicists	21	38	65	79,270
17,357	95	Microbiologists	18	29	50	60,680
20,091	95	Zoologists and wildlife biologists	17	26	43	55,100
29,067	95	Biological scientists, all other	18	30	47	63,340
1,671,829	95	Postsecondary teachers	22	33	50	48,350
1,540,159	95	Elementary school teachers	22	32	50	48,940
658,060	95	Middle school teachers	23	33	52	49,640
64,876	94	Health practitioners	17	31	#	63,730
22,416	93	Statisticians	18	34	54	69,900
83,697	93	Chemists	18	31	52	63,490
83,267	93	Environmental scientists and specialists	17	28	48	58,380
31,061	93	Geoscientists	20	36	69	75,800
40,743	93	Natural sciences managers	30	50	#	104,040
33,809	92	Urban and regional planners	18	28	43	57,970
30,444	91	Chemical engineers	25	39	59	81,500
98,858	90	Occupational therapists	20	31	45	63,790
35,994	90	Social scientists	18	32	49	67,200
172,948	89	Physical therapists	23	34	48	69,760
131,873	88	Architects	19	33	54	67,620
27,839	88	Landscape architects	17	28	46	57,580
256,330	87	Civil engineers	22	34	52	71,710
220,568	87	Financial analysts	20	34	66	70,400

Figure 24.1. Jobs filled by those with "college or more" with numbers of jobs (column 1), sorted in descending order by percent filled by education level (columns 2), common job description (column 3), hourly compensation (column 4-6) and annual income (column 7). Wages in excess of $70 an hours or $140,000 annually are indicated by an "#" (pound sign).

(1) Total Positions 2006	(4) College or moe	(5) College or More — Job Description	(6) 10th	(7) 50th	(8) 90th	(9) Median Annual Compensation
			\$ Hourly Wage by percentile			
485,916	87	Special education teachers	22	33	50	48,350
89,831	87	Aerospace engineers	29	44	62	90,930
54,341	86	Environmental engineers	21	35	52	72,350
158,373	86	Librarians	15	25	37	50,970
19,777	86	Conservation scientists	16	27	39	56,150
59,212	85	Reporters and correspondents	9	17	37	34,690
506,751	85	Computer applications engineers	25	40	60	83,130
350,048	85	Computer software engineers	27	43	63	89,070
135,246	84	Writers and authors	13	24	48	50,660
187,089	84	Engineering managers	34	53	#	111,020
34,562	83	Therapists, all other	13	24	39	50,120
170,305	82	Engineers, all other	23	41	61	85,260
234,354	82	Market research analysts	16	29	55	60,300
26,853	82	Survey researchers	8	18	38	36,820
15,790	82	Soil and plant Scientists	17	28	48	58,000
60,032	82	Surveyors	14	25	40	51,630
121,511	81	Editors	13	23	44	48,320
243,275	81	Public relations specialists	14	24	45	49,800
153,375	81	Electrical engineers	25	38	58	79,240
137,868	81	Electronics engineers	26	40	60	83,340
176,220	81	Personal financial advisors	16	33	#	67,660
17,355	80	Petroleum engineers	28	50	#	103,960
1,274,357	79	Accountants and auditors	17	27	47	57,060
129,430	79	Instructional coordinators	15	27	44	55,270
99,216	79	Education and library workers	8	16	31	33,030
75,795	79	Sales engineers	23	39	63	80,270
56,064	78	Education admin, preschool	12	19	34	38,580
225,905	78	Education admin, K-12	33	52	76	80,580
131,293	78	Education admin, post HS	20	36	#	75,780
29,714	78	Education admin, all other	18	33	57	69,300
225,797	78	Mechanical engineers	22	35	52	72,300
61,858	78	Budget analysts	20	31	47	63,440
678,188	78	Management analysts	20	34	63	71,150
282,424	77	Child, family, and school social workers	12	19	31	38,620
123,643	77	Medical & public health social workers	14	21	32	44,670
122,272	77	Mental health-substance abuse	11	18	29	36,640
66,220	77	Social workers, all other	13	22	35	45,800
21,616	77	Materials engineers	23	37	56	77,170
25,115	77	Recreational therapists	10	18	28	36,940
25,588	76	Financial examiners	18	32	59	66,670
47,296	76	Advertising managers	18	38	#	78,250
49,575	75	Public relations managers	22	42	#	86,470
404,396	75	Clergy	10	19	34	40,460

Figure 24.1. Continued

Helping Your Child Think Through Career Decisions

Controlling parents often try to dictate their child's career, and their child usually finds a way to sabotage the plan or successfully rebel. At the other end of the spectrum, "laissez faire" parents send their child off to college hoping, in some black-box sort of way, that their child will somehow pair up an appropriate course of study with a career.

Occupations by Industry Requiring University Degree or More	Number of Jobs	Percent of Each Industry
Professional and related occupations	19,566,278	66%
Management, business, and financial	8,215,987	53%
Sales and related	4,524,386	28%
Office and administrative support	4,337,074	18%
Service	3,261,366	11%
Installation, maintenance, and repair	383,750	7%
Transportation and material moving	581,203	6%
Production	569,000	5%
Farming, fishing, and forestry	53,036	5%
Construction and extraction	422,749	5%
Total	41,914,829	

Figure 24.2 Concentration of jobs requiring a four-year university degree or more by industry.

Effective parenting should strike a balance between these extremes. Helping your child prepare a four-year college class schedule (like the high school class schedule) is a useful way to organize information with your child. Once you and your child organize 40 semester classes and the 180 credits that fulfill the general requirements, get your child into her selected department or program, and finally lead her to degree completion based on actual interest and aptitude data, several things will happen.

- First, your child will actually see a path, however dimly, from her freshman to her senior year.
- Second, she will be one of the few freshmen who actually made a four-year plan (even though you know it may change).
- Third, your student will either take these classes, refining her choice of classes and professors each year, or the courses will

start feeling like a mountain of undesirable work (meaning major class changes are forthcoming).

- Fourth, you will have dramatically increased the probability of your child completing her degree in four years (or even less) instead of five years or more.

Completing a four-year college degree plan while your child is a high school senior living at home is a good time to develop a structure and to provide your initial input. Any subsequent course corrections are more likely to result in both of you sitting down and jointly revising the plan.

The first two years are often similar as students complete general or core requirements. During the second two years, your student declares a major and takes required classes to earn her particular degree. Increasingly, many departments are establishing competitive admission processes to get into and take upper division classes in their department.

Don't get attached to the contents of the plan. Perhaps 70% of the benefit of the plan comes from getting one done, regardless of its content. This result is highly preferable to your child mindlessly wandering from one major to another.

Dropping Out

It is probably becoming increasingly clear that your real goal for your child is not university *enrollment*. It is university *graduation*. About one in three first-year students who enroll in four-year universities will not re-enroll in that university their sophomore year. This percentage varies significantly by university.[1] Catalog-size books like the *U.S. News and World Report Ultimate College Guide and Barron's Profiles of American Colleges* list these re-enrollment and graduation rates for various universities. Obviously, there will be some necessary slippage between enrollment and graduation as students enlist in the military, drop out to start a family, or find that the size, location, or flavor of a particular university is not a good match for them.

While it is not uncommon for students to flunk out of college, the risk of your student leaving is often the result of other major forces for

---

[1] This is over 421,000 students (33% x 1,277,700 admitted freshman students = 421,000). The return rate is as low as 55% for Idaho State University and as high as 98% for Yale, Harvard, Dartmouth, and Columbia. There is a similar range in the number of students who initially enroll at and actually graduate from that university. The four-year graduation rate of initial enrollees is as low as 4% for the University of Texas-El Paso and as high as 90% for the University of Notre Dame and Duke University. Anne McGrath, editor, *U.S. News and World Report Ultimate College Guide 2008* (Naperville, Illinois: Sourcebooks, Inc, 2007), 109-126.

which you can prepare your child during his high school years. Smart parenting and flexible universities can reduce the risk of dropping out down to the 12-15% range. Here are some issues you may consider managing.

Your child's competitive level is going to drop. Nothing magical happens to math and reading skills between graduating from high school and enrolling in college. If your child was a yellow or blue band student (one or two years behind dark-blue band students) in reading and math as a high school senior, he still is. The difference is the new makeup of the competitive mix. Only a few high school C students and virtually no D and F students make it to four-year universities.

Students who were in the top 10% of their high school class now fill most of the seats from the 78th to 99th percentile of most college student bodies. If your student was in the *bottom* of the dark blue band in high school, she is now only in the top 50% at college. If she was a blue band

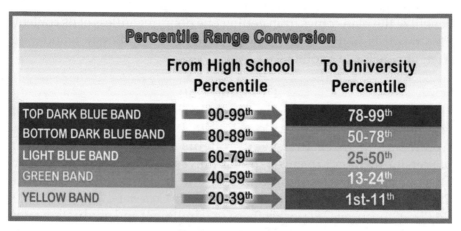

Percentile Range Conversion		
	From High School Percentile	**To University Percentile**
TOP DARK BLUE BAND	90-99th	78-99th
BOTTOM DARK BLUE BAND	80-89th	50-78th
LIGHT BLUE BAND	60-79th	25-50th
GREEN BAND	40-59th	13-24th
YELLOW BAND	20-39th	1st-11th

Figure 24.3 Big frogs in little ponds become little frogs in bigger ponds.

student in high school, she will be in the 25th to 50th percentile and if she was a green band student in high school, she is now likely to be in the lowest 25% of her college. These shifts are even more dramatic at high-end universities. At very selective universities, high school students in the 90th percentile may be in the bottom 25% of their student body. Of course, these shifts will be less dramatic in less competitive universities.

Your child is going to experience real stress. Your student, used to getting A's but now getting C's, either has to accept these grades or begin to work like a dog to maintain the same grades he had in high school. Some students may view their college experience as a pleasant leisure-filled alternative to the full time jobs that some of their friends are now stuck with. Yet college is their job. It should take at least forty hours a week and perhaps more. Dark-blue band students may have gone through their entire public school experience studying only one or two hours a night. For these students, it is nearly incomprehensible that they must now study seven to ten hours a day to remain competitive. Either way, it is a lot of new stress.

College Grants and Loans

1. Sixty percent of undergraduate students fund a portion of their higher education using loans.

2. The federal government makes low-interest loans available to encourage enrollment and lower economic barriers. Often student loans are called "grants," but they still require repayment with interest.

3. Your student will be responsible for repaying the loans regardless of graduation or unemployment after graduation so the loans should be used carefully and wisely. About three-quarters of students who default on the loans do so after withdrawing from school and failing to complete their education.Consequences of defaulting on a federal student loan are:
     - Loss of eligibility for further Title IV aid.
     - Loss of eligibility for payment relief.
     - Notification of default is sent to national credit bureaus and drops your child's credit score.

4. Defaulting students are subject to collection activity commencing with a demand for the entire amount due, then a lawsuit, followed by a judgment, and seizure and sale of any assets, with up to an additional 25% of the judgment in collection fees. Discharge of student loans in bankruptcy is rare, occurring only on proof of "undue hardship" (demonstrating a good-faith effort to repay the debt, current inability to maintain a minimal standard of living and still repay the debt using the lowest monthly payment under any of the repayment plans, and proof that conditions that prevent repaying the debt now will likely persist for most of the full term of the loan). The result, even upon the unlikely proof of "undue hardship" is often just a partial discharge or reduction of debt.

Your child, at the same time, is going to experience unfettered freedom. The first weeks at a university come with a sense of carefree independence. There is no required study schedule, no curfew, and no one checking up. The first major papers or tests (the first real evidence of the sudden step-up in academic competition) may not occur for a month at which point the new, playful (sloppy) habits are already entrenched. A thoughtful phase-in of increasing responsibility and added responsibility during the high school years can go a long way toward reducing the shock and awe of freshman freedom and its accompanying irresponsible behavior. Frank discussions about this change, setting some clear expectations and regular checking with your child may be preferable to the inevitable alternative.

Depression, despondency, and loneliness may hollow out her will. Depression and despondency often result from increased academic competition, loss of an appropriate and stable peer group, sense of inadequacy growing from lack of caring relationships, being the object of shallow and predatory sexual behavior, and simple loneliness from being away from home. Cell phones with weekly calls will help. Doling out the money monthly with frequent discussions also keeps her in contact. Suicidal urges stemming from chemical imbalances are not uncommon, and good medical help should be one of the first responses.

There are few silver bullets for the transition between the cocoon of high school and college. That said, having your student pay for a substantial part of his educational expense (especially if it is earned during the middle and high school years and summers) is an effective way to link undisciplined behaviors to their economic cost.

Working and Credit Hours

The next page has a lot of numbers on it, but it is worth plowing through it. It suggests that it may be less expensive for your child to take as many credits each quarter as he can handle and only work during the summer unless it is absolutely necessary. Here is the math.

It takes about 180 credit hours to graduate. If your child earns 180 credits and graduates in four years, she will average 45 credits a year or 15 credits each quarter. Fifteen to sixteen credits a quarter are considered "carrying a full load." One of the ways you can (and should) adjust for your child's academic proficiency in relationship to the rigor of her university, is to increase or decrease the number of credits she carries, especially during the first year until you both have a feel for what she can handle.

At state colleges where current costs are about $17,650, credits run about $392 each ($17,650 /45 = $392 which is $222 per credit for tuition plus another $170 for books, fees and living costs). By contrast, typical on-line universities tuition charges run anywhere from $290 to $530 a credit hour.

Yet for that same flat quarterly tuition at most four-year universities, your child can take as few as 10 or as many as 18 credits. Some universities do not limit the amount of credits that you can carry. Now some of you are probably way ahead of me. At 30 credits a year (10 credits a semester), each credit will

cost $588. At 54 credits a year (18 credits a semester) each credit will cost $327. At 18 credits a semester, he will only take 3.3 years, a savings of about $14,000. So does working during the school year make sense if your child can save $14,000 by taking a heavier load?

The Light at the End of the Tunnel

If it were an easy job, everyone's child would graduate from college. All parents would watch their children "walk:" walk with the graduates, walk across the stage and get their diploma. After all the planning, all the scheduling, and all the nurturing, it is done. It is a huge accomplishment. It is easier for parents from families where college graduation is a repeated, multi-generation accomplishment, and expectation—harder for those parents who never went themselves.

> *"Those who never dream can never have a dream come true."*
>
> Andy Andrews
> The Traveler's Gift

The great irony, of course, is that fewer numbers of students actually "walk" at graduation, even though they've earned a diploma. Not walking is a way of saying it is not a big deal, especially for those who still have graduate school ahead of them.

But for those extraordinary moms and dads who set their child on this path more than two decades ago, and who played and read and nurtured her every day through the first five years as her wise and playful teacher, it is a big deal.

For those X-moms and dads who kept checking real data for evidence of where she really was in terms of national norms, kept checking homework, and grades and refused to be content to delivering their child to the hands of the system, resigned to whatever the academic proficiency levels turned out to be, it has been a huge investment.

> "If I see farther than most men, it is because I stand on the shoulders of giants."
> - Sir Isaac Newton

For extraordinary parents who have embedded this vision in the neurons of their child, who helped form his little hands around the oar, and helped him row until he could row himself, encouraged, and cheered him on, it has been a huge psychological feat.

As parents who went without in order to make a monthly deposit in the college savings account, who enlisted grandparents to contribute in lieu of (or in addition to) birthday and Christmas presents, who helped fill out scholarship applications and grant forms and signed bank loans for her, you know better. It is a big deal. And for your child, it's a great deal.

So thank you. Thank you for holding the vision. Thank you for your sacrifice and giving your child as good or a better economic future than you had. Thank you for allowing your child to stand on your shoulders.

Your second thanks may come when the cycle starts again. When you own daughter starts to hold a vision for her little one. When your son begins to spend the 25 minutes in reading and purposeful play and saving for his child. That is a real plus-when you realize that you have smoothed the path not only for your child but for your grandchildren and possibly succeeding generations.

CHAPTER TWENTY FIVE

THE EXTRAORDINARY PARENTING MAXIMS

"The best way to predict the future is to create it."

— Peter Drucker

Maxim 1. Extraordinary Moms and Dads. Extraordinary moms and dads are not born. You are a result of choice supported by vision, endurance, and patience. Parents like you are made by what you do over the initial two decades of your child's life.

Maxim 2. Achievement. Most babies, including yours, start life capable of similar levels of achievement.

Maxim 3. Early Growth. You have little impact on aspects of your baby's development affected by innate levels of intelligence. You have a potentially huge impact on aspects controlled by your baby's environment.

Maxim 4. Range in Growth. Your child could make as much as seven years of language, literacy and math growth during her first five years of life. On the other hand, she could make as little as two years of growth in her first five years of life.

Maxim 5. Targets, Tools, and Activities. Your child can make accelerated growth when you read 20 minutes a day to her, talk to her 30 times an hour, and utilize everyday moments in purposeful play to achieve clear targets.

Maxim 6. Choice. Your child's early cognitive growth is parent-dependent. You pretty well get to decide whether your child enters kindergarten one or two years ahead, at grade level, or one, two or three years behind.

Maxim 7. Early is Easier. You can make a greater difference with less effort from birth to five than during any other period of your child's education.

Maxim 8. Achievement by Kindergarten. Only 20% of students enter kindergarten on grade level (green band).
Some enter ahead.
- The top 20% enter two years ahead (dark-blue band)
- The next 20% enter one year ahead (blue band)

Others enter behind.
- 20% enter a year behind (yellow band)
- 10% enter two years behind (orange band)
- 10% enter three years behind (red band)

Maxim 9. Annual Growth. When your child starts two years ahead and makes a year of academic growth each year, he will stay two years ahead. When your child starts three years behind and makes a year of growth each year, he will stay three years behind.

Maxim 10. Goal. You want to move your child into the dark-blue band of achievement by the beginning of kindergarten or as soon thereafter as possible.

Maxim 11. Persistence of the Range in Reading Achievement. There is a one-year difference between the bands at elementary school, for a total of a five-year range between the top and bottom bands. This range in reading achievement persists from kindergarten through 12th grade.

Maxim 12. Growth in the Range in Math Achievement. There is a three-year difference in math ability at kindergarten that grows to five years by the end of elementary school and persists thereafter.

Maxim 13. Parent Duties. Part of your job is to determine where your child is, assure that he makes annual growth each year, and catch-up growth if he needs it. You can best determine your child's actual level of achievement by using national percentiles.

Maxim 14. Annual Growth and Staying Ahead. When your child starts ahead, it is easy to stay ahead. All she has to do is make a year of academic growth each year in reading and math.

Maxim 15. Catching Up and Starting Behind. When your child starts behind, catching up is fairly difficult. Not only must she make a year of growth each year, she must also make some additional part of a year of growth. If she only makes annual growth, she will remain in the same band. For a red band kindergarten child to move to the dark-blue band, she must make 17 years of growth in 12 years.

Maxim 16. Movement Between Bands. Student growth varies over time. Without conscious effort to accelerate growth, the chances are that your child will end in that band she was in third grade plus or minus a band 70% to 80% of the time. Rarely, some students make dramatic growth from the red to the blue (4%) and the dark-blue bands (2%).

Maxim 17. Parenting and Movement Between Bands. Consistent parental expectations, student buy-in, effective teacher instruction, and substantial increases of time on task will create more than a year of academic growth each year.

Maxim 18. High School Graduation Rates. About 68-72% of students graduate from high school each year. About 30% of students drop out, most during high school. When high schools drop 7.5% of students each year, over a four-year period this equals 30%.

Maxim 19. Post-Secondary Training. There are 1,420 four-year universities, 1,166 community and technical colleges, and innumerable trade schools, apprenticeships and online institutions. Academic proficiency during K-12 affects access to these post-secondary training opportunities.

Maxim 20. University Seats. There are about 3.7 million students at each age level. There are 1.2 million freshman university seats. Your child has a one-in-three chance of getting one of those seats.

Maxim 21. University Enrollment by Achievement Band. The odds of your child getting into a four-year university vary with their achievement proficiency. Enrollment varies by band as follows:
- Upper half of dark-blue band   98%
- Lower half of dark-blue band   63%
- Blue band students   44%
- Green band students   25%
- Yellow band students   12%

Maxim 22. Community College Graduation Rates. Of community college students who have declared their intention to get a degree, only 11% graduate with a two-year (AA) degree. An additional 4% complete a 3-18 month certificate program.

Maxim 23. Jobs. When the current 150.6 million U.S. jobs are broken down by the education level of those holding them,
- 41% are held by workers with a "high school or less,"
- 31% are held by persons with "some college," and
- 28% are held by persons with "college or more" education.

Maxim 24. Legacy. Extraordinary parents smooth the path for their children, and often the path of their grandchildren, with opportunities and benefits that last a life time.

APPENDIX   A
ORDER FORM

For additional copies of
Extraordinary Parents

Please FAX your order to: (509) 783.5237
Mail to: The New Foundation Press, Inc
114 Vista Way, Kennewick, WA 99336 or
Order online at NewFoundationPress.com
Questions? Call (509) 551-3226

Quantity		Price	Total
1 – 10	_____	x ($17.95 + S&H of $4.00)= $21.95 ea.	_____
11 – 50	_____	x ($14.95 + S&H of $3.00)= $17.95 ea.	_____
51 +	_____	x ($10.95 + S&H of $2.00)= $12.95 ea.	_____

WA residents: Add 8.7% for sales tax   _____
Expedited or shipping outside continental US:*   _____
                    TOTAL $ _____

Please print clearly.

Name [ ] Mr. [ ] Mrs. [ ] Ms. [ ] _____
Organization_____
Address_____
City_____State_____Zip_____
Telephone_____E-mail_____

[ ] Check or money order enclosed
    (Payable To: The New Foundation Press, Inc.)

[ ] Charge my Visa or MasterCard (circle one)
    Account #_____
    Signature_____
    Exp. Date:_____
[ ] Book Store purchase order attached:
[ ] School District purchase order attached:
    P.O. #_____

You may also order copies of *Annual Growth for All Students,
Catch-Up Growth for Those Who Are Behind* **or** *The 90% Reading
Goal* **at the same quantity discounts and at the above address.**

**Orders shipped outside the 48 states or rushed will be for charged
actual shipping plus $1.50 per book handling.*

Northwest Evaluation Association (NWEA) Data

Northwest Evaluation Association (NWEA) is a not-for-profit organization that provides beginning, middle, and end-of-year online assessments of student achievement and growth. The assessments, called Measures of Academic Progress (MAPs), are currently used in over 2,500 of the nation's 13,862 school districts.

The Northwest Evaluation Association developed and has provided computer-based assessments to school districts and others for the last thirty years. Using a bank of 20,000 test questions in language usage, reading, mathematics, and science, the questions are weighted according to difficulty from the beginning of second grade through high school. Each question is assigned a difficulty level along an equal interval growth scale where each point of growth along the interval is substantially equal to every other point of growth. Using the scale, a student's growth can be measured over a decade, or this year's third graders in a single elementary school can be compared against the last decade of third-grade class scores.

The original work on the scale was done in the mid-'70s from third through tenth grades. In the last decade, the scale was extended to second grade, and, in the last few years, further extended to kindergarten and first grade. For the three grades 4-7 where the scale was completed in the early '70s, the average RIT growth between the midpoints of the percentile bands is 5.3 RIT points. Data for students are currently being collected for K-3. Where the scale was completed in the last five to ten years, the average RIT growth is 13.6. When average K-3 growth is deflated to average elementary growth, the growth lines extend downward to kindergarten at the same rate that they appear in Figure 2.3.

Figures 14.2 and 14.3 were developed by identifying 20,500 students who were both in the third and eighth grade spring data sets. Students whose scores then clustered around the mid-points of the bands were then selected. That is, students with RIT scores equivalent to the 90th, 70th, 50th, 30th, 15th and 5th percentiles and those students with a RIT score one RIT point above and one below these mid-points were selected.This is roughly equivalent to selecting students plus or minus one percentile above or below the 90th, 70th, 50th, 30th, 15th and 5th percentiles. This process resulted in a sample of 7,520 third grade students whose eighth grade scores were then tabulated, converted to percentiles, and formatted to appear as Figures 14.2 and 14.3.

Available Freshman Seats By State With Odds of Enrolling in the State's Four Year Universities As Percentages

	Seats	Students	Odds		Seats	Students	Odds
Nevada	5,510	30,727	18%	Tennessee	27,916	71,504	39%
California	90,650	484,639	19%	Colorado	23,202	58,485	40%
Arizona	15,839	75,028	21%	Kansas	14,533	36,076	40%
Alaska	2,325	10,866	21%	Virginia	38,544	93,745	41%
Wyoming	1,518	7,036	22%	Georgia	49,535	119,020	42%
Mississippi	8,519	38,053	22%	Maine	7,130	17,068	42%
Texas	72,887	323,396	23%	Kentucky	21,059	49,602	42%
Washington	19,227	80,484	24%	New York	96,514	215,948	45%
New Jersey	24,612	102,063	24%	Louisiana	26,625	59,217	45%
Florida	49,535	203,765	24%	Nebraska	10,123	22,151	46%
Hawaii	3,635	14,048	26%	Iowa	17,331	37,813	46%
New Mexico	6,952	25,739	27%	Wisconsin	31,385	67,425	47%
Maryland	19,669	68,226	29%	Utah	17,126	36,771	47%
Illinois	46,670	158,312	29%	New Hampshire	8,150	17,302	47%
Oregon	13,271	44,141	30%	Delaware	5,066	10,113	50%
Oklahoma	14,251	46,978	30%	Pennsylvania	75,881	148,965	51%
Arkansas	11,943	36,625	33%	Montana	6,289	12,215	51%
Missouri	24,333	72,442	34%	South Dakota	5,164	9,884	52%
Michigan	47,842	135,473	35%	Indiana	43,332	80,516	54%
Connecticut	16,010	44,796	36%	Massachusetts	43,259	76,962	56%
South Carolina	20,142	54,994	37%	West Virginia	12,689	22,115	57%
Idaho	7,371	20,061	37%	North Dakota	5,775	8,251	70%
Alabama	21,760	58,552	37%	Vermont	5,846	7,910	74%
North Carolina	40,119	107,768	37%	Rhode Island	11,333	12,707	89%
Ohio	54,505	144,867	38%	District of Columbia	9,078	4,762	191%
Minnesota	25,753	66,627	39%	National	1,277,733	3,752,237	34%

	Kindergarten	First Grade
Vocabulary	Add, subtract, equal, two dimensional, three dimensional, squares, rectangles, circles, triangles, morning, afternoon, evening, days of week, calender, today, yesterday, tomorrow, clock	Even and odd numbers, greater than, less than, patterns, doubles, addendums, bar graph
Number Sense	Count: from one to 20 Count: from 20 to 25 Count: from 25-30 Touch, count and color numbers from 1 to 100 Place value: write these numbers as tens and ones; 12; 21; 20 Compare: which is more 4 or 7? 22 or 18? 8 or 30? Write the missing numbers, 13, 13, __, 15, 16, __ Estimate students in class: 15, 25, 50 Patterns: create a pattern out of blocks	Count by ones to 100, count by 2s, 5s, 10s, by even and odd. Circle even and odd numbers on a chart Use a chart to count by 2s, 5s, and 10s. Read and write the number and its name for numbers 0-10, then 10-15, then 15-20 Place value: write 12 as 10 and some 1s Compare: 12 is >, <, or = 3 Patterns: extend a two step pattern Patterns: create a three step pattern
Addition	Make 4: use blocks to make number 2 + 2, 1 + 3 Make 5: use blocks to make number 2 + 3, 1 + 1 + 3 Make 6 use blocks to make number 5 + 1 Make 7: use blocks to make number 2 + 5; 4 + 3 Make 8: use blocks to make number 2 + 6 Make 9: use blocks to make number 3 + 6 Add: use blocks to add 4 + 1 Add: use blocks to add 3 + 2 Equal: write a number sentence using the equal Equal: circle two objects showing equal parts	Add: add 2 and 1 Add: say, then write 2 + 2 Add: find the sum of 0 + 8 Add: use blocks to make 4, 5, then 6 Add: use blocks to make 7, 8, then 9 Add: use blocks to make 10, 11, the 12 Add: use block or number line to find 2 + 6 Complete the sentence 3 + 3 =; 6 + 6 = Complete 3 + 3; 3 + 4 Change order of addendums Start with greater number; count to add Write and add vertically 5 + 1 = 6
Subtraction	Takeaway from 4: model 4 - 2 using blocks Takeaway from 5: model 5 - 3 using blocks Takeaway from 6: model 6 - 2 using blocks Takeaway from 7: model 7 - 3 using blocks Takeaway from 8: model 8 - 1 using blocks Takeaway from 9: model 9 - 2 using blocks	Subtract: subtract 2 - 1 Write 8 - 3 = 5 Subtract zero: find 8 - 0 Subtract to zero: find 8 - 8 Subtract small numbers: 4 - 1 Subtract larger numbers: 7 - 2 Subtract 2 digit numbers: 11 - 4
Application	Squares: identify a square Triangles: identify a triangle Circles: identify a circle 2 dimentional: identify two dimentional objects 3 dimentional: identify a three-dimensional object Time: know morning, afternoon, and evening Time: know today, yesterday and tomorrow Time: identify the correct day of the week Time: which hand of a clock shows the hour Time: which number on a digital clock shows hour?	Write and subtract vertically 6 - 1 = 5 Count back to subtract 8 - 3 Use number line to subract 8 - 2 Add doubles 2 + 2 = 4; subtract 4 - 2 + 2 Time: order morning, afternoon, evening Time: write the time to the hour Time: write the time to the half hour Time: write the time to the hour and half Sort: sort items by shape Graph: make a bar graph

Grade K-5 adopted from the Math Connects series of MacMillan, McGraw-Hill

	Second Grade	Third Grade
Vocabulary	Number, digit, second, minute, hour, day, week, month, penny, nickel, dime, quarter, half dollar, dollar, thermometer	Dollar, is equal to, pattern, place value, round, array, commutative property of multiplication, associative property of multiplication, factor, product, divide, dividend, divisor, quotient
Number Sense	Place value: value of each digit in 29	Place value: through hundred thousands and billions
	Place value: group 10 1s to make 10	Compare 679 and 686
	Write out 35; write fifteen as a number	Order from least to greatest. 7,541; 5,300; 6,108
	Round: round 18 to nearest tenth	Estimate 679 - 325; round to nearest hundred
	Estimate: 21 + 26	Round 5,357 to nearest hundred, then thousand
	Estimate: how many beans in a can	Identify a pattern in 140, 135, 130, ___ . 120,
	Compare: use >, < or = to compare	Add two digit: 25 + 3
	Pattern: continue 2, 4, 6, __ __	Add three digit: 377 + 26
Addition	Add: find the sum of 4 + 5	Add four digit: 1,003 + 7,927
	Use a number line to find 7 + 3	Add money: $0.74 + $0.58
	Use double facts to find 6 + 7; 6 + 5	Why does 2 + 7 = 7 + 2
	Add three: find 7 + 4 + 7	Subtract two digit: 23-15
	Add: 4 tens + 2 tens = _ tens	Subtract three digit: 213 - 155
	Count on to add 47 + 2	Subtract across zero: 400 - 39
	Carrying: find 27 + 5	Subtract money: $0.74 - $0.58
	Add one and two digits: find 15 + 5	Multiply by 0: 0 x 3
	Add two digits: find 18 + 25	Multiply by 1: 1 x 5
	Add three two digits: 32 + 42 + 16	Multiply by 2: 2 x 3
	Subtract all: find 3 - 3	Multiply by 3: 3 x 5
	Subtract zero: find 5 - 0	Multiply by 4: 4 x 6
	Count back to subtract 10 - 3	Multiply by 5: 5 x 3
Subtraction	Use addition: 6 + 7 = ; 13 - 6 = ; 13 - 7 =	Multiply by 6: 6 x 5
	Use doubles to find 16 - 8	Multiply by 7: 7 x 3
	Subtract: find 9 +__= 15	Multiply by 8: 8 x 4
	Subtract 6 tens - 4 tens = __ tens	Multiply by 9: 2 x 9
	Count back to subtract 37 - 2	Multiply by 10: 10 x 3
	Carrying: find 24 - 8 =	Multiply by 11: 4 x 11
	Subtract two and one digit: 34 - 6	Multiply by 12: 12 x 4
	Subtract two digit numbers: 52 - 17	Multiply by 10's, and 100's
Application Conversion	Estimate time to eat	Divide by 0 and 1:
	Time: write the time to hour and half	Divide by 10
	Time: write time to quarter hour	Divide by 2, 3, 4
	Time: write time to five minutes	Divide by 5, 6, 7
	Money: count pennies, nickles, dimes	Divide by 8, 9, 11, 12
	Money: count dimes, quarters	Know customary units of length (US and metric)
	Money: add $0.72 + $0.19	Know customary units of weight (US and metric)
	Money: subtract $0.57 - $.028	Know customary units of volume
	Temperature: read a thermometer	Know customary units of mass and capacity
	Chart: use a tally chart	Time: 80 minutes after 3:30
	Graph: make bar graph from tally chart	Temperature: read a thermeter in Fahrenheit
Geometric Algebraic		Identify common two and three dimensional figures
		Identify and extend geometric patterns
		Identify congruent figures

Grade K-5 adopted from the Math Connects series of MacMillan, McGraw-Hill

	Fourth Grade	Fifth Grade
Vocabulary	Associative property of addition, commutative property of, angle, polygon, 2 or 3-dimensional figures, estimate, dividend, divisor, quotient, decimal, decimal point, difference, estimate, sum, area, convert, customary, metric, perimeter	Bar graph, line graph, median, mode, range,parallel lines, perpendicular lines, reflection, rotation, numerator, denominator, fraction, improper fraction, mixed number, certain, impossible, outcome, probability
Number Sense	Place value: through billions Compare 1,278 1,500. use >,<, or = Estimate 4 x 8,596 Order 54,282; 65,820, and 52,466 Extend the pattern. 26,23,20,17, ___ Round 12.18 to nearest tenth	Place value: through trillions Compare 65 is (>,< or = to) 45 Compare 6.67 is (>,<, or = to) 6.81 Estimate 34/4=? Order 50.13, 50 and 55.01 Round: 4.719 to the nearest tenth
Addition	Add: 714 + 249; 2.7 + 12.38 Add 3,459 = 6,267; 8.139 + 15.39	Add: 4.8 + 5.7 = ? 7.013 - 2.21 = ? Add: 561 + 23 =? , 6702 - 913 = ?
Sub-traction	Subtract: 4,274 - 249; 2,005 - 593 Subtract $125 - 19; 1.2-.007	Subtract: 7 1/5 - 2 4/5 (estimate 7-3=4)
Multiplication	Multiply 3 numbers: 3 x 5 x 4 = Find all factors of 9; 16 Two digits: 18 x 14 Three digits: 806 x 39 Four digits: 5,331 x 25 Money: $1,273 x 4 By 10, 100, 1000: 29 x 30; 7 x 6,000 What 6 coins equal 72 cents	Mentally multiply 14 x 2 x 5 =? 7 x 54 = ? 12 x 14 = ? 108 x 55 = ? 70 x 50 = 35 00 or 3500 Understand: 2 x (40 + 1) = (2 x 40) + (2 x 1)
Division	Divide by 10, 100, 1000 Remainders: find 59/3 Two digit: find 93/4 Three digit: find 426 /5 Four digit: find 6,313/3	Mentally divide 15000/5 = ? Divide 825/20 =? 893/8 = ? 586/62 = ? In 86/5 = 17 R1 what does 1 mean? Write 17/6 as a mixed number Write 5 3/7 as an improper fraction Round 6/13 to 0, 1/2, or 1 Find the common factors of 6 and 21 Find two fractions equivalent to 2/9
Application and Conversion	Estimate height to nearest 1/2 inch Measure length to nearest centimeter Find perimeter of rectangle Find minutes between 4:45pm and 6:15pm Order 6.34, 6 1/4, 6.5, and 6 21/100 Compare 7.26 and 7.62. use <, >, or = Write 7 52/100 as a decimal Find: 5 pounds is ___ ounces	Find two fractions equivalent to 2/9 Find 11/12 - 5/12; find 11/12 - 5/12; Find 2/3 + 1/2; find 4/5 - 1/4 Convert oz to lbs, pints to gallons Convert liters to millilters, meters to cm Convert 54 inches to feet.
Geometric and Algebraic	Tell whether each shape is a polygon Find: rectangle area 7 x 4 meters Find the perimeter Find the volume of the prism Classify the triangle. use acute, right, or obtuse and isosceles, equilateral, or scalene. Evaluate 8 + a if a = 4 Find the value of 5 x n if n = 3 Solve 4 + x = 10	Find congruent sides of a triangle. Find congruent sides of a quadrilateral. Graph: rotation a triangle about a point. Graph: reflection of figure across a line. Find the perimeter of the rectangle Is a transformation a translation, reflection, or rotation? Find the area of the rectangle Find the value of 3 x (4 + 5) 2 x (40 + 1) = (2 x 40) + (2 x 1)

Grade K-5 adopted from the Math Connects series of MacMillan, McGraw-Hill

6th Grade

Comparing and ordering: order of operations, associative property, commutative property, distributive property, base, exponent, exponential form, numerical expression, overestimate, underestimate, sequence, term, clustering, front-end estimate.
Equations: algebraic expression, constant, equation, solution, variable

Estimate a sum by rounding to specified place value	Order of operations: evaluate 9 x 8 - 13
Exponents: write 5 x 5 x 5 in exponent form	Mental math: add 9 + 5 + 1 + 15
Patterns: extend the pattern 4, 9, 14, 19,___,___,___	Equations: is n + 11 a solution for 28 + n = 39
Place value: write 5.68 in expanded form and words	Dividing by whole numbers: 6.18 / 6=
Estimating: add 8.095 + 3.218; round to hundredth	Dividing by decimals: 4.86 / 0.6 =
Adding and subtracting: 7.08 + 4.5 + 13.27 =	Converting: how many .25 L in 3.6 liters?
Converting to scientific notation: 12.6 x 10,000	Solving decimals: a - 6.2 = 7.18
Multiplying decimals: 4 x 2.36 =	

Divisibility and fractions: equivalent, improper, like, unlike and proper fractions, composite number, divisible, common denominator, greatest common factor, improper fraction, like fraction, proper fraction, unlike fraction, mixed number, factor, prime factor

Divisibility: is 96 divisible by 2,3,4,5,6,9 or 10	Add/subtract: 1/5 + 5/8; 1 3/10 + 3 2/25; x - 12 3/4 = 7 2/5
Factors: list all factors of 144	Multiplying: 5 x 1/7; 5/6 x 2/5; 2/5 x 2 1/4
Greatest common factor: find GCF of 144 and 432	Dividing: 8 7/8 / 2 1/4
Conversion: write .37 as fraction; 7/8 as decimal	Multiplying: 4a = 1/2
Equivalent fractions: write 14/16 in simplest form	Compare: 6/8 is <, =, or > 3/8
Estimate: find 3/5 + 3/7 by rounding to 1/2 then 1	Add: 1/5 + 4/5=
Least common multiple: find the LCM of 3,5, and 10	

Data: bar graph, coordinate grid, double-bar graph, double-line graph, frequency table, histogram, line graph, line plot, mean, median, mode, ordered pair, outlier, range, stem-and-leaf plot

Understand mean, median, mode, and range	Use ordered pairs to describe location
Understand outliers and misleading graphs	Make stem-and-leaf plots
Use bar graphs	Make line plots, frequency tables, and histograms

Ratios and percents: corresponding angles, corresponding sides, discount, equivalent ratio, indirect measurement, percent, proportion, rate, ratio, sales tax, scale, scale drawing, similar, tip, unit rate

Ratios examples	Percent: write 25% as a fraction
Proportions: 3/5 = n/15	Convert: .896, 7/1 to percents, decimals, fractions
Indirect measurements: h/6 = 12/4	Percent: find 30% of 85
Scale drawings and maps: 1 cm/35 m = 3 cm/x m	Percent: find sales tax of 5% on $24.95

Geometry: acute angle, acute triangle, adjacent angles, angle, complementary angles, congruent, equilateral triangle, isosceles triangle, line, line of reflection, line of symmetry, line segment, line symmetry, obtuse angle, obtuse triangle, parallel lines

Classify angle: acute, right, obtuse, or straight	Polygons: name and classify as regular or irregular
Lines: classify a pair of lines	Congruence: determine if figures are congruent
Triangles: name and classify common triangles	Transformation: determine if pairs are congruent
Quadrilaterals: name common quadrilaterals	Symmetry: determine if line is in line of symmetry

Measurement: center, circle, circumference, customary system, diameter, metric system, perimeter, pi, radius, area, base, cone, cylinder, face, net, polyhedron, prism, pyramid, surface area, vertex, volume

U.S. unit of measure providing best estimate?	Find the area of a rectangle; parallelogram
Metric unit of measure providing best estimate?	Find the area of a triangle; trapezoid
Convert 5 yards to feet; 29 cm = __ meters	Find the area of a polygon; circle
Convert 14 hours = ___minutes	Find how area changes when dimensions change
Measure and classify an angle	Identify faces, edges, vertices on solid figure
Find the perimeter of a rectangle; a circle	Find the volume of a rectangular prism; cylinder
How perimeter changes when dimensions change	Find the surface area of solids

Probability: complement, compound event, equally likely, experiment, experimental probability, fair, outcome, population, prediction, probability, sample, sample space, theoretical probability

Probability: event is impossible, unlikely, as likely, not as likely, or certain	Compound event: determine probability of event
	Prediction: of a 1 in 4 event with 30 tries
Theoretical probability: of rolling a 3 on a dice	

Grade 6-11 adopted from Mathematics by Holt, Rinehart and Winston

7th Grade

Integers and decimals: additive, subtractive, multiplication and division property of equality, associative, communitive, identity property, algebraic expression, base, coefficient, constant, equation, exponent, inverse operation, numerical expression

Patterns: extend the pattern 64, 32, 16, 8, __ , __	Properties: which property is $2 + (7 + 8) = (2 + 7) + 8$
Order of operations: simplify $27 - 18 \div 6$;	Expressions: evaluate $n + 7$ when $n = 3$; $n = 5$
Conversion: 510 cm to meters; 2.3 L to milliliters	Simplify: $7x + 2x$; $5x^3 + 3y + 7x^3 - 2y - 4y^2$
Exponents: multiply 137×10^3	Does $18 = s - 7$ when $s = 11$; $w + 17 = 23$ when $w = 6$
Write 9,580,000 in scientific notation	Solve: $x - 8 = 17$; $a + 5 = 11$; $102 = v - 66$; $987 = 16 + m$

Integers, rational numbers and decimals: absolute value, composite number, equivalent fractions, greatest common factor (GCF), improper fraction, integer, least common multiple (LCM), mixed number, multiple, opposite, prime factorization, prime number

Add: $-7 + (-11)$; $-8 + 5$; $12 + (-18)$; $4.99 + 22.89$	Solve: $x - 12 = 4$; $7y = 70$; $-13 + p = 8$; $0.8n = 0.0056$
Find product/quotient: $12 \times (-3)$; $-16 \div (-4)$; -3×4	Multiple: 7×0.5; 7.88×7.65; 63.4×1.22
Write prime factorizations: 56; 162; 88; 27	Divide: $2.8 \div 7$; $16.1 \div 7$; $8.25 \div (-5)$; $102.9 \div (-21)$
Find GCF of 32, 12; 120, 210; 36, 60, 96	Add/subtract: $1/3 + 2/5 = 5/15 + 6/15$
Find LCM of 8, 10; 5, 12; 5, 7, 9; 4, 32	Add/subtract: $1/5 + 5/8$; $1\ 3/10 + 3\ 2/25$; $x - 12\ 3/4 = 7\ 2/5$

Patterns and functions: arithmetic sequence, coordinate plane, function, geometric sequence, input, linear equation, linear function, ordered pair, origin, output, quadrant, sequence, term, x-axis, y-axis

Plot points on coordinate plane: M(-3,1); R(3,-4)	Find output for each input: $y = 2x - 1$; $y = 3x + 4$
Graph the ordered pairs (-2,0); (1,1); (3,-4)	Graph: $y = -x + 2$; $y = 2x - 1$; $y = -3x$; $y = 3x - 9$

Ratios and percents: corresponding angles, corresponding sides, cross product, equivalent ratios, indirect measurement, proportion, rate, ratio, scale, scale drawing, scale factor, scale model, similar, slope, unit rate, interest, percent, percent of change

Write ratio of 3 red, 7 blue, 5 white balloons	Write as a percent: 7/8; 0.82
Average 540 ft in 90 secs and 436 ft in 4 hrs	Estimate 26% of 77; 22% of 44; 31% of 97
Find n w/ cross products: $p/8 = 10/12$; $4/6 = n/3$	Find 15% of 425; 130% of 21
Convert 5 mi to feet; 32 fl oz to pints	Find % of change when 54 is increased to 84
Write as fraction and decimal: 78%; 89%; 5%	Find I when $P = \$545$, $r = 1.5\%$, $t = 2$ years, $I = \_\_$

Data: bar graph, biased sample, box-and-whisker plot, circle graph, convenience sample, cumulative frequency, double-bar graph, double-line graph, frequency table, histogram, interquartile range, line graph, line plot, lower quartile, mean, median, mode

Using 35, 29, 14, 19, 32, 25, 27, 16, and 8, make a cumulative frequency table, a stem-and-leaf plot, and a line plot.

Choose the type of graph that would best represent the population of a town over a 10-year period.

Make a bar graph with the chess club's results: W,L,W,L,W,L,L,W,W,W,L,W.	Use the data to make a box-and-whisker plot: 14, 10, 23, 16, 21, 26, 17, and 25.

Geometry: acute angle, acute triangle, adjacent angles, angle, arc, asymmetry, center of a circle, center of rotation, central angle, chord, circle, complementary angles, congruent, corresponding angles, diameter, equilateral triangle, image, isosceles

Measurement: accuracy, area, circumference, hypotenuse, leg, perfect square, perimeter, precision, base, cone, cylinder, edge, face, net, polyhedron, prism, pyramid, surface area, vertex, volume

Find area of a triangle when L = 14 in, W = 8.6 in	Find the volume of prisms, cylinders, pyramids, cones
Estimate square root of $\sqrt{71}$; $\sqrt{106}$; $\sqrt{92}$	Find the surface area of cylinders

Probability: combination, complement, dependent events, event, experiment, experimental probability, factorial, Fundamental Counting Principle, independent events, outcome, permutation, probability, sample space

Permutations: how many different 4-digit numbers can you make from the numbers 2, 4, 6, and 8 using each once?

Theoretical probability: find the probability of drawing a 4 from a standard deck of 52 playing cards.

Multi-Step Equations and Inequalities: algebraic inequality, compound inequality, inequality, solution set

Two-step equations: solve $6a - 3 = 15$; $-5y + 6 = -34$	Multi-step equations: solve $7a + 4 - 13a = 46$
Variables on both sides: solve $8a = 3a + 25$; $-6b + 9 = 12b$	Inequalities: solve and graph each set. $b + 6 > -10$; $r - 16 > 9$
Inequalities: solve $8b < -48$; $-5p > -25$	Two-step inequalities: solve and graph. $-7b - 16 > -2$

Grade 6-11 adopted from Mathematics by Holt, Rinehart and Winston

8th Grade

Integers and decimals: absolute value, additive inverse, algebraic expression, algebraic inequality, coefficient, constant, evaluate equation, least common denominator, rational number, reciprocal, relatively prime inequality, integer, inverse operation

Expressions: write in words 25 + 13t	Evaluate: $4x + 9y$ for $x = 2$ and $y = 5$
Absolute value: evaluate: [-9] - [3]	Integers: add/subtract -6 + 4; -3 - (-5); 7(-5), 72 / -4
Solve and graph: h - 3 < 7; 5z - 12 > -7	Add/subtract: 3/4 + 2/5 Solve: y + 7.8 = -14; 3m + 5 = 35
Write <, >, or = for 5/7__9/10	Multiply/divide: 3/4 / 1/8; 3(-2/5)

Vocabulary: least common denominator, rational number, reciprocal, relatively prime

Vocabulary: arithmetic sequence, common difference, coordinate plane, domain, function, graph of an equation, input, ordered pair, origin, output, quadrant, range, sequence, term, vertical line test, x-axis, x-coordinate, y-axis, y-coordinate

Add/subtract: 1/5 + 5/8; 1 3/10 + 3 2/25; x - 12 3/4 = 7 2/5	Exponents: write in exponential form(7)(7)(7)
Squares: find 2 square roots of the number 16	Write in scientific notation 0.000000008
Pythagorean Theorem: solve for the unknown side of right triangle if a = 6 and b = 8	

Vocabulary: base, density property, exponent, exponential form, hypotenuse, irrational number, let, perfect square, power, principal square root, Pythagorean Theorem, scientific notion

Geometry: acute angle, acute triangle, angle, center of rotation, complementary angles, congruent, correspondence, equilateral triangle, image, isosceles triangle, line, line of symmetry, line symmetry, obtuse angle, obtuse triangle, parallel lines

Know how to find points, lines, planes, and angles	Find the angle measures in each regular polygon
Know parallel and perpendicular lines	Graph quadrilateral Q(2,0), R(-1,1), S(3,3), T(8,3)
Know polygons, congruence and symmetry	Draw image with transformations, reflection, translation

Measurement: area, capacity, circle, circumference, cone, cylinder, diameter, edge, face, great circle, hemisphere, lateral face, lateral surface, orthogonal views, perimeter, prism, pyramid, radius, regular pyramid, right cone, slant height, sphere, surface area

Find perimeter and area of rectangles; parallelograms	Find perimeter and area of triangles and trapezoids
3-D figures: draw the top view of each figure	Circle: find area, circumference, and volume in terms of Pi

Data: back-to-back stem-and-leaf plot, biased sample, box-and-whisker plot, convenience sample, correlation, double-bar graph, double-line graph, frequency table, histogram, line of best fit, line plot, mean, median, mode, outlier, population, quartile

Organize: use line plot to organize the data	Use the given data to make a box-and-whisker plot
Display: make a histogram of each data set	Misleading: explain why a graph is misleading
Vocabulary: equivalent expression, like term, simplify, solution of a system of equations, system of equations, term	
Simplify 5(3m - 2) + 4m	Solve: 12s = 8 + 2(5s + 3)
Solve the system of equations y = x + 3; y = 2x + 5	Inequalities: solve and graph -8 < t/2

Vocabulary: boundary line, constant of proportionality, direct variation, linear equation, linear inequality, point-slope form, slope-intercept form, x-intercept, y-intercept

Write the point-slope form of the line given conditions	Graph exponential and quadratic functions
Find a given term in the arithmetic sequence	Simplify 4(5mn - 3m); solve (p - 6)(p - 2)

Vocabulary: common ratio, exponential decay, exponential function, exponential growth, Fibonacci sequence, first differences, function notation, geometric sequence, inverse variation, linear function, parabola, quadratic function, second differences

Ratios and Percents: benchmark, commission, commission rate, estimate, interest, percent, percent change, percent decrease, percent increase, principal, rate of interest, sales tax, simple interest

Find two ratios that are equivalent to 8/16	Determine the better buy 50 for $14.99 or 75 for $21.50
Solve: 3/5 = 9/x; 15/5 = f/6; 3/5 = 7.5/t	Use conversion factors to find the rate: 90 km/h to m/h

Probability: Addition Counting Principle, certain, combination, dependent events, disjoint events, equally likely, event, experiment, experimental probability, factorial, fair, Fundamental Counting Principle, impossible, independent events, mutually exclusive

Vocabulary: center of dilation, congruent angles, conversion factor, cross product, dilation, enlargement, equivalent ratio, indirect measurement, proportion, rate, ratio, reduction, scale, scale drawing, scale factor, scale model, similar, unit price

Grade 6-11 adopted from Mathematics by Holt, Rinehart and Winston

ALGEBRA I

Expressions: absolute value, additive inverse, algebraic expressions, axes, base, coefficient, constant, coordinate plane, evaluate, exponent, input, integers, irrational numbers, like terms, multiplicative inverse, natural numbers, numerical expression

Expressions: evaluate b - a for a = 7 and b = 15	Simplify: $18 - 3(15 - 7 \div 4)^2$; Evaluate $-5\sqrt{40} - x + 12$ for x=4
Add/subtract: -4+(-9) ; -8-(-3)	Simplify: $-6f^2 - 8f + 3f^2$; $3x - 4y$; $5x^2 - 3(x - 2) - x$
Multiply/divide: -12(9); -⅛ ÷ (-¾)	Functions: graph the ordered pairs $y = x + 2$; x = -3, -2, -1, 0

Equations: commission, contradiction, conversion factor, corresponding angles, corresponding sides, cross products, discount, equation, formula, identity, indirect measurement, interest, literal equation, markup, percent, percent change, percent decrease

Solve by addition/subtraction: x - 12 = -8.3; -7.8 = 5 + t	Two-step: solve $3x/5 - x/4 + 1/2 = 6/5$
Solve by multiplication/division: 4z = 12; -8x = 148	Solve: -3r - 8 = -5r - 12; 0.2(7 + 2t) = 0.4t + 1.4

Inequalities: Compound inequality, inequality, intersection, solution of an inequality, union

Graph the inequality: y > -3; x > -3; r ≥ 9.5; 2(3 - 5) < k	Divide: solve p/-3 ≤6; -18 < 6t; -2k < 14
Solve and graph: x + 6 > 2; n - 1.3 < 3.2; -3 < c + 5 ≤ 11	Functions

Understand and Use Functions: arithmetic sequence, common difference, continuous graph, correlation, dependent variable, discrete graph, domain, function, function notation, function rule, independent variable, negative/positive correlation, no correlation

Add/subtract: 1/5 + 5/8; 1 3/10 + 3 2/25; x - 12 3/4 = 7 2/5

Linear Functions: constant of variation, direct variation, family of functions, linear equation, linear function, parallel lines, parent function, perpendicular lines, rate of change, reflection, rise, rotation, run, slope, transformation, translation

Using intercepts: find the x- and y-intercepts of 2x + 5y = 10; -x + 6y = 18; 3x - 4y = 1; -2x + y = 1	Slope formula: find the slope of line describe by 2x - 3y = 6; 4x + 3y = 24; y = -3x + 6
Rate of change and slope	Slope-intercept form, point-slope form

Equations and Inequalities: consistent system, dependent system, inconsistent system, independent system, linear inequality, solution of a linear inequality, solution of a system of linear equations, solution of system of linear inequalities

Solve each system by substitution: y = x + 3; y = -4x; x = y - 7	Solve y = 2x - 2 by graphing; solve y = 3x + 2 by graphing
Solve each system by elimination: 4x + y = -1; x + 2y = -1	Solve each system of linear equations: y = -x + 4; y = 3x + 2

Exponents and Polynomials: binomial, cubic, degree of a monomial, degree of a polynomial, difference of two squares, leading coefficient, monomial, perfect-square trinomial, polynomial, quadratic, scientific notation, standard form of a polynomial, trinomial

Exponents: evaluate $r^3s - 4$ for r = -3 and s = 2	Multiply: $(2x - 4)(3x + 5)$; $(b - 2)(b^2 + 4b - 5)$; $(2r)(4r)$
Find the value of 386.21×10^5	Multiply: simplify $5^3 \cdot 5 - 2$; $a^4 \cdot b - 3 \cdot b \cdot a - 2$; $(a - 3b2)-2$

Factoring Polynomials: greatest common factor, prime factorization

Factor $3t^3 - 9t2$; $-12s - 6s^3$; $5(x - 7) + 3x(x - 7)$	Factor: $x^2 + 14x + 45$; $x^2 + 6x - 27$; $x^2 + 6x + 5$; $x^2 - 3x - 28$

Quadratic Functions and Equations: axis of symmetry, completing the square, discriminant, maximum, minimum, parabola, quadratic equation, quadratic function, vertex, zero of a function

Find the zeros of: $y = 2x^2 - 4x - 6$; $y = x^2 + 3x - 10$	Solve $4x^2 - 8x + 4 = 0$; $x^2 - 5x - 6 = 0$; $x^2 + 4x + 4 = 0$
Graph: $y = 2x^2 - 8x - 10$; $y = x^2 + 6x + 6$; $3x^2 + 6x = y - 3$	Solve by factoring: $x^2 + 6x + 5 = 0$; $3x^2 - 6x = 24$

Understand and Use Data: bar graph, box-and-whisker plot, circle graph, combination, complement, compound event, cumulative frequency, dependent events, equally likely, event, experiment, experimental probability, fair, frequency, frequency table, histogram

Exponential and Radical Functions: common ratio, compound interest, exponential decay, exponential function, exponential growth, extraneous solution, geometric sequence, half-life, like radicals, radical equation, radical expression, radicand, square-root

Find 10th term of sequence -6400, 3200, -1600, 800	Exponential functions and decay
Simplify: $\sqrt{50x} - \sqrt{2x} + \sqrt{12x}$; $6\sqrt{7} + 3\sqrt{7}$; $9\sqrt{5t} - 8\sqrt{5t}$	Solve: $\sqrt{4x} + 1 - 8 = -3$; $3\sqrt{-x} = 27$; $12 = 4\sqrt{2x} + 1$

Functions and Equations: asymptote, discontinuous function, excluded value, inverse variation, rational equation, rational expression, rational function

Add/subtract: $\dfrac{7x}{3xy} - \dfrac{x^2-3x}{3xy}$; $\dfrac{3b+4}{-b} - \dfrac{5-2b}{7-b}$; $\dfrac{h^2+2h}{h-5} - \dfrac{3h-1}{5-h}$	Divide: $(6x^4 - 9x^3 + 3x^2) \div 3x$; $(5x^3 - 10x - 25) \div (5x^2)$

Grade 6-11 adopted from Mathematics by Holt, Rinehart and Winston

GEOMETRY	
Foundations for Angles: acute angles, adjacent angles, angle, angle bisector, area, base, between, bisect, circumference, collinear, complementary angles, congruent angles, congruent segments, construction, coordinate, coordinate plane, coplanar, degree	
Understanding points, lines, and planes	Using formulas in geometry
Measuring and constructing segments and angles	Pairs of angles
Geometric Reasoning: biconditional statement, conclusion, conditional statement, conjecture, contra positive, converse, counterexample, deductive reasoning, definition, flowchart proof, hypothesis, inductive reasoning, inverse, logically equivalent statement	
Using inductive reasoning to make conjectures	Flowchart and paragraph proofs
Conditional and biconditional statements	Algebraic proof
Using deductive reasoning to verify conjectures	Geometric proof
Parallel and Perpendicular Lines: alternate exterior angles, alternate interior angles, corresponding angles, distance from a point to a line, parallel lines, parallel planes, perpendicular bisector, perpendicular lines, point-slope form, rise, run	
Lines and angles	Perpendicular lines
Angles formed by parallel lines and transversals	Slopes of lines
Proving lines parallel	Lines in the coordinate plane
Triangle Congruence: acute triangle, auxiliary line, base, base angle, congruent polygons, coordinate proof, corollary, corresponding angles, corresponding sides, CPCTC, equiangular triangle, equilateral triangle, exterior, exterior angle, included angle	
Classifying triangles	Triangle congruence: CPCTC
Angle relationships in triangles	Isosceles and equilateral triangles
Triangle congruence: SSS, SAS, ASA, AAS, and HL	Introduction to coordinate proof
Properties and Attributes of Triangles: altitude of a triangle, centroid of a triangle, circumcenter of a triangle, circumscribed, concurrent, equidistant, in center of a triangle, indirect proof, inscribed, locus, median of a triangle, midsegment of a triangle	
Perpendicular and angle bisectors	Indirect proof and inequalities in one triangle
Bisectors, medians and altitudes of triangles	Inequalities in two triangles
The triangle midsegment theorem	The Pythagorean theorem
Polygons and Quadrilaterals: base of a trapezoid, base angle of a trapezoid, concave, convex, diagonal, isosceles trapezoid, kite, leg of a trapezoid, midsegment of a trapezoid, parallelogram, rectangle, regular polygon, rhombus, side of a polygon, square	
Properties and attributes of polygons and parallelograms	Properties and conditions of special parallelograms
Conditions for parallelograms	Properties of kites and trapezoids
Similarity: cross products, dilation, extremes, indirect measurement, means, proportion, ratio, scale, scale drawing, scale factor, similar, similar polygons, similarity ratio	
Ratio and proportion	Applying properties of similar triangles
Ratios in similar polygons	Using proportional relationships
Triangle similarity: AA, SSS, and SAS	Dilations and similarity in the coordinate plane
Right Triangles and Trigonometry: angle of depression, angle of elevation, component form, cosine, direction, equal vectors, geometric mean, magnitude, parallel vectors, resultant vector, sine, tangent	
Similarity in right triangles	Angles of elevation and depression
Trigonometric ratios, solving right triangles	Law of sines and law of cosines, vectors
Extending Perimeter, Circumference, and Area: apothem, center of a circle, center of a regular polygon, central angle of a regular polygon, circle, composite figure, geometric probability	
Developing formulas for triangles and quadrilaterals	Perimeter and area in the coordinate plane
Developing formulas for circles, regular polygons	Effects of changing dimensions proportionally
Composite figures	Geometric probability
Spatial Reasoning: altitude, altitude of a cone, altitude of a pyramid, axis of a cone, axis of cylinder, center of a sphere, cone, cross section, cube, cylinder, edge, face, great circle, hemisphere, horizon, isometric drawing, lateral edge, lateral face	
Solid geometry	Volume of prisms, cylinders, pyramids, cones and sphere
Representation and formula of three-dimensional figures	Surface area of prisms, cylinders, pyramids and cones

Grade 6-11 adopted from Mathematics by Holt, Rinehart and Winston

ALGEBRA 2

Functions: compression, dependent variable, domain, element, empty set, finite set, function, function notation, independent variable, infinite set, interval notation, like radical terms, parent function, principal root, radicand, radical symbol, range

Estimate to the nearest tenth $\sqrt{12}$; $\sqrt{74}$; simplify $\sqrt{3} \cdot \sqrt{21}$; $\sqrt{32}$

Simplify: evaluate $6c - 3a2 + d3$ for $c = -1$ and $d = 3$ Write in scientific notation $(4.5 \times 10^{-2})(1.2 \times 10^{3})$

Linear Functions: absolute value, absolute-value function, boundary line, conjunction, contradiction, correlation, correlation coefficient, disjunction, equation, identity, indirect measurement, inequality, line of best fit, linear equation in one variable

Solve the proportion $\dfrac{x+2}{12} = \dfrac{15}{20}$ Solve $5(x + 4) = 3x - 2$; $35 = 7(2x - 8)$; $3x + 12 - 9x = 12 - 6x$

Graph the solution: $3x - 5y < 10$; $y > -3$; $2x + 4y > -12$

Linear Systems: consistent system, constraint, dependent system, elimination, feasible region, inconsistent system, independent system, linear programming, linear system, objective function, ordered triple, parameter, parametric equations, substitution

Graph: $x + y = 6$; $x - 3y = 6$; $x - 6y = 2$; $x - y = 2$; $3x - y = 2$ Graph each feasible region, $x < 3$, $y < 2x + 1$; $x > 2$, $x^2 - 1$

Graph inequalities: $y + 1 > 4x$; $y - 3x < 3$; $y \leq x + 1$ Solve: $\{3x + 2y - z = -1, x + 3y - z = -10, 2x - y - 3z = -3\}$

Matrices: address, augmented matrix, coefficient matrix, constant matrix, Cramer's rule, determinant, dimensions, entry, main diagonal, matrix, matrix equation, matrix product, multiplicative identity matrix, multiplicative inverse matrix

Understand multiplying matrices   Determinants and Cramer's rule

Using matrices to transform geometric figures   Add/subtract: $1/5 + 5/8$; $1\ 3/10 + 3\ 2/25$; $x - 12\ 3/4 = 7\ 2/5$

Quadratic Functions: absolute value of a complex number, axis of symmetry, binomial, completing the square, complex conjugate, complex number, complex plane, discriminant, imaginary number, imaginary unit, maximum value, minimum value, parabola

Factor: $x^2 - 7x - 8 = 0$; $2x^2 + 8x + 6 = 0$; $x^2 = 144$ Solve each equation: $x2 - 22x + 133 = 0$; $6x^2 + 150 = 0$

Solve: $x^2 - 8x = 12$; $x^2 + 20x + 84 = 0$ Solve and graph: $X2 - 4x - 9^3 = 3$; $y > x^2 + 3x + 4$

Polynomial Functions: degree of a monomial, degree of a polynomial, end behavior, leading coefficient, local maximum, local minimum, monomial, multiplicity, polynomial, polynomial function, synthetic division, turning point

Subtract $(6x - 2x^2 + 1) - (4x - 5x^2)$; $(x^4 - x^2 + 4) + (x^2 - x^3 - 5x^4 - 7)$ Divide $(x^3 - 5x^2 + 2x - 7) \div (x + 2)$; $(8x^4 + 6x^2 - 2x + 4) \div (2x - 1)$

Exponential and Logarithmic Functions: asymptote, base, common logarithm, exponential decay, exponential equation, exponential function, exponential growth, exponential regression, inverse function, inverse relation, logarithm, logarithmic equation

Write in logarithmic form: $3^5 = 243$; $1 = 9^0$; $9^{1.5} = 27$ Solve $5^x = 50$; $\log_9 x^2 = 5$

Simplify: $\log_2 8 + \log_2 16$; $\log_3 8^2$; $\log_5 125 - \log_5 25$ Simplify $e^{\ln(2s + 1)}$

Rational and Radical Functions: Combined variation, complex fraction, constant of variation, continuous function, direct variation, discontinuous function, extraneous solution, hole (in a graph), index, inverse variation, joint variation, radical equation

Multiply: $\dfrac{x+5}{3x+1} \cdot \dfrac{9x+3}{x^2-25}$ Divide $\dfrac{x^3 y}{4xy^4} \div \dfrac{x}{8y^2}$ Add $\dfrac{4}{x^2+4} + \dfrac{x^2+8}{x^2+4}$ Subtract $\dfrac{2x}{x+4} - \dfrac{3}{x+4}$

Solve each equation. $\dfrac{30}{x+1} + x = 10$; $\dfrac{3x}{x+2} = \dfrac{2x+2}{x+2}$

Properties of Functions: composition of functions, one-on-one function, piecewise function, step function

Multiple representations of functions   Operations with functions and their inverses

Piecewise and transforming function   Modeling real-world data

Sequences and Series: arithmetic sequence, arithmetic series, converge, diverge, explicit formula, finite sequence, geometric mean, geometric sequence, geometric series, infinite geometric series, infinite sequence, iteration, limit, mathematical induction

Introduction to sequences   Find the first 5 terms of the sequence with $a_1 = -52$; $a_n = 0.5a_{n-1} + 2$

Understand and Use Trigonometric Functions: angle of rotation, cosecant, cosine, cotangent, coterminal angle, initial side, inverse cosine function, inverse sine function, inverse tangent function, radian, reference angle, secant, sine, standard position

The law of sines and cosines   Inverse of Trigonometric functions

Trigonometric Graphs and Identities: amplitude, cycle, frequency, period, periodic function, phase shift

Grade 6-11 adopted from Mathematics by Holt, Rinehart and Winston

Blue Band Writing Answers (Chapter 21)

Evaluate this statement. [1]

"Events on the frontier between 1763 and 1788 and the development of government policies in response to them were more significant for the development of the United States than the events that took place in the settled areas of the eastern seaboard between 1763 and 1788."

Example answer.

The role of the historian is to determine what events of the past are significant and explain to his or her generation why they are. For many years, American historians have concentrated on the events that took place on the eastern seaboard between 1763 and 1788, suggesting that for American history they were the most significant events of those decades. These historians have often ignored the events on the western frontier in those years - events that were "more significant for the development of U.S. history" than happenings in the East.

Granted, many significant events from the Stamp Act Crisis of 1765 to Shay's Rebellion of 1786 took place in the East. Granted also that the Declaration of Independence was signed, the Continental Congress met, and many battles of the Revolutionary War were fought in the East, but *all of these events were affected by occurrences in the West*. It must be remembered that the Peace of Paris in 1763 ended a war fought for control of the Northwest Territory (Ohio, Michigan, etc.) and of the Mississippi Valley. It was in this war that George Washington gained his colonial reputation that allowed him to become the leader of the colonial army. Without his western military experience, where would the colonial armies have been? More significantly, the entire taxation issue that was argued in the East was precipitated by the need of the British to pay the expenses they incurred in the French and Indian War. Without that war, *a result of British policy on the frontier*, there would have been no need for the taxes – Stamp Act, Townshend Acts, Tea Act —which stirred up the East and led to the cry, "No taxation without representation" and ultimately to independence.

---

[1] William O. Kellogg, *Barron's AP United States History, viii edition* (New York: Barron's, 2008), 222.

One often-forgotten event leading to American independence is the British Proclamation Line of 1763, which closed the Northwest Territory to colonial settlement. American leaders such as Washington and Benjamin Franklin had committed money to companies to organize this territory. When the British stopped this settlement on the frontier, colonists had an important motive for leading an anti-British movement in the East. In 1774 the English made matters worse for colonial leaders when, by the Quebec Act, they extended the boundaries of the former French province of Quebec to include the Northwest and established a form of government for the area, putting it under different laws than the British colonies.

Many of these colonies, such as Virginia and Connecticut, claimed control of the Northwest. After the Declaration of Independence, as the Continental Congress struggled to govern the colonies, Maryland refused to ratify the new government arrangement – the Articles of Confederation – until all colonies gave up their claims to western lands. When Virginia finally did cede its claim in 1781, the articles were ratified, and so, again, the West played a significant role in Eastern events.

Many other illustrations could be given of the *significance* of the West: the British plan to split the West from the seaboard colonies, which was frustrated by the colonial victory at Saratoga, and victories on the frontier in Carolina, which led to Yorktown. Also, during the negotiations for peace, the United States won control over the land from the Appalachians to the Mississippi because of the victories of George Rogers Clark in the Northwest. The British refused to evacuate forts, and the resulting diplomatic struggle to gain control of the frontier region was the major foreign policy issue between 1783 and 1788.

This chart displays 747 job descriptions with number of jobs in 2006, the percentage filled by workers by educational level ("high school or less," "some college," or "college or more,") the hourly wage of the jobs (for those in the 10th percentile, 50th percentile, and 90th percentile), and the median annual wage. Wages in excess of $70 an hour or $140,000 annually are indicated by an "#" (the pound sign). The information is adapted from *Employment by Industry, Occupation, and Percent Distribution 2006 and Projected 2016* from the U.S. Department of Labor National Employment Matrix.

(1) Total Positions 2006	(2) HS or Less	(3) Some College	(4) College or more	(5) Job Description	(6) 10th	(7) 50th	(8) 90th	(9) Median Annual Compensation
127,260,082				TOTAL, ALL OCCUPATIONS	$8	$15	$36	$31,410
				Management, business, and financial				
				Management occupations	20	41	#	84,440
402,246	13	22	65	Chief executives	31	#	#	#
1,720,460	20	33	48	General and operations managers	21	43	#	88,700
64,507	13	22	65	Legislators	•	•	•	16,220
47,296	7	18	76	Advertising and promotions managers	18	38	#	78,250
167,464	9	22	69	Marketing managers	26	50	#	104,400
318,329	9	22	69	Sales managers	22	46	#	94,910
49,575	9	16	75	Public relations managers	22	42	#	86,470
247,103	21	39	40	Administrative services managers	17	34	60	70,990
263,695	5	23	73	Computer and information systems	32	52	#	108,070
506,347	13	27	60	Financial managers	25	46	#	95,310
49,087	15	28	58	Compensation and benefits managers	22	39	68	81,410
28,878	15	28	58	Training and development managers	22	41	69	84,340
58,233	15	28	58	Human resources managers, all other	26	45	#	92,710
157,341	25	32	43	Industrial production managers	23	39	65	80,560
69,526	15	28	57	Purchasing managers	23	41	67	85,440
94,012	39	36	25	Transportation, storage, and distribution	22	37	61	76,310
258,156	45	29	26	Farm, ranch, and other agricultural	15	26	50	53,720
1,058,444	54	30	16	Farmers and ranchers	10	16	38	33,360
487,077	40	31	29	Construction managers	21	37	68	76,230
56,064	6	15	78	Education administrators, preschool	12	19	34	38,580
131,293	6	15	78	Education administrators, postsecondary	20	36	#	75,780
29,714	6	15	78	Education administrators, all other	18	33	57	69,300
187,089	4	12	84	Engineering managers	34	53	#	111,020
350,259	40	36	24	Food service managers	14	21	36	44,570
28,770	9	51	41	Funeral directors	14	24	45	50,370
3,997	34	42	24	Gaming managers	18	31	51	64,410
70,988	23	32	45	Lodging managers	13	21	40	44,240
261,925	11	32	57	Medical and health services managers	23	37	64	76,990
40,743	0	0	93	Natural sciences managers	30	50	#	104,040
25,870	17	27	55	Postmasters and mail superintendents	19	28	38	57,900
328,928	27	37	36	Property, real estate, and community	10	21	47	43,670
130,018	9	20	72	Social and community service managers	16	26	45	54,530
869,558	17	27	55	Managers, all other	22	42	#	86,680

				Business and financial operations occupations				
24,870	18	23	59	Agents, managers of artists, performers	15	32	#	66,440
15,904	36	43	0	Purchasing agents, buyers, farm products	13	23	42	48,410
156,568	28	36	36	Wholesale and retail buyers, except farm	13	23	42	46,960
287,429	22	36	42	Purchasing agents, retail, farm	16	25	42	52,460
305,169	18	35	47	Claims adjusters, examiners, investigators	16	26	39	53,560
13,399	18	35	47	Insurance appraisers, auto damage	17	25	34	51,500
237,035	14	28	58	Compliance officer, health & safety	14	23	40	48,400
221,100	28	40	32	Cost estimators	16	26	44	54,920
11,725	18	33	49	Emergency management specialists	13	23	40	48,380
196,892	14	30	56	Employment, recruitment specialists	13	21	41	44,380
109,916	14	30	56	Compensation, benefit, job analysis specialist	16	25	40	52,180
210,342	14	30	56	Training and development specialists	14	24	40	49,630
214,383	14	30	56	Human resources, labor relations specialists	13	26	44	54,280
83,443	19	38	43	Logisticians	18	31	47	64,250
678,188	7	16	78	Management analysts	20	34	63	71,150
50,962	11	22	67	Meeting and convention planners	13	21	36	43,530
1,043,120	18	33	49	Business operation specialists, all other	15	27	48	57,090
1,274,357	4	17	79	Accountants and auditors	17	27	47	57,060
101,125	17	39	44	Appraisers and assessors of real estate	12	22	42	46,130
61,858	4	18	78	Budget analysts	20	31	47	63,440
67,132	15	25	60	Credit analysts	15	26	51	54,580
220,568	3	10	87	Financial analysts	20	34	66	70,400
176,220	4	15	81	Personal financial advisors	16	33	#	67,660
104,477	16	32	53	Insurance underwriters	16	26	46	54,530
25,588	0	15	76	Financial examiners	18	32	59	66,670
33,396	16	35	49	Loan counselors	12	18	31	36,550
372,544	16	35	49	Loan officers	15	25	51	53,000
80,726	23	34	43	Tax examiners, collectors, revenue agents	13	23	42	46,920
100,415	15	31	54	Tax preparers	8	14	30	28,510
129,135	17	34	50	Financial specialists, all other	16	27	47	55,380
				Professional and related occupations				
				Computer and mathematical science	18	33	55	69,070
25,261	7	25	68	Computer, information scientists, research	27	47	#	97,970
435,076	6	22	73	Computer programmers	19	33	53	68,080
506,751	2	13	85	Computer software engineers, applications	25	40	60	83,130
350,048	2	13	85	Computer software engineers	27	43	63	89,070
552,458	13	44	43	Computer support specialists	12	20	33	42,400
503,631	7	25	68	Computer systems analysts	21	35	55	73,090
119,415	5	24	72	Database administrators	19	32	51	67,250
309,201	8	42	50	Network,computer systems administrators	19	31	49	64,690
261,793	8	35	57	Network systems and data analysts	19	33	51	68,220
135,949	7	25	68	Computer specialists, all other	18	34	52	71,510
18,137			99	Actuaries	23	41	#	85,690
3,033	0	6	93	Mathematicians	25	44	64	90,870
58,353	7	23	71	Operations research analysts	19	32	54	66,950
22,416	0	6	93	Statisticians	18	34	54	69,900
1,302	0	6	93	Mathematical technicians	13	19	37	38,560
10,390	0	6	93	Mathematical scientists, all other	15	26	47	53,860
				Architecture and engineering occupations	17	31	52	64,780
131,873	2	10	88	Architects, except landscape and naval	19	33	54	67,620
27,839	2	10	88	Landscape architects	17	28	46	57,580
12,184	0	18	82	Cartographers and photogrammetrists	16	24	40	49,970
60,032	0	18	82	Surveyors	14	25	40	51,630
89,831	3	10	87	Aerospace engineers	29	44	62	90,930

(1)	(2)	(3)	(4)	(5)	(6)	(7)	(8)	(9)
					\$ Hourly Wage			
					by percentile			
Total Positions 2006	HS or Less	Some College	College or moe	Job Description	10th	50th	90th	Median Annual Compensation
3,133	0	18	76	Agricultural engineers	22	33	49	67,710
14,379	0	18	76	Biomedical engineers	22	36	58	75,440
30,444	0	6	91	Chemical engineers	25	39	59	81,500
256,330	3	10	87	Civil engineers	22	34	52	71,710
78,525	7	23	70	Computer hardware engineers	27	44	67	91,860
153,375	3	17	81	Electrical engineers	25	38	58	79,240
137,868	3	17	81	Electronics engineers, except computer	26	40	60	83,340
54,341	0	10	86	Environmental engineers	21	35	52	72,350
25,380	8	19	74	Health and safety engineers	20	33	50	69,580
201,311	8	19	74	Industrial engineers	22	34	50	71,430
9,196	0	18	78	Marine engineers and naval architects	23	37	55	76,200
21,616	0	19	77	Materials engineers	23	37	56	77,170
225,797	4	18	78	Mechanical engineers	22	35	52	72,300
7,070	0	18	80	Mining, safety, and geological engineers	21	36	61	74,330
15,273	3	15	82	Nuclear engineers	32	45	64	94,420
17,355	0	18	80	Petroleum engineers	28	50	#	103,960
170,305	3	15	82	Engineers, all other	23	41	61	85,260
115,522	13	62	25	Architectural and civil drafters	13	21	31	43,310
34,848	13	62	25	Electrical and electronics drafters	15	24	37	49,250
78,340	13	62	25	Mechanical drafters	14	22	33	44,740
24,521	13	62	25	Drafters, all other	14	21	35	44,690
90,650	27	54	18	Civil engineering technicians	12	20	31	42,580
170,433	27	54	18	Electrical, electronic engineering techs	15	25	37	52,140
15,739	27	54	18	Electro-mechanical technicians	15	22	34	46,610
21,126	27	54	18	Environmental engineering technicians	12	20	33	40,690
74,915	27	54	18	Industrial engineering technicians	15	23	38	47,490
47,792	27	54	18	Mechanical engineering technicians	15	23	35	47,280
81,824	27	54	18	Engineering technicians, except drafters	15	27	38	56,060
75,555	42	51	7	Surveying and mapping technicians	10	16	27	33,640
				Life, physical, and social science occupations	14	27	50	55,300
5,371	0	18	82	Animal scientists	15	23	42	48,360
11,782	0	18	82	Food scientists and technologists	15	28	49	57,870
15,790	0	18	82	Soil and plant scientists	17	28	48	58,000
20,131	0	5	95	Biochemists and biophysicists	21	38	65	79,270
17,357	0	5	95	Microbiologists	18	29	50	60,680
20,091	0	5	95	Zoologists and wildlife biologists	17	26	43	55,100
29,067	0	5	95	Biological scientists, all other	18	30	47	63,340
19,777	0	14	86	Conservation scientists	16	27	39	56,150
13,188	0	14	86	Foresters	17	25	37	52,440
4,507	0	0	99	Epidemiologists	19	29	44	60,010
87,402	0	0	99	Medical scientists, except epidemiologists	18	31	60	64,200
14,027	0	0	99	Life scientists, all other	17	28	54	59,010
1,656	0	0	95	Astronomers	21	48	#	99,020
16,516	0	0	95	Physicists	25	47	#	96,850
8,759	0	0	85	Atmospheric and space scientists	18	38	59	78,390
83,697	0	7	93	Chemists	18	31	52	63,490
9,695	0	7	93	Materials scientists	21	37	57	76,160
31,061	0	7	93	Geoscientists and geographers	20	36	69	75,800
8,314	0	7	93	Hydrologists	20	33	49	68,140
23,881	0	2	98	Physical scientists, all other	21	42	65	87,660
14,792	0	0	100	Economists	21	39	68	80,220
234,354	4	14	82	Market research analysts	16	29	55	60,300

				Occupation				
26,853	4	14	82	Survey researchers	8	18	38	36,820
152,381	0	0	99	Clinical, counseling, school psychologists	18	30	50	62,210
1,943	0	0	99	Industrial-organizational psychologists	19	39	66	80,820
11,591	0	0	99	Psychologists, all other	17	38	62	79,570
3,702	0	10	90	Sociologists	18	29	52	61,140
33,809	0	0	92	Urban and regional planners	18	28	43	57,970
5,545	0	10	90	Anthropologists and archeologists	15	26	41	53,080
1,095	0	10	90	Geographers	19	32	47	65,690
3,446	0	10	90	Historians	12	24	45	50,790
4,694	0	10	90	Political scientists	18	44	68	91,580
35,994	0	10	90	Social scientists, related workers,all other	18	32	49	67,200
25,804	43	26	32	Agricultural and food science technicians	10	16	25	33,630
78,690	14	26	60	Biological technicians	12	18	29	37,810
61,228	30	33	37	Chemical technicians	12	20	30	40,740
11,818	34	35	32	Geological and petroleum technicians	12	25	45	50,950
6,502	19	35	46	Nuclear technicians	19	32	45	66,140
17,777	19	35	46	Social science research assistants	11	17	28	35,870
36,500	19	35	46	Environmental and health technicians	12	19	31	39,370
13,051	19	35	46	Forensic science technicians	14	23	37	47,680
33,829	19	35	46	Forest and conservation technicians	11	16	25	33,520
66,177	19	35	46	Life, physical, and social science technicians	11	18	31	38,130
				Community and social services occupations	10	18	31	37,170
83,343	9	18	73	Substance abuse, behavioral counselors	11	17	27	35,580
259,543	9	18	73	Educational, vocational,school counselors	14	24	38	49,450
24,701	9	18	73	Marriage and family therapists	13	21	33	43,600
99,794	9	18	73	Mental health counselors	11	17	30	36,000
140,732	9	18	73	Rehabilitation counselors	9	14	26	29,630
27,306	9	18	73	Counselors, all other	11	19	30	38,680
282,424	7	16	77	Child, family, and school social workers	12	19	31	38,620
123,643	7	16	77	Medical and public health social workers	14	21	32	44,670
122,272	7	16	77	Mental health,substance abuse social	11	18	29	36,640
66,220	7	16	77	Social workers, all other	13	22	35	45,800
61,546	16	26	58	Health educators	12	21	37	42,920
94,445	16	26	58	Probation officers, correctional treatment	14	21	36	44,510
338,743	16	26	58	Social and human service assistants	8	13	20	26,630
118,012	16	26	58	Community and social service specialists	10	18	29	36,420
404,396	9	17	75	Clergy	10	19	34	40,460
99,230	10	26	64	Directors, religious activities, education	10	17	32	35,370
39,194	16	29	56	Religious workers, all other	7	13	26	26,660
				Legal occupations	16	34	#	69,760
760,672	0	1	99	Lawyers	25	51	#	106,120
15,479	0	1	99	Law judge, adjudicator, hearing officer	17	36	65	74,170
8,469	0	1	99	Arbitrators, mediators, and conciliators	14	23	48	48,840
27,192	0	1	99	Judges, magistrate judges, magistrates	15	52	#	107,230
237,703	13	43	45	Paralegals and legal assistants	14	22	34	44,990
19,101	23	39	38	Court reporters	11	22	38	45,330
36,689	23	39	38	Law clerks	11	18	30	37,550
69,009	23	39	38	Title examiners, abstractors, searchers	11	18	30	37,200
47,878	23	39	38	Legal support workers, all other	14	23	45	48,460
				Education, training, library occupations	9	20	37	42,580
437,088	20	38	43	Preschool teachers	10	15	20	23,130
170,234	20	38	43	Kindergarten teachers	20	30	38	45,120
1,540,159	0	5	95	Elementary school teachers	22	32	40	47,330
658,060	0	5	95	Middle school teachers	22	32	40	47,900

(1) Total Positions 2006	(2) HS or Less	(3) Some College	(4) College or moe	(5) Job Description	(6) 10th	(7) 50th	(8) 90th	(9) Median Annual Compensation
					\$ Hourly Wage by percentile			
15,805	0	5	95	Vocational teachers, middle school	21	31	38	46,290
1,037,547	1	4	96	Secondary school teachers	22	32	52	62,980
95,534	1	4	96	Vocational teachers, secondary school	22	32	52	62,310
218,850	5	8	87	Sp. Ed,preschool,kindergarten,elementary	22	32	41	48,350
102,165	5	8	87	Special education teachers, middle school	22	33	41	48,940
137,901	5	8	87	Special education teachers, secondary	23	33	42	49,640
75,847	17	29	54	Adult literacy, GED teachers, instructors	12	22	37	44,710
261,496	17	29	54	Self-enrichment education teachers	9	17	32	34,580
740,916	17	29	54	Teachers and instructors, all other	*	*	*	30,020
6,449	5	9	86	Archivists	13	21	35	43,110
10,362	5	9	86	Curators	13	22	39	46,000
10,676	5	9	86	Museum Technicians and Conservators	10	17	30	35,350
158,373	5	9	86	Librarians	15	25	37	50,970
121,256	46	28	27	Library technicians	8	13	21	27,680
7,305	4	17	79	Audio-visual collections specialists	11	20	33	42,480
14,969	4	17	79	Farm and home management advisors	10	20	34	41,830
129,430	4	17	79	Instructional coordinators	15	27	44	55,270
1,312,222	37	45	18	Teacher assistants	*	*	*	21,580
99,216	4	17	79	Education,training,library workers,all other	8	16	31	33,030
				Arts, design, entertainment, sports, media	9	19	41	40,100
				Art and design occupations				
77,898	14	29	58	Art directors	19	35	69	72,320
8,816	14	29	58	Craft artists	7	13	25	26,200
30,323	14	29	58	Fine artists,painters, sculptors, illustrators	9	20	40	42,070
87,296	14	29	58	Multi-media artists and animators	15	26	47	54,550
13,799	14	29	58	Artists and related workers, all other	9	22	44	44,790
47,978	14	32	55	Commercial and industrial designers	15	27	46	56,550
20,411	14	32	55	Fashion designers	15	30	58	62,810
86,909	14	32	55	Floral designers	8	11	17	22,540
260,831	14	32	55	Graphic designers	12	20	35	41,280
71,856	14	32	55	Interior designers	12	21	39	43,970
87,001	14	32	55	Merchandise displayers, window trimmers	8	12	20	24,830
12,205	14	32	55	Set and exhibit designers	11	21	38	43,220
16,041	14	32	55	Designers, all other	11	21	43	43,710
70,030	16	22	62	Actors	8	14	58	*
93,074	6	19	75	Producers and directors	14	29	#	61,090
17,524	14	26	60	Athletes and sports competitors	*	*	*	38,440
216,780	14	26	60	Coaches and scouts	*	*	*	27,840
18,699	14	26	60	Umpires, referees, other sports officials	*	*	*	24,770
19,767	41	38	22	Dancers	7	11	28	*
20,429	41	38	22	Choreographers	8	17	31	35,580
68,005	19	28	53	Music directors and composers	8	19	54	40,150
196,330	19	28	53	Musicians and singers	7	20	58	*
77,075	31	38	30	Entertainers, performers, sports workers	8	14	28	*
58,905	26	36	38	Radio and television announcers	7	13	36	26,060
11,960	26	36	38	Public address system and other announcers	7	12	34	25,860
7,724	1	14	85	Broadcast news analysts	11	24	#	49,060
59,212	1	14	85	Reporters and correspondents	9	17	37	34,690
243,275	5	14	81	Public relations specialists	14	24	45	49,800
121,511	4	15	81	Editors	13	23	44	48,320
49,151	7	18	74	Technical writers	18	29	45	60,390
135,246	4	12	84	Writers and authors	13	24	48	50,660

41,193	16	36	48	Interpreters and translators	10	18	32	37,490
35,660	16	36	48	Media, communication workers, all other	11	20	36	41,740
49,881	21	44	35	Audio and video equipment technicians	10	17	30	36,050
37,881	21	44	35	Broadcast technicians	8	16	32	32,230
1,548	21	44	35	Radio operators	10	19	29	40,210
16,124	21	44	35	Sound engineering technicians	11	22	47	46,550
122,480	19	36	46	Photographers	8	13	29	27,720
26,897	13	29	58	Camera operators, television,video, motion	10	20	38	41,850
20,544	13	29	58	Film and video editors	12	23	55	47,870
18,779	21	44	35	Media,communication equipment workers	11	25	44	51,860
				Healthcare practitioners and technical	13	26	54	54,440
52,725	0	0	98	Chiropractors	16	32	#	65,890
136,323	0	0	100	Dentists, general	34	66	#	137,630
7,698	0	0	100	Oral and maxillofacial surgeons	31	#	#	#
9,179	0	0	100	Orthodontists	46	#	#	#
999	0	0	100	Prosthodontists	36	#	#	#
6,928	0	0	100	Dentists, all other specialists	20	51	#	105,440
57,126	15	14	72	Dietitians and nutritionists	15	24	34	49,010
32,740	0	0	100	Optometrists	23	45	#	93,800
243,482	0	3	97	Pharmacists	35	48	61	100,480
633,292	0	3	97	Physicians and surgeons				
65,628	8	26	67	Physician assistants	22	38	51	78,450
11,944	0	0	99	Podiatrists	22	53	#	110,510
2,504,664	1	43	56	Registered nurses	20	29	42	60,010
12,253	0	0	91	Audiologists	18	29	46	59,440
98,858	0	9	90	Occupational therapists	20	31	45	63,790
172,948	2	9	89	Physical therapists	23	34	48	69,760
14,627	0	55	42	Radiation therapists	22	34	47	70,010
25,115	0	14	77	Recreational therapists	10	18	28	36,940
102,406	1	71	28	Respiratory therapists	18	24	32	50,070
109,677	0	0	98	Speech-language pathologists	19	29	46	60,690
34,562	3	14	83	Therapists, all other	13	24	39	50,120
62,196	0	0	100	Veterinarians	21	36	65	75,230
64,876	0	0	94	Health diagnosing, treating practitioners	17	31	#	63,730
167,207	14	35	51	Medical, clinical laboratory technologists	17	25	35	51,720
151,366	14	35	51	Medical and clinical laboratory technicians	11	16	25	34,270
167,017	3	64	33	Dental hygienists	20	31	43	64,740
45,378	7	68	25	Cardiovascular technologists, technicians	12	22	34	44,940
45,668	7	68	25	Diagnostic medical sonographers	20	29	39	59,860
19,850	7	68	25	Nuclear medicine technologists	23	31	41	64,670
196,200	7	68	25	Radiologic technologists and technicians	16	24	34	50,260
201,099	18	68	14	Emergency medical technician,paramedic	9	14	23	28,400
25,083	27	57	16	Dietetic technicians	8	12	19	24,750
285,035	27	57	16	Pharmacy technicians	9	13	18	26,720
62,098	27	57	16	Psychiatric technicians	10	14	23	29,670
19,167	27	57	16	Respiratory therapy technicians	13	20	29	40,590
86,197	27	57	16	Surgical technologists	13	18	25	37,540
71,178	27	57	16	Veterinary technologists and technicians	9	13	20	27,970
748,605	21	72	7	Licensed practical, vocational nurses	13	18	25	37,940
169,742	37	51	12	technicians	9	14	23	29,290
65,904	29	56	15	Opticians, dispensing	10	15	24	31,430
5,706	28	45	27	Orthotists and prosthetists	15	29	48	60,520
79,344	28	45	27	Healthcare technologists and technicians	11	18	29	36,630
45,206	9	18	72	Occupational health and safety specialists	17	29	43	60,140
10,468	9	18	72	Occupational health, safety technicians	12	21	34	44,020

(1) Total Positions 2006	(2) HS or Less	(3) Some College	(4) College or moe	(5) Job Description	(6) 10th	(7) 50th	(8) 90th	(9) Median Annual Compensation
					\$ Hourly Wage by percentile			
17,117	9	18	72	Athletic trainers	*	*	*	38,360
52,768	9	18	72	Healthcare practitioners, technical worker	11	19	42	40,550
				Service occupations				
				Healthcare support occupations	8	11	18	23,820
787,315	55	37	7	Home health aides	7	10	13	20,010
1,447,233	55	37	7	Nursing aides, orderlies, and attendants	8	11	16	23,160
61,735	55	37	7	Psychiatric aides	8	12	18	25,470
24,981	0	86	13	Occupational therapist assistants	13	22	30	45,050
8,235	0	86	13	Occupational therapist aides	9	13	22	26,080
60,296	12	65	23	Physical therapist assistants	13	21	29	44,130
46,242	12	65	23	Physical therapist aides	8	11	16	22,990
117,696	19	49	32	Massage therapists	8	17	34	34,870
279,828	34	58	9	Dental assistants	10	15	22	31,550
416,882	31	59	10	Medical assistants	10	13	19	27,430
45,247	31	59	10	Medical equipment preparers	9	13	18	27,040
98,454	31	59	10	Medical transcriptionists	11	15	21	31,250
50,394	31	59	10	Pharmacy aides	7	9	14	19,530
74,534	31	59	10	Veterinary assistants, animal caretaker	7	10	15	20,770
204,428	31	59	10	Healthcare support workers, all other	9	14	20	28,330
				Protective service occupations	8	16	33	33,510
39,584	26	49	25	Supervisor/manager of correctional officers	15	27	40	55,720
93,018	18	49	33	Supervisor/manager of police, detectives	21	35	52	72,620
52,468	18	64	17	Supervisor/manager fire fighting,prevention	18	31	49	65,040
48,019	26	47	28	Supervisor, protected service workers	12	21	36	43,010
292,876	23	59	18	Fire fighters	10	21	33	43,170
13,805	21	52	27	Fire inspectors and investigators	15	24	38	50,830
1,815	21	52	27	Forest fire inspectors,prevention specialist	9	15	29	31,420
18,608	40	49	11	Bailiffs	9	18	29	36,900
441,761	40	49	11	Correctional officers and jailers	12	18	30	36,970
106,336	10	35	54	Detectives and criminal investigators	17	29	46	59,930
8,030	32	26	42	Fish and game wardens	15	23	39	47,830
10,520	32	26	42	Parking enforcement workers	10	15	24	31,470
648,418	16	52	33	Police and sheriff's patrol officers	14	24	36	49,630
5,551	16	52	33	Transit and railroad police	15	22	37	46,360
15,202	33	55	12	Animal control workers	9	14	23	29,320
51,693	18	30	52	Private detectives and investigators	10	18	35	37,640
8,658	46	42	13	Gaming investigators, surveillance officers	9	13	22	27,440
1,040,287	46	42	13	Security guards	8	11	18	22,570
69,320	67	28	5	Crossing guards	7	11	16	22,140
114,189	35	34	31	Lifeguards, ski patrol, all other	7	9	13	17,980
82,703	35	34	31	Protective service workers, all other	8	14	25	28,240
				Food preparation and serving related	7	8	14	17,150
114,784	48	39	14	Chefs and head cooks	10	18	31	37,160
817,108	51	35	14	Supervisor of food preparation, servers	9	13	22	28,040
629,405	77	19	5	Cooks, fast food	6	8	10	16,130
401,027	77	19	5	Cooks, institution and cafeteria	7	10	15	21,340
4,927	77	19	5	Cooks, private household	7	12	23	24,270
850,343	77	19	5	Cooks, restaurant	7	10	15	21,220
195,495	77	19	5	Cooks, short order	7	9	13	18,630
15,588	77	19	5	Cooks, all other	7	11	17	22,120
901,660	74	19	7	Food preparation workers	7	9	13	18,150
495,307	42	41	17	Bartenders	7	8	15	17,090

2,502,891	71	24	5	Combined food preparation, serving worker	6	8	10	15,750
532,840	73	19	8	Counter, cafeteria,concession,coffee shop	7	8	11	16,890
2,360,630	51	35	14	Waiters and waitresses	6	8	14	15,850
189,234	64	27	9	Food servers, nonrestaurant	7	9	14	18,850
416,276	76	18	6	Dining room, cafeteria attendants	6	8	11	16,040
517,358	87	10	3	Dishwashers	7	8	10	15,410
351,188	51	33	17	Hosts, hostesses, restaurant, lounge, coffee	7	8	11	16,790
56,326	76	18	6	Food preparation, serving workers, all other	7	9	14	18,580
				Building, grounds cleaning, maintenance	7	10	17	21,170
282,237	58	32	11	Manager of housekeeping,janitorial worker	10	16	26	32,850
201,840	54	31	15	Supervisor of landscaping, lawn service	12	19	30	38,720
2,386,570	75	20	4	Janitors, cleaners	7	10	16	20,800
1,469,519	81	15	5	Maids and housekeeping cleaners	7	9	13	18,350
15,649	75	20	4	Building cleaning workers, all other	8	13	25	27,080
69,722	58	33	9	Pest control workers	9	14	21	29,030
1,220,054	78	17	6	Landscaping and groundskeeping workers	8	11	17	22,240
30,605	78	17	6	Pesticide handlers, sprayers, vegetation	9	14	21	28,560
40,560	78	17	6	Tree trimmers and pruners	9	14	22	29,800
27,873	78	17	6	Grounds maintenance workers, all other	8	10	21	21,350
				Personal care and service occupations	7	10	19	19,760
33,887	34	36	30	Gaming supervisors	13	21	31	42,960
19,658	34	36	30	Slot key persons	8	11	19	23,760
214,810	37	36	26	Managers of personal service workers	10	16	28	33,900
42,924	49	28	24	Animal trainers	8	13	23	26,190
156,624	47	37	16	Nonfarm animal caretakers	7	9	15	18,890
83,523	45	44	11	Gaming dealers	6	8	13	15,610
18,463	45	44	11	Gaming, sports book writers and runners	7	9	17	19,280
14,644	45	44	11	Gaming service workers, all other	8	11	19	23,070
11,493	24	47	29	Motion picture projectionists	7	9	15	18,380
103,166	53	30	18	Ushers, lobby attendants, ticket takers	6	8	12	16,340
291,199	46	32	22	Amusement and recreation attendants	7	8	12	16,850
4,328	46	32	22	Costume attendants	7	13	28	26,290
19,383	46	32	22	Locker, coat, dressing room attendants	7	9	14	19,090
9,028	37	33	29	Embalmers	10	18	29	36,800
32,807	37	33	29	Funeral attendants	7	10	15	20,950
60,034	62	34	4	Barbers	7	11	19	23,510
617,452	51	42	6	Hairdressers, hairstylists, cosmetologists	7	11	20	22,210
2,146	60	31	10	Makeup artists, theatrical, performance	8	17	36	35,250
78,121	60	31	10	Manicurists and pedicurists	7	10	16	19,960
29,428	60	31	10	Shampooers	7	8	11	16,500
38,209	60	31	10	Skin care specialists	7	13	25	27,190
49,319	51	33	17	Baggage porters and bellhops	7	9	18	19,240
19,753	51	33	17	Concierges	8	12	19	25,540
40,381	36	36	29	Tour guides and escorts	7	11	18	22,110
4,672	36	36	29	Travel guides	9	15	25	30,650
96,730	25	44	31	Flight attendants	*	*	*	***
20,830	25	44	31	Transportation attendants	7	10	15	20,310
1,388,168	48	38	15	Child care workers	7	9	14	18,350
767,257	59	32	10	Personal and home care aides	6	9	12	18,480
234,841	21	32	47	Fitness trainers and aerobics instructors	7	13	28	27,680
319,818	21	32	47	Recreation workers	7	10	18	21,220
56,845	26	46	28	Residential advisors	7	11	18	23,050
86,431	46	33	21	Personal care and service workers	7	9	17	19,180
				Sales and related occupations	7	11	34	23,740

(1) Total Positions 2006	(2) HS or Less	(3) Some College	(4) College or moe	(5) Job Description	(6) 10th	(7) 50th	(8) 90th	(9) Median Annual Compensation
					\$ Hourly Wage by percentile			
				Supervisors, sales workers				
1,675,937	39	37	25	Supervisor/manager of retail sales workers	10	17	29	34,470
529,958	31	31	38	Supervisor/Manager non-retail sale worker	17	32	64	67,020
				Retail sales workers				
				Cashiers				
3,500,169	63	28	10	Cashiers, except gaming	7	8	12	17,160
27,109	63	28	10	Gaming change persons, booth cashiers	7	10	15	20,890
				Counter ,rental clerks, parts salespersons				
476,623	53	30	16	Counter and rental clerks	7	10	19	20,070
238,015	59	35	6	Parts salespersons	8	14	23	28,130
4,476,942	38	37	25	Retail salespersons	7	10	19	20,150
				Sales representatives				
170,479	14	30	56	Advertising sales agents	11	21	45	42,820
436,100	18	36	45	Insurance sales agents	12	21	54	44,110
319,943	10	23	67	Securities, commodities, financial sales	15	33	#	68,430
101,167	25	49	26	Travel agents	9	14	23	30,130
539,732	19	32	48	Sales representatives, services, all other	12	23	49	48,550
410,948	21	28	51	Sales Rep., technical, scientific products	17	33	62	68,270
1,562,254	21	28	51	Sales Rep., wholesale, manufacturing	13	24	50	50,750
104,769	38	36	26	Demonstrators and product promoters	8	11	20	22,570
2,003	38	36	26	Models	8	11	18	22,530
131,239	18	37	45	Real estate brokers	13	28	#	58,860
432,291	18	37	45	Real estate sales agents	10	20	51	40,600
75,795	0	16	79	Sales engineers	23	39	63	80,270
394,783	50	36	14	Telemarketers	7	10	18	21,390
199,552	47	32	21	Door-to-door, news, street vendors	7	9	22	19,400
179,564	15	24	62	Sales and related workers, all other	8	17	36	34,940
				Office and administrative support occupations workers	8	14	23	28,920
1,418,494	28	43	29	Supervisor of office, administrative support	13	21	35	44,650
177,485	39	51	10	Switchboard operators, answering service	8	11	16	23,460
26,681	40	49	11	Telephone operators	8	15	24	31,570
4,346	21	50	29	Communications equipment operators	8	16	27	33,760
				Financial clerks				
434,200	38	48	13	Bill and account collectors	10	14	22	29,990
541,869	36	49	15	Billing, posting clerks, machine operators	10	14	21	29,970
2,113,780	34	50	16	Bookkeeping, accounting, auditing clerks	10	15	23	31,560
18,033	47	40	0	Gaming cage workers	8	11	16	23,510
213,612	33	50	18	Payroll and timekeeping clerks	11	16	23	33,810
77,798	28	48	24	Procurement clerks	11	16	23	34,120
607,609	39	45	16	Tellers	8	11	15	22,920
				Information and record clerks				
73,309	24	45	31	Brokerage clerks	12	18	28	37,360
17,445	47	37	16	Correspondence clerks	10	14	21	29,500
114,584	27	49	24	Court, municipal, and license clerks	10	16	24	32,330
68,975	35	37	28	Credit authorizers, checkers, and clerks	9	14	22	29,640
2,202,271	34	44	22	Customer service representatives	9	14	23	29,040
112,418	17	45	38	Eligibility interviewers, government	13	19	25	39,110
233,808	36	43	20	File clerks	8	11	17	23,010
218,776	44	42	14	Hotel, motel, and resort desk clerks	7	9	13	18,950
220,911	28	48	24	Interviewers, except eligibility and loan	9	13	19	27,320
116,009	19	44	37	Library assistants, clerical	7	11	17	22,270

256,023	32	45	24	Loan interviewers and clerks	10	15	23	31,680
81,422	37	35	28	New accounts clerks	10	14	19	29,610
270,869	47	37	16	Order clerks	8	13	21	26,920
168,201	25	46	29	Human resources assistants, no payroll	11	17	24	34,970
1,172,666	42	46	13	Receptionists and information clerks	8	11	17	23,710
165,345	29	43	29	Reservation, ticket agents, travel clerks	9	14	22	29,820
244,584	27	52	21	Information and record clerks, all other	10	15	23	32,110
				Material recording, scheduling, dispatch				
85,985	43	42	16	Cargo and freight agents	11	18	28	37,060
133,770	46	42	12	Couriers and messengers	8	11	17	22,360
99,053	44	45	11	Police, fire, and ambulance dispatchers	10	16	24	32,660
190,231	44	45	11	Dispatchers	10	16	26	33,140
46,574	50	45	6	Meter readers, utilities	9	15	25	31,810
79,505	43	46	11	Postal service clerks	19	22	24	45,050
337,768	42	48	11	Postal service mail carriers	17	21	25	44,500
197,714	41	47	12	Mail sorter, processors, machine operator	13	21	24	43,700
292,794	30	40	30	Production, planning, expediting clerks	12	19	29	39,690
768,974	64	30	6	Shipping, receiving, and traffic clerks	8	13	20	26,990
1,704,921	63	29	8	Stock clerks and order fillers	7	10	16	20,490
79,021	55	33	13	Weigher, measurer, checker, sampler	8	13	20	26,120
				Secretaries and administrative assistants				
1,618,018	33	49	18	Executive secretaries, administrative	13	19	28	38,640
275,269	33	49	18	Legal secretaries	12	19	29	38,810
408,369	33	49	18	Medical secretaries	10	14	20	28,950
1,939,837	33	49	18	Secretaries	9	14	20	28,220
				Office and administrative support workers				
129,997	27	46	27	Computer operators	10	17	26	34,610
313,355	35	47	18	Data entry keyers	8	12	18	25,370
178,998	29	52	19	Word processors and typists	10	15	22	30,380
31,833	25	44	32	Desktop publishers	10	17	27	35,510
253,949	31	48	22	Insurance claims, processing clerks	11	15	23	32,040
152,064	56	35	9	Mail clerks, mail machine operators	8	12	18	24,410
3,200,245	36	45	19	Office clerks, general	7	12	19	24,460
93,926	49	37	14	Office machine operators, not computer	8	12	18	25,230
17,856	22	31	47	Proofreaders and copy markers	8	14	23	28,920
22,507	24	47	30	Statistical assistants	10	16	24	32,540
319,970	25	43	32	Office and administrative support workers	8	14	23	28,500
				Farming, fishing, and forestry occupations	7	9	18	18,590
				Agricultural workers				
53,219	63	25	13	Supervisor,farming, fishing,forestry worker	7	14	26	29,920
16,176	38	37	26	Agricultural inspectors	12	19	27	39,780
10,505	86	10	4	Animal breeders	8	13	26	26,580
42,091	85	10	0	Graders and sorters, agricultural products	7	9	13	17,980
				Miscellaneous agricultural workers				
59,451	86	10	4	Agricultural equipment operators	7	10	16	21,180
603,083	86	10	4	Farmworker, laborer, nursery, greenhouse	7	8	11	17,020
106,843	86	10	4	Farmworkers, farm and ranch animals	7	10	15	20,350
20,350	86	10	4	Agricultural workers, all other	8	12	20	25,890
				Fishing and hunting workers				
38,372	67	23	11	Fishers and related fishing workers	8	13	21	27,930
474	67	23	11	Hunters and trappers				
				Forest, conservation, and logging workers				
19,844	63	15	22	Forest and conservation workers	7	10	19	20,510
13,085	84	14	2	Fallers	9	14	28	29,980
40,496	84	14	2	Logging equipment operators	10	15	22	30,850

(1) Total Positions 2006	(2) HS or Less	(3) Some College	(4) College or more	(5) Job Description	(6) 10th	(7) 50th	(8) 90th	(9) Median Annual Compensation
					$ Hourly Wage by percentile			
7,115	84	14	2	Log graders and scalers	10	15	23	32,140
7,935	84	14	2	Logging workers, all other	9	16	22	32,290
	84	14	2	Construction and extraction occupations	10	18	32	36,540
				Construction trades and related workers				
771,796	60	30	10	Manager of construction trade extraction	17	27	43	55,950
17,571	75	25	0	Boilermakers	16	24	36	50,700
158,316	82	15	3	Brickmasons and blockmasons	13	21	34	44,070
23,844	82	15	3	Stonemasons	11	18	30	36,950
1,462,071	73	22	6	Carpenters	11	18	32	37,660
				Carpet, floor, tile installers and finishers				
73,205	80	17	3	Carpet installers	10	17	33	36,040
14,319	80	17	3	Floor sanders and finishers	10	15	24	31,290
79,183	80	17	3	Tile and marble setters	11	19	31	38,720
221,539	86	12	2	Cement masons and concrete finishers	11	16	29	33,840
6,769	86	12	2	Terrazzo workers and finishers	11	17	29	34,390
1,232,002	79	17	5	Construction laborers	8	13	25	27,310
64,255	84	15	0	Paving, surfacing, and tamping equipment	10	16	26	32,360
5,584	78	20	3	Pile-driver operators	14	23	39	47,550
424,152	78	20	3	Operating engineers, equipment operators	12	18	32	38,130
185,864	85	13	2	Drywall and ceiling tile installers	11	18	30	36,520
54,312	85	13	2	Tapers	12	20	32	42,050
705,015	51	42	7	Electricians	13	22	37	44,780
54,992	72	25	0	Glaziers	10	17	31	35,230
32,414	80	16	0	Insulation workers, floor, ceiling, and wall	9	15	26	31,280
28,446	80	16	0	Insulation workers, mechanical	11	18	33	36,570
462,833	76	17	6	Painters, construction and maintenance	10	15	26	32,080
9,899	66	32	0	Paperhangers	11	17	32	34,580
66,590	68	29	4	Pipelayers	10	15	26	31,280
502,201	68	29	4	Plumbers, pipefitters, and steamfitters	13	21	36	44,090
61,148	87	10	0	Plasterers and stucco masons	11	18	29	36,430
30,162	83	15	0	Reinforcing iron and rebar workers	11	18	34	37,890
156,284	86	11	3	Roofers	10	16	27	33,240
188,655	63	32	4	Sheet metal workers	11	19	34	39,210
71,736	68	29	4	Structural iron and steel workers	12	20	36	42,130
				Helpers, construction trades				
65,364	84	13	3	Brickmason, stonemason, tile, marble	9	13	20	26,260
109,060	84	13	3	Helpers—Carpenters	8	12	17	24,340
105,340	84	13	3	Helpers—Electricians	8	12	17	24,880
24,455	84	13	3	Painters, paperhangers, plasterers, stucco	8	11	15	22,300
84,643	84	13	3	Pipelayer, plumber, pipefitter, steamfitter	9	12	18	25,350
21,769	84	13	3	Helpers—Roofers	8	11	15	22,810
37,564	84	13	3	Helpers, construction trades, all other	8	11	18	23,900
				Other construction and related workers				
109,730	31	46	23	Construction and building inspectors	15	23	36	48,330
21,830	48	42	10	Elevator installers and repairers	19	33	45	68,000
32,470	79	18	3	Fence erectors	9	13	21	26,720
39,497	63	27	9	Hazardous materials removal workers	11	17	29	36,330
145,216	69	26	5	Highway maintenance workers	10	16	24	32,600
14,635	61	32	0	Rail-track laying, equipment operators	13	20	27	42,120
23,774	75	21	4	Septic tank servicers, sewer pipe cleaners	10	16	24	32,740
957	75	21	4	Segmental pavers	8	13	19	26,320
62,455	75	21	4	Construction and related workers, all other	9	15	25	31,220

				Extraction workers				
18,784	77	19	0	Derrick operators, oil and gas	13	18	27	37,790
19,923	77	19	0	Rotary drill operators, oil and gas	13	21	32	43,480
27,905	77	19	0	Service unit operators, oil, gas, mining	11	17	28	34,790
21,681	78	18	0	Earth drillers, except oil and gas	12	17	28	36,310
5,333	63	34	0	Explosive worker, ordnance handling	14	20	29	41,520
10,043	71	27	0	Continuous mining machine operators	14	21	28	43,860
7,918	71	27	0	Mine cutting, channeling machine operator	13	19	24	39,930
2,989	71	27	0	Mining machine operators, all other	12	19	30	40,350
3,883	74	24	0	Rock splitters, quarry	9	13	23	28,050
4,291	74	24	0	Roof bolters, mining	17	21	25	43,270
44,085	77	19	0	Roustabouts, oil and gas	9	14	22	28,510
25,016	74	24	0	Helpers—Extraction workers	10	14	22	29,890
9,750	74	24	0	Extraction workers, all other	11	19	32	38,960
				Installation, maintenance, repair	10	18	30	37,520
464,881	43	43	13	Supervisor of mechanic, installer,repairer	16	27	41	55,380
				Electrical equipment mechanics, installers				
174,961	23	53	25	Computer, automated teller, repairer	11	18	28	37,100
6,533	36	51	9	Radio mechanics	12	19	30	39,280
197,993	36	51	13	Telecommunications equipment installers	15	26	33	54,070
15,709	31	65	0	Avionics technicians	16	23	30	48,100
25,474	45	43	0	Electric motor, power tool, related repairer	10	16	26	34,130
21,079	46	46	0	Electrical, electronic installer, transportation	13	21	29	43,940
80,226	46	46	0	Commercial, industrial equipment repairer	14	23	32	47,110
22,300	46	46	0	Powerhouse, substation, relay repairers	20	28	36	58,970
20,017	54	39	7	Electronic installer, repairer, motor vehicle	9	14	22	28,130
56,959	48	44	8	Security and fire alarm systems installers	11	17	27	35,390
				Vehicle, mobile equipment mechanics				
122,472	33	57	11	Aircraft mechanics, service technicians	15	24	32	49,010
182,676	74	23	3	Automotive body and related repairers	10	17	29	35,690
23,610	76	22	0	Automotive glass installers and repairers	9	15	23	31,470
772,675	62	34	4	Automotive service technicians, mechanic	9	16	28	34,170
274,876	66	31	3	Bus, truck, diesel engine special	12	19	27	38,640
30,672	62	35	3	Farm equipment mechanics	10	15	22	30,690
130,570	62	35	3	Mobile heavy equipment mechanics	13	20	30	41,450
26,578	62	35	3	Rail car repairers	14	22	29	44,970
24,114	64	32	5	Motorboat mechanics	10	16	25	34,210
21,211	64	32	5	Motorcycle mechanics	9	15	23	30,300
32,892	64	32	5	Outdoor power equipment, small engine	9	13	20	28,060
8,644	74	20	6	Bicycle repairers	8	10	16	21,820
13,998	74	20	6	Recreational vehicle service technicians	10	15	24	31,760
105,842	74	20	6	Tire repairers and changers	8	11	16	21,880
				Other installation, maintenance, repair				
15,399	55	38	7	Mechanical door repairers	10	15	24	31,880
42,991	55	38	7	Control and valve installers and repairers,	12	22	32	46,140
291,861	58	39	3	Heating, air, refrigeration mechanic	12	18	30	38,360
57,364	50	43	7	Home appliance repairers	10	16	26	33,560
260,727	56	39	5	Industrial machinery mechanics	13	20	31	42,350
1,390,952	58	36	6	Maintenance and repair workers, general	9	16	25	32,570
84,291	57	39	0	Maintenance workers, machinery	11	17	27	35,590
54,884	54	43	0	Millwrights	14	22	36	46,090
3,478	56	39	5	Refractory materials repairers	12	20	30	41,060
112,183	56	38	6	Electrical power-line installer, repairers	14	25	36	52,570
162,317	48	44	8	Telecommunications line installer, repairer	12	23	33	47,220
4,403	28	57	15	Camera, photographic equipment repairers	9	17	28	35,850

(1) Total Positions 2006	(2) HS or Less	(3) Some College	(4) College or moe	(5) Job Description	(6) 10th	(7) 50th	(8) 90th	(9) Median Annual Compensation
					\$ Hourly Wage by percentile			
37,645	28	57	15	Medical equipment repairers	12	19	32	40,320
5,998	28	57	15	Musical instrument repairers and tuners	9	15	26	32,030
3,814	28	57	15	Watch repairers	9	16	27	33,110
16,327	28	57	15	Precision instrument, equipment repairers	14	23	34	47,410
47,928	63	29	8	Coin, vending, amusement servicer	8	14	22	29,060
3,133	61	30	9	Commercial divers	14	20	44	41,610
1,809	61	30	9	Fabric menders, except garment	9	13	19	28,060
26,018	56	33	0	Locksmiths and safe repairers	9	16	25	33,230
11,803	79	17	0	Mobile home installer	9	13	19	26,680
12,315	76	21	0	Riggers	11	19	29	39,420
7,165	61	30	9	Signal and track switch repairers	19	25	31	51,120
163,379	77	18	0	Helpers--Installation, maintenance, repair	7	11	18	22,920
168,431	61	30	9	Installation, maintenance, repair workers	9	16	27	33,010
				Production occupations	8	14	24	28,130
				Assemblers and fabricators				
699,259	53	32	15	Supervisor of production, operating worker	14	23	38	48,670
28,083	59	35	0	Aircraft structure, surface, rigging	12	22	30	45,420
22,835	69	26	6	Coil winders, tapers, and finishers	9	13	19	27,100
213,381	69	26	6	Electrical, electronic equipment assemblers	8	13	21	26,540
60,298	69	26	6	Electromechanical equipment assemblers	9	14	21	28,560
45,265	69	28	0	Engine and other machine assemblers	10	15	24	31,500
103,008	57	34	0	Structural metal fabricators and fitters	10	15	22	31,030
33,294	71	25	5	Fiberglass laminators and fabricators	9	13	18	26,630
1,274,303	71	25	5	Team assemblers	8	12	19	24,630
2,527	71	25	5	Timing device, adjusters, and calibrators	9	14	22	28,420
291,591	71	25	5	Assemblers and fabricators, all other	8	13	28	27,910
				Food processing occupations				
149,266	70	22	8	Bakers	8	11	17	22,590
131,352	83	15	2	Butchers and meat cutters	8	13	21	27,480
144,228	83	15	2	Meat, poultry, fish cutters and trimmers	8	10	14	21,050
122,074	83	15	2	Slaughterers and meat packers	8	11	14	22,500
18,876	69	28	0	Food, tobacco roasting, drying operators	8	12	19	25,330
94,921	72	23	5	Food batchmakers	8	11	19	23,730
44,393	70	26	0	Food cooking machine operators, tenders	8	11	17	22,420
				Metal workers and plastic workers				
140,510	50	45	6	Computer-controlled machine tool operator	10	16	23	32,550
17,980	50	45	6	Numerical, process control programmers	13	20	31	42,520
93,869	79	18	0	Extruding, drawing machine setter	9	14	21	28,750
31,068	72	26	0	Forging machine setter, operator, tender	9	15	22	30,250
35,853	82	16	0	Rolling machine setter, operator, tender	10	16	24	32,590
271,745	77	22	0	Cutting, punching, press setter, operator	9	13	20	27,240
42,686	71	0	0	Drilling, boring machine setter, operator	10	15	23	30,240
101,441	73	24	0	Grinding, lapping, polishing, buffing setter	9	14	22	28,640
67,760	77	23	0	Lathe, turning machine tool setter, operator	10	16	23	32,470
29,211	73	24	3	Milling, planing machine setter, operator	10	15	23	31,950
396,539	60	37	3	Machinists	10	17	26	35,230
18,386	77	20	0	Metal-refining furnace operators, tenders	11	17	24	34,580
14,791	77	20	0	Pourers and casters, metal	10	15	22	31,610
8,791	69	24	0	Model makers, metal and plastic	11	20	36	40,580
7,429	69	24	0	Patternmakers, metal and plastic	11	17	29	36,270
				Molders, molding machine setter, operator				
14,523	72	25	0	Foundry mold and coremakers	9	14	20	29,200

156,842	72	25	0	Molding, coremaking, casting, operator	8	13	20	26,430
96,553	72	25	0	Multiple machine tool setter, operator	9	15	24	30,390
100,788	43	52	5	Tool and die makers	14	22	33	45,090
409,024	73	25	2	Welders, cutters, solderers, and brazers	10	16	24	32,270
52,803	73	25	2	Welding, soldering,brazing machine setter	10	15	24	30,980
27,122	69	24	0	Heat treating equipment setter, operator	10	15	22	31,270
10,153	73	24	0	Lay-out workers, metal and plastic	10	17	27	35,210
41,898	79	21	0	Plating, coating machine setter, operator	9	13	21	27,870
21,930	60	38	0	Tool grinders, filers, and sharpeners	10	15	23	30,990
48,661	73	24	3	Metal worker, plastic worker, all other	10	16	29	32,750
				Printing occupations				
64,859	70	23	7	Bindery workers	8	13	21	26,470
7,211	70	23	7	Bookbinders	8	14	24	28,740
48,240	62	31	7	Job printers	10	16	24	32,630
70,899	46	38	16	Prepress technicians and workers	10	16	26	33,990
197,594	66	28	6	Printing machine operators	9	15	25	31,490
				Textile, apparel, and furnishings occupations				
238,681	79	16	5	Laundry and dry-cleaning workers	7	9	13	18,420
77,182	88	9	3	Presser, textile, garment, related material	7	9	12	18,440
232,810	82	13	5	Sewing machine operators	7	9	14	19,370
15,575	79	0	0	Shoe and leather workers and repairers	8	10	16	21,570
4,089	82	0	0	Shoe machine operators and tenders	7	12	17	24,390
23,440	62	24	14	Sewers, hand	7	10	15	21,010
53,910	62	24	14	Tailors, dressmakers, and custom sewers	8	12	19	24,100
19,420	84	12	0	Textile bleaching, dyeing machine	8	11	16	23,630
18,687	84	12	0	Textile cutting machine setters, operators	8	11	16	22,450
40,145	84	14	0	Textile knitting, weaving machine setter	8	12	16	24,510
43,340	81	19	0	Textile winding, twisting, drawing	9	11	15	23,370
17,682	75	15	10	Extruding, forming,tenders,synthetic,glass	10	14	21	29,830
9,209	75	15	10	Fabric and apparel patternmakers	9	17	35	35,740
54,809	77	19	0	Upholsterers	9	14	21	28,070
24,379	75	15	10	Textile, apparel, and furnishings workers	8	11	20	23,880
				Woodworkers				
149,047	72	24	4	Cabinetmakers and bench carpenters	9	13	21	27,970
31,326	72	23	0	Furniture finishers	8	12	19	25,820
1,888	69	21	10	Model makers, wood	10	14	33	30,060
2,279	69	21	10	Patternmakers, wood	10	16	27	32,510
65,032	84	14	0	Sawing setter, operator, tender, wood	8	12	18	24,830
99,518	82	15	0	Woodworking setter, operator, tender	8	12	18	24,190
20,486	69	21	10	Woodworkers, all other	8	11	19	23,400
				Plant and system operators				
3,794	36	44	20	Nuclear power reactor operators	26	34	45	70,410
8,571	36	44	20	Power distributors and dispatchers	20	30	40	63,320
34,759	36	44	20	Power plant operators	18	27	38	56,640
45,389	56	34	10	Stationary engineers and boiler operators	14	23	34	47,640
110,840	52	41	8	Water, liquid waste treatment, operators	11	18	27	37,090
53,243	52	41	7	Chemical plant and system operators	16	24	34	50,860
12,261	52	41	7	Gas plant operators	17	26	36	54,640
41,970	52	41	7	Petroleum pump, refinery, operators	16	25	36	53,010
14,132	52	41	7	Plant and system operators, all other	13	22	32	46,740
				Other production occupations				
52,737	53	33	14	Chemical equipment operators, tenders	13	21	30	44,050
44,289	53	33	14	Separating, filtering, clarifying, setters	10	17	27	35,940
42,485	75	20	4	Crushing, grinding, polishing setter	9	14	22	28,680
44,776	75	20	4	Grinding and polishing workers, hand	8	12	18	24,850

Total Positions 2006	HS or Less	Some College	College or more	Job Description	10th	50th	90th	Median Annual Compensation
(1)	(2)	(3)	(4)	(5)	(6)	(7)	(8)	(9)
					\$ Hourly Wage by percentile			
142,842	75	20	4	Mixing, blending machine setter, operator	9	15	23	30,340
28,633	81	16	3	Cutters and trimmers, hand	8	11	18	23,280
78,794	81	16	3	Cutting, slicing machine setter, operator	9	14	22	28,500
81,193	76	21	0	Extruding, forming, pressing,compacting	9	13	21	28,000
31,596	59	34	0	Furnace, kiln, oven, drier, kettle operators	10	15	22	30,750
491,417	53	33	14	Inspector, tester, sorter, sampler, weigher	9	15	25	30,310
52,219	53	31	16	Jeweler, precious stone, metal workers	9	15	26	31,200
53,439	43	46	12	Dental laboratory technicians	9	16	27	33,480
12,323	43	46	12	Medical appliance technicians	10	16	28	32,640
29,064	43	46	12	Ophthalmic laboratory technicians	8	13	21	26,550
385,988	80	15	5	Packaging, filling machine operator	8	11	19	23,760
106,426	75	21	4	Coating, painting, spray setter, operator	9	13	20	27,550
54,322	75	21	4	Painters, transportation equipment	11	17	29	36,000
30,885	75	21	4	Painting, coating, and decorating workers	8	11	18	23,180
23,684	42	39	19	Photographic process workers	8	12	22	24,940
49,304	42	39	19	Photographic processing machine operators	7	9	15	19,710
42,397	72	23	5	Semiconductor processors	10	15	25	31,870
23,362	79	19	0	Cementing, gluing machine operators	8	13	20	26,300
15,914	69	30	0	Clean, wash, metal pickling operators	8	11	18	23,040
10,677	72	23	5	Cooling, freezing equip operator, tender	8	11	18	23,670
13,625	59	24	0	Etchers and engravers	8	13	21	26,540
55,928	69	21	10	Molder, shaper, caster, no metal, plastic	8	13	20	26,650
113,107	72	24	0	Paper good machine setter, operator	10	15	23	32,050
22,664	71	27	0	Tire builders	10	20	27	41,720
541,605	81	15	4	Helpers--Production workers	7	10	16	21,090
304,906	72	23	5	Production workers, all other	8	12	25	25,640
				Transportation, material moving occupations	8	13	24	26,320
				Supervisors, transportation, material moving				
5,792	47	37	17	Aircraft cargo handling supervisors	12	18	37	37,760
181,954	47	37	17	Supervisor of helper, laborer, movers, hand	12	20	31	40,640
226,065	47	37	17	Manager of transportation, material-moving	14	24	38	49,850
				Air transportation occupations				
79,444	6	21	74	Airline pilots, copilots, and flight engineers	*	*	*	***
27,596	6	21	74	Commercial pilots	*	*	*	61,640
25,223	13	55	32	Air traffic controllers	23	54	#	112,930
4,891	13	55	32	Airfield operations specialists	9	18	32	38,320
				Motor vehicle operators				
21,538	53	38	0	Ambulance driver, attendant, no EMT	7	10	15	21,140
198,488	61	35	4	Bus drivers, transit and intercity	9	16	25	33,160
454,800	61	35	4	Bus drivers, school	7	12	18	25,860
445,092	71	25	4	Driver/sales workers	7	10	21	21,380
1,859,848	71	25	4	Truck drivers, heavy and tractor-trailer	11	17	26	36,220
1,051,159	71	25	4	Truck drivers, light or delivery services	8	13	23	26,380
228,531	57	27	15	Taxi drivers and chauffeurs	7	10	16	20,810
75,942	70	24	0	Motor vehicle operators, all other	7	12	22	24,190
				Rail transportation occupations				
46,588	49	42	9	Locomotive engineers and operators				
24,609	45	50	0	Railroad brake, signal, switch operators	16	25	38	51,140
40,152	38	52	11	Railroad conductors and yardmasters	18	28	45	58,650
6,936	40	49	0	Subway and streetcar operators	16	24	28	50,520
6,772	40	49	0	Rail transportation workers, all other	12	19	25	39,260

				Water transportation occupations				
32,981	57	26	17	Sailors and marine oilers	9	16	24	32,570
33,617	55	24	21	Captains, mates, pilots of water vessels	14	28	48	57,210
2,978	55	24	21	Motorboat operators	10	16	28	32,570
14,797	57	26	17	Ship engineers	17	27	46	56,090
				Other transportation workers				
3,926	50	43	7	Bridge and lock tenders	10	19	25	39,230
135,204	57	30	14	Parking lot attendants	7	9	13	18,020
96,199	68	26	6	Service station attendants	7	9	13	18,290
6,916	50	43	7	Traffic technicians	12	19	28	38,880
26,400	45	40	15	Transportation inspectors	13	25	47	51,440
43,608	50	43	7	Transportation workers, all other	8	16	26	32,270
				Material moving occupations				
49,677	64	32	0	Conveyor operators and tenders	9	13	20	28,060
46,393	72	26	0	Crane and tower operators	12	19	31	40,260
2,142	79	18	4	Dredge operators	11	16	28	34,240
80,157	79	18	4	Excavating, loading, dragline operators	11	16	27	34,050
3,085	79	18	4	Loading operators, underground mining	13	19	27	39,080
3,017	64	32	0	Hoist and winch operators	11	17	32	34,770
637,034	79	19	2	Industrial truck and tractor operators	9	13	21	28,010
368,216	83	15	3	Cleaners of vehicles and equipment	7	9	15	18,680
2,416,034	72	24	5	Laborer,freight, stock, material mover,hand	7	11	17	21,900
147,763	73	24	0	Machine feeders and offbearers	8	11	18	23,880
833,812	83	14	3	Packers and packagers, hand	7	9	14	18,310
4,154	73	25	0	Gas compressor, gas pumping operators	13	22	29	45,390
10,544	73	25	0	Pump operators, except wellhead pumpers	11	19	30	39,000
14,411	73	25	0	Wellhead pumpers	11	18	27	36,700
135,970	77	20	3	Refuse and recyclable material collectors	8	14	24	29,420
2,886	70	24	6	Shuttle car operators	16	20	24	40,920
16,295	70	24	6	Tank car, truck, and ship loaders	9	16	28	33,140
53,588	70	24	6	Material moving workers, all other	8	15	25	30,650

A

accelerated growth, 64, 80, 95, 99, 109
    in reading and math, 112-17
ACT. *See* university application
achievement bands. *See* bands
adjust. *See* rules
age level targets, 42, 54, 68, 86, 107,
    108, 110
    listening and speaking targets 34,
        42, 44-45, 59-60, 75-76, 88, 101-02
    math and reasoning targets, 34, 46,
        62, 76-78, 92-93, 103-05
    physical development, 41, 43,
        44, 53, 67, 69, 85, 87, 97, 99
    reading and writing target,
        45-46, 60, 74, 75, 87-88, 101-03
    social and emotional targets,
        34, 47-48, 62- 64, 79-80, 93, 95,
        105-06, 109
    visual matching and naming
        targets, 34, 44, 55, 69, 73, 90-92,
        99-100
algebra, 153, 157
    predictive at 8th grade, 150
annual growth. *See also* catch-
    up growth
    assuring, making, 35, 129, 153,
        156, 186, 192, 225
    defined, 129
    failure to make, 129
    maintaining relative position, 130,
        153
    variance in schools, 130-31
ash breeze, 166
assessments, 38, 111, 127-286
    Lexiles, 125
    national percentiles, 154
    of interests. *See* Kuder
    rarely available, 124
    state, 154
ASSET test, 192

B

bands
    and dropping out, 194, 196
    and IQ, 141
    and university enrollment, 26, 28
    at kindergarten, 225
    colors defined, 12, 15, 18, 21, 30
    conversion from Lexiles, 149
    conversion from state tests, 154
    dark blue, 150, 151, 166
    determined using curriculum,
        147, 152, 231-39
    determined using national
        percentiles, 154
    determined using targets, 64, 80, 95,
        99
    in high school, 22, 23, 187-88
    in middle school, 157
    movement within, 122, 132- 33, 225
        more fluid k-3, 124
    need for parents to
        determine, 122, 153
    one year between, 23
    through high school, 22, 23
body language, 47
Bond, Dave, 147
Buchwald, Emile, 61

C

catch-up growth. *See* also
    annual growth
    assuring, making, 35, 132, 134, 136,
        153, 192, 225
    best shots, 138
    calculating, 14, 119, 137
    dead zone, 134-36, 157
    how to achieve, 137-40
    line of sight, 122
    long shots, 140
    mistaken belief, 20, 118
    need for, 14, 122
    school system, 124, 140, 134
    seventeen years in 12 years, 20

targeted accelerated growth, 139
celebrate, 38, 192
Children's Reading Foundation, 33
  website, 74, 87
class schedule
  college, 220
  high school, 186-88
community college
  assessment, 206
completion rate, 205, 226
  offerings, 209
  remedial classes, 119
  student profile, 212
consequences, 39
costs. *See* also financing
  postsecondary education
  preschool, 83
  credit hours, 221,
  college, 117
crafts, 200, 204
Crosby, Olivia, 213

D
daily routines, 49, 50
dark blue band. *See* bands
data, 29
data in graphs and charts
  band and ACT/SAT
    achievement, 171
  competitive drop from high
    school to college, 218
  converting reading Lexiles to
    bands, 149
  costs, four year university, 177
  costs, two year, then four
    year, 177
  disproportionate growth
    birth to five, 19
  dropout at high school by
    achievement band, 195
  odds of university enrollment
    by band, 27
  odds of university enrollment,
    national, 25

state, 25, 229
math curriculum at grade level
  231-39
math scores from grade 2 to 10, 151
movement within bands
  in reading, 133
  in math, 133
range in annual growth of
  elementary schools, 131
reading, 135
reading scores from grade 2 to 10,
  22-23
state standards in
  3rd grade math, 135
  3rd grade reading, 135
  8th grade math, 155
  8th grade reading, 155
  jobs and income,
    Associates degree, 207
    by industry, 242-57
    Certificate, 211
    college or more, 214-15
    crafts, 210
    unskilled, 197
dead zone. *See* catch-up growth
dance. *See* rules
Dorman, 35
  accelerated reading and math,
    112-16
  Glenn, 117
  Janet, 117
dropping out
  of college, 217
  of high school, 192-95, 226
  predict at 3rd grade, 194, 196

E
English, 185
extraordinary
  parents, 221-22
  effort, 121
extrinsic rewards, 166

F

Fielding
  Autumn, 164
  Jared, 163
  Lynn, *viii*, 112
    email, *viii*
  Shalom, 165
  Sonnet, 164
  Wendy, *viii*, 163
financing postsecondary
  education
  bubble, 182,
  completion in four years, 176, 220
  costs, 175, 177, 179, 220
  loans, 180, 219
  frugality, 176, 181
  saving, 178-79, 182
  scholarships, 180, 190-91, 219
  splitting, 176, 178
fun. *See* rules

G

Gates, Bill, 141
genetics, 37
gifted and talented
  advantage, 143
  IQ, 141
  program description, 141, 143
Gladwell, Malcom, 98
goals,
  achieve annual growth, 30
  start as high as possible, 30-31, 35
  move up, 225
  setting, 183
grades, 126-27, 130, 154, 188
grandparents, *xi*, 39, 122

H

Hart, Betty. *See* vocabulary

I

Institute of the Achievement of
  Human Development, 117
IQ, 37-38, 78, 141, 145

J

jobs by training, 226
  all, 242-257
  high school or less, 196-202
  some college, 203-12
  university or more, 213-15

K

Kerr, Nancy, 12, 37
kindergarten
  first step to college, 31
  incoming targets, 32
  responsibility for entering
    scores, 124
  when to start, 109
Kuder testing, 167-68, 192, 213

L

Lakeini, Alan, 175
Landers, Ann, 163
learning by imitation and
  repetition, 4
Lexiles, 123, 125, 148-49
  conversion to bands, 149
  limitations, 37-39
Lipton, Bruce, 41
listening and speaking. *See* targets
Lloyd, Norman, 194

M

math
  algebra, 150, 153, 157-58
  calculus, 125, 157-58
  curriculum to band, 149-151
  geometry, 158
  grade level, 98, 107, 111, 230, 238
  range in achievement, 2, 10, 150
  trigonometry, 157-58
  years behind, 150
math and reasoning. *See* targets
Mindy, 12, 13, 15
  modest proposal, 174
mnemonics, 153, 159, 192
Moncarz, Roger, 21

Montague, Dave, *i*
more instructional time, 134, 138
movement within bands. *See* bands, movement
myelination, 37

N
national percentiles, 130, 170, 186, 192
Newton, Isaac, 222
Northwest Evaluation Association
  about, 124
  assessment, 127-28
  math longitudinal data, 151
  most weight should be given, 126
  necessity for numbers and statistics, 20
  RIT scale, 19, 22, 23
NWEA. *See* Northwest Evaluation Association

O
odds of university enrollment
  at birth, 17, 28
  by band, 22, 27, 28

P
parenting, 38-39, 147, 225, 226
  engaging your child, 140, 163, 166
  extraordinary, x, 222, 226
  planning with, 167-68, 216
Pelletier, Evelyn, *ii*
percentile ranges. *See* bands
phonemic awareness, 34, 89
physical development. *See* targets
postsecondary education
  high school or less, 182, 193-202
    crafts, 200-202
    unskilled, 196-99
  some college, 182, 203, 210
    Associates degree, 202, 204-07
    applied associates, degree 203, 208
    certificate, 203, 210-11

defined, 203
dropout of college, 203
university degree, 213-222
  adjustment to, 217, 220
  alternatives to, 173
  jobs, 214-15
Powell, Dave, 153
predicting future performance, 145, 170-70
preschool, 82-83
PTAs, 131, 140
purposeful play, 35

R
race analogy, 12-15
range, *xi*, 12, 18, 144, 244, 255
rate of learning, 13-15, 18
  different from birth to five, 18, 20, 224-25
  reading bands, 18, 19. *See* bands
  slowing at middle school, 24, 156
  slowing at high school, 24
reading
  and math and IQ, 139, 145
  and other subjects, 119
  fundamental skill, 32
  Lexiles. *See* Lexiles
  20 minutes a day, 33-34, 119
reading and math, 144-45, 186
reading and writing. *See* targets
READY! For Kindergarten, 33, 35
  website, 35, 73, 102
regret, 118-19
resigned to eventual outcome, 128
Riley, Jeni, 18, 19, 104, 123
Risley, Todd R. *See* vocabulary
RIT scale. *See* NWEA
Rosier, Paul, 31
  in math at kindergarten, *xi*
  in reading at kindergarten, *xi*
  in reading and math, *xi*, 20, 119, 123, 144
rules
  adjust, 36, 39

dance, 36
fun, 29, 36

S
SAT. *See* university application
Saving. *See* finances postsecondary
scholarships. *See* finances
science, 187
Scully, John, 85
Shaw, Bernard, 185
signing, 45
skill continuum, 33, 51, 64-65, 81, 94, 107
social and emotional. *See* targets
speed reading, 153, 159, 160, 192
start ahead, stay ahead, *x*, 20, 24, 132-33. *See* also predicting finishing ahead, 24
start behind, stay behind, 124, 127, 132-33
run just as far, 13
starting points, 12, 14, 118-19, 225
as a choice, *xi*, 18, 119, 121, 224
state standards
in math, 134-35, 155
in reading, 134-35, 155
Stone, Elizabeth, 82
summer reading loss, 24
Sylvan, *i*, 138

T
targeted accelerated growth, 139
See also catch-up growth
targets, tools, and activities, *ix*, 33, 34, 42, 54, 68, 86, 98, 107, 109-100
thinking critically, 153, 160-62, 85, 189
Trelease, Jim, 74

U
University. *See also*
postsecondary education
application, 160, 183, 189-90, 192

common, 168
alternatives to, 173-74
aspirations, 17
credit hours, 220
dropping out. *See* dropping out
impacted by family culture, 121
odds, 17, 24, 26, 27-28, 226
by state, 25
by band, 27
seats, 24, 25, 229
stress, 218-19
university assessment, 169
ACT/SAT, 26, 168-73, 192,
prediction bases on bands, 171
costs, 172
taking multiple times, 172
unskilled jobs. *See* jobs, high school or less

V
VanHoff, Carl, 129
video gaming, 153, 162
vision, *x*, 222
visual matching. *See* targets
vocabulary, 60, 78, 101

W
Winfrey, Oprah, 191
where is my child? 123-25, 132, 153-54
work, 172, 174
writing, 186-87, 240-41

Y
Yankelovich, Dan, 17